Media and Technology in Emerging African Democracies

Cosmas U. Nwokeafor and Kehbuma Langmia

Foreword by Chuka Onwumechili

University Press of America,® Inc.
Lanham · Boulder · New York · Toronto · Plymouth, UK

TABLE OF CONTENTS

FOREWORD: Dr. Chuka Onwumecheli   vii
INTRODUCTION TO THE BOOK   xi
ACKNOWLEDGMENTS   xv

1. ICT AND MEDIA PLURALISM IN AIDING DEMOCRACY

Chapter 1
From Handmaid to Goad of the Governing Elite? ICT Orientations
  of Broadcast Media Professionals in Metropolitan Lagos, Nigeria
Victor A. Aluma   1

Chapter 2
Media, Technology, and Democracy in Niger: What Did the
Advent of ICTs Change?
Gado Alzouma   23

2. NEW TECHNOLOGIES AND THE PRINT MEDIA IN AFRICA

Chapter 3
Role of ICT in Election Coverage by the Nigerian Print Media: A
Study of the 2007 General Elections
Solomon O. Akinboye and Ibitayo S. Popoola   43

Chapter 4
The Role of Online Media Technology and Democratic Discourse
in Cameroon: A Case Study of *The Post* and *Cameroon Tribune*
Kehbuma Langmia   65

3. RADIO AND TELEVISION: ASSUMING NEW ROLES IN AFRICAN DEMOCRACY

Chapter 5
Localism in the South African Media Context: A Comparison of
the South African Local Content and Canadian Content Rules
Adele M. Mda   83

Chapter 6
The New Public Sphere: Radio and Democracy in Kenya
George W. Gathigi and Duncan H. Brown   105

Chapter 7
The Phasing of Analog to Digital Technology in Nigerian Movie
and Broadcasting Industries: A Review of Nollywood and Nigerian
Television Authority (NTA)
Cosmas U. Nwokeafor   125

Chapter 8
Media and Peace-building in Sudan
Hala A. Guta   155

4. NEW MEDIA AND POLITICS

Chapter 9
Media and Conflict: A System Analysis of Mass Media
Technology's Impact on Africa's Democratic and Economic
Systems
Cosmas U. Nwokeafor   177

Chapter 10
Communication, Civil Society, and Democratization in Africa:
Perspectives on Political Development
Ephraim Okoro   199

5. **HEALTHCARE AND THE INFLUENCE OF NEW
    MEDIA TECHNOLOGY**

Chapter 11
The Use of Techno-media Strategies in Effective Healthcare
Service Delivery in Nigeria and the Implications for Democracy
Sustenance
Matthew Uzukwu   225

6. **NEW TECHNOLOGY AS A WEAPON AGIANST
    CRIMES**

Chapter 12
Concepts, Dimensions in New Media Technology: Reinforcing the
Contest Against Financial Crimes in Nigeria
Isika G. Udechukwu and Assay B. Enahoro   249

CONTRIBUTORS   269
THE AUTHORS/EDITORS   275

FOREWORD

The importance of Information and Communication Technologies (ICT) cannot be overstated, particularly in an emerging continent like Africa. Unfortunately, the academic literature fails to keep pace with development of ICT in the region. Thus, it is remarkable that the editors of this text are able to bring together a number of diverse scholars, some outside Africa and others in Africa, to contribute to this important book on ICT in the continent titled *Media and Technology in Emerging African Democracies*. That singular effort is commendable particularly during a period when books on African ICT issues are rare and yet such issues continually demand the attention of African governments, policy makers, and corporations.

The book demonstrates how the old mass media – print, radio, and television – interact with emerging technologies to impact African nations and communities. While it is true that the old divisions of print, radio, and television media are quickly disappearing with increasing convergence of old and new media via Voice Over the Internet Protocol (VOIP) and mobile telephones, as well as other platforms, it is also important to record how new technologies continue to intersect with existing technologies in making a difference in the lives of people in Africa. For instance, local newspapers in Africa are widely available today on the web. In essence, citizens of Tanzania, in the diaspora, no longer have to wait for weeks to learn about events in Dar es Salaam or Arusha, nor do they have to wait for the one paragraph of home news hidden in the depths of a newspaper in the West. Today, such news can be read in detail by browsing the web. The same applies to television where people in the West can now access African television stations including Eritrea TV, Nigerian Television Authority (NTA) and South African Broadcasting Corporation (SABC) through cable or even access many more via the web. In addition, several African radio stations are available through the web. The ubiquity of these media has produced a positive impact on democracy on the continent making it more difficult for despots to mute opposition voices.

The book has various strengths found in the various chapters. For instance, it recognizes that discussions of nationalism goes beyond existing borders of nation states to include transnationalism of citizenship demonstrated in the impact on the state by citizens from the diaspora. Second, it discusses some issues and subjects often ignored in existing communication texts on the continent. For instance, the discussion of the impact of new technology on movie-making in places like Nigeria is an important one focusing on a key industry responsible for a significant percentage of private labor in the country. It also focuses a chapter on the Niger Republic, a country rarely discussed in English-language communication texts. Third and significantly, the book goes beyond publication of essays to provide us with empirical research on important media issues in the continent. Just as important is the variety of methods used in the research studies including survey research, historicism, and frame analysis.

The book makes its greatest contribution in alerting us that in spite of the potential of ICT in the continent, the reality of their usage must be our focus.

After all, what use is it to dedicate time discussing what ought to be while ignoring what is? There are large numbers of journalists who continue to be unaffected by the introduction of new technologies in their craft, while a few have made tremendous impact using new technologies to access news sources, craft, submit, and deliver stories to the public. Usage issues go beyond traditional journalists to include the wider public. For instance, the book's discussion about the use of new ICT, particularly the Internet, for health communication and for crime, presents us with the conundrum surrounding new technology. It is the same dialectic that points to new technologies creating new vistas for democracy, and at the same time leading ethnocentric-charged crises in countries such as Rwanda and Kenya, or helping mask existing forms of social control. Ultimately, while technology brings us positive developments, it can also lead to developments that are adverse to the public.

The Internet is perhaps the most widely covered ICT in the book, and for good reasons. It remains the ICT with arguably the most visible impact in the continent. Thus, we see why scholars have cited it in their discussion of journalism's impact, democracy, conflict, health, and crime. Clearly, ICT's impact is largely vivid but it is also beyond just the Internet. The availability of new forms of ICT have a much wider impact as demonstrated by this book and experienced by Africans in their daily lives. New communication technologies are increasingly helping the widespread of regional multinational companies in Africa as network communications become much easier. Examples are everywhere. Socketworks, an ICT company, operates in both Ghana and Nigeria; MTN offers telephone services across the continent in countries like South Africa, Cameroon, Congo Republic, Rwanda, and Zambia; Arik Airlines that originated in Nigeria is today a prominent airline flying domestically into five cities in the Niger Republic; and EcoBank does business in over 25 African countries. In fact, these new multinationals have spread beyond the continent with MTN Group offering services in Cyprus, Iran, Syria, and Yemen. But just as these services are spreading internally and, at times, externally, so also we recognize that external media from other regions of the world are taking grip on Africa. While those external influences are not the focus of this book, the book provides us with an example of reactions to such external influences. The chapter on content regulation through the concept of localism in South Africa focuses on such reactions. To be sure there are several other African countries that have also introduced such responses including Tanzania and Nigeria.

Obviously, the growth of ICT in Africa has been remarkable over the last two decades. Take Nigeria for example; in 2001, very few Nigerians had a telephone even in the office. In fact, one of the country's Information Ministers infamously explained that telephones were not meant for everyone. In essence, only the wealthy could have it. After all, they were the only ones who could afford to pay for it. Five years later, even the market trader has a telephone in Nigeria following the liberalization of the country's telephone service. It was a remarkable turnaround, but a reminder to all of us that the impact of ICT, its potential, and the future of Africa lay in adopting ICT. Remarkably, the

Nigerian story is not isolated. Similar stories exist from Cape Town to Cairo and from Dakar to Dire Dawa.

Therefore, Dr. Cosmas Nwokeafor and Dr. Kehbuma Langmia are to be commended for editing an important book that reminds us of a need to evaluate ICT's contributions to Africa and its people. In doing so, they also allude to other trends in Africa and the world in the area of transnationalism of citizenship.

Chuka Onwumechili, Ph.D.
Professor
Communication & Culture
John. H. Johnson School of Communications
Howard University. Washington, DC 20059

Introduction to the Book

Media technology is increasingly becoming an essential strategic information tool that has continued to facilitate the process of information and communication dissemination in Africa. It has changed the way people in the continent of Africa exchange information among themselves and with various government, nongovernmental agencies, and established organizations. It is, of course, obvious to say that the advancement in technology has surely changed the way mass media in Africa collects, processes, and disseminates news and information. In today's changing society driven by technological innovation, the use of information and communication technology seems to have made some dynamic changes in the way media houses function. The move from old media systems (print, radio, and television) to a new, technology-driven media which includes Internet access, voice-over protocol, and mobile telephones, has considerably changed the way and style of information dissemination in the continent of Africa. A clear review of African newspapers, radio, and television systems of contemporary time has shown tremendous improvement because most of them could be easily accessed through the web and cable network (in the case of television).

While there have been several research articles and conference panel presentations on media technology, most importantly on information and communication technologies (ICT) in Africa, there is a lack of documentation and books that address the significant impact of the fascinating role media technology plays on emerging African democracies. This book is designed primarily for students and university professors engaging in discourse relevant to the impact of media technology to African democracies. It is also a major contribution to governments, policy makers, non-governmental agencies, private business conglomerates, communication consultants, professionals, diplomats and various corporations in both Africa and global communities who engage in media and technological discourse.

Media and Technology in Emerging African Democracies is a standard text that will give students an opportunity to familiarize themselves with some of the best literature in media technology impact in emerging African democracies with relevant concentration on information and communication technology (ICT). As described fully in the entire book, most importantly in the introductory chapters, this textbook is a collection of essays that may be used as primary reading for courses on mass media technology, and information communication technology (ICT). It is also suitable as supplementary reading in media and politics, political science and courses that focus on political communication, and business communication. In addition, the book can serve as a reference guide to mass media scholars, development communication experts, government leaders and diplomats interested in media review, most importantly as it pertains to African democratic dispensations. The book includes contributions by scholars whose research interest on media and its relevant impact on African democratic system has stirred considerable academic discourse. The chapters span several social science disciplines, which gives students, professionals, and government agencies an opportunity to see challenges from an interdisciplinary perspective.

Several principles guided the choice of specific strengths in editing this book. Most important among these were the crucial strength a reader would derive from this book with all the contributing chapters authored and co-authored by African scholars whose research interests dealt with the area of their chapters. Inasmuch as media scholars have engaged in various research discourses on media technology and sometimes information communication technology (ICT), very few of their scholarly ideas have been documented in a text. In some instances also, textbooks on information communication technology (ICT) are rare, which makes this text a must-have for courses in undergraduate and graduate programs in the United States, Asia, South America, and across the continent of Africa. Furthermore, the significance and quality of the research and its ability to shed light on diverse aspects of information communication technology (ICT), and media impact on emerging African democracies, makes this text a gem among other books in the same category.

Attractiveness and clarity of presentation and ease of reading also were other major strength criteria. Several African countries' specific media systems and their media practices are clearly presented in various chapters. The authors' most crucial intent has been to include the most recent and thought-provoking scholarship from the perspective of their forte in bringing about validity to the textbook. To stimulate critical thinking about the processes of knowledge acquisition, along with thinking about substantive media related issues in Africa, several of the readings contain information about ICT, new technologies and the print media in Africa, and new technology as a weapon against crime in the continent of Africa. In keeping the readers' interest, each author's work has an abstract that serves as an introductory excerpt to the entire chapter.

Each of the six sections into which the chapters have been grouped discusses media and technology in emerging African democracies. The six sections consist of twelve chapters written by thirteen African scholars. The chapters cover a wide array of relevant media technology and information communication technology (ICT) issues.

Part 1 of the book consists of two chapters which deal with ICT and media pluralism in aiding democracy in Africa. The tenet of this part hinges on two broad areas which are: (1) to provide the reader with the understanding that broadcast media tends to play the role of handmaid to the governing elite in Nigeria. This role is supported by Nigeria's history of undemocratic colonial and military government and the hegemonic nature of the mass media, in keeping with the social shaping of technology perspective, and argues that broadcast professionals' ICT comprehension and appropriation is significant for their political role change from handmaid to goad of the governing elite; (2) to significantly demonstrate that the use of ICT's is fostering democratic participation, weakening the state control over media and citizens, and expanding civic engagements in Niger Republic, a country rarely discussed in English language communication textbooks.

Part 2, titled "New Technologies and the Print Media in Africa" explores the impact of ICT in election coverage with specific reference to the 2007 general election in Nigeria. With the use of survey instrument to gather information from senior journalists in the Nigerian print media, the authors arrived at a conclusion that ICT has assisted the Nigerian print media in reporting information timely to their audience. The next chapter on this part examined two online newspapers in Cameroon with opposing views on how their contents have been able to reflect the influence of technology in shaping the way people discuss the pressing political needs in Cameroon.

Part 3 consists of four chapters and deals with Radio and Television assuming new roles in African democracy. This section carefully compared the progress of Canadian and South African media regulations and provides an insight in the two countries' similarities and differences. It also provides clarity as to their efforts toward stimulating the production of local content and their effectiveness. The authors of the second chapter in this part found in their research that the number of full-fledged radio stations has grown from two stations in 1993 to about 110 stations in 2008. It examined how radio in Kenya has functioned as a public sphere which allows for political participation and the formation of diverse opinions by the citizens. In this part also, one of the authors of the chapters examined the impact the transition from analog to digital technology has had in the movie and broadcasting industries in Nigeria. Media and peace-building in Sudan informed how radio was effectively used to bring about peace and social cohesion in a country ravaged by civil war.

Part four examines, in two chapters, new media politics. In an attempt to explore media coverage of conflict in Africa, the author reviewed conflict and conflict types and explores the role media plays in reporting conflicts, and to what extent they have been successful in covering the conflicts without interference. The author finds in his research that the old media system in Africa may have been controlled in the process of covering conflict issues, but the contemporary media systems — some of which are independent establishments — experience less interference from government regulations. This part of the book also reviewed perspectives on political development by looking at communication, civil society, and democratization in Africa. It focuses on the instrumentality of the press in advancing and promoting political practice and democratic reforms in Africa.

Part five, titled "Healthcare and the Influence of New Media Technology" focuses on the use of technomedia strategy as a tool in effective healthcare service health delivery and the implications for democracy sustenance. The author argues that the healthcare system in Nigeria is a two-way dimensional system consisting of the public and private sectors, and has been ineffective in delivering healthcare services to its users. Using historical data analysis methodologies, we examine the problem associated with this ineffectiveness, their potential impact on Nigeria's nascent democracy, and how a technomedia strategy can be successful in achieving effective, systemic healthcare services delivery with positive implications for democratic sustenance.

Part six examines concepts, dimensions in new media technology, and how it would be used in reinforcing the contest against financial crimes by proposing appropriate strategies, including techniques to discourage and check fraudulent practices, especially among the youth.

The flexibility of *Media and Technology in Emerging African Democracies* springs from its diverse and rich content and from the considerable enriched backgrounds and experiences of the scholars who contributed chapters to this groundbreaking textbook. The importance of the issues we raise in the twelve chapters of this book and the fascinating examples and critical research perspectives in exploring this new area in the study and publication of an information communication technology (ICT) text will attract media scholars, undergraduate and graduate students, government agencies, diplomats, policy makers, and corporations all over the world as we continue to support the advancement of academe.

Cosmas U. Nwokeafor
Kehbuma Langmia

Acknowledgments

There are several individuals who have assisted in the development of this book in different essential ways. We use this medium to sincerely express our appreciation and thank them for the wonderful jobs they have done in making our hard work come to fruition. We sincerely extend our gratitude to the editorial team at the University Press of America, who saw the need and timeliness of this book at this crucial time when technology and media systems form a useful alliance in information dissemination across the globe, and accepted to publish it. Our special gratitude goes to Dr. Chuka Onwumechili, full professor of communication at Howard University, Washington, DC who, in spite of his busy professional schedules, wrote the foreword and found time to review the book when it was in manuscript form, and provided us with constructive critical guidance and comments.

We are very thankful to Dr. Benjamin Arah, assistant professor of philosophy at Bowie State University in the Department of History and Government, whose words of encouragement kept us in good spirits when the burden of putting this book together weighed down on us. To Dr. Mathias Mbah, assistant dean at Bowie State University Graduate School, we sincerely appreciate your encouragement and support.

To Dr. George Chinonyerem Ego-Osuala, an internist and CEO of Edge Medical Care PLC in the State of Maryland, whose encouragement and motivation spurred us to working conscientiously in making the dream of this book a reality. We remain grateful to Stephanie Key of the office of the Graduate School at Bowie State University who carried out some of the secretarial work for this book in spite of her full administrative responsibilities. We are very thankful to Cris Wanzer of Manuscripts to Go, who formatted and did some editing work on this book, and worked painstakingly to make sure that we met the deadline for the publication of this book in spite of her numerous formatting engagements.

We would like to express our sincere and deepest appreciation to our families, whose strong encouragement motivated us tremendously. We thank them for their understanding of the importance of this book to communication and media scholars around the world as they gave us the deserving support to accomplish our hearts' desires. As we take full responsibility of errors or omissions that our readers may find in this book, we rejoice on the completion of this book project that will add to scholarship and the need for information communication technology (ICT) text in African region and diaspora. We remain grateful to all the scholars whose work we have cited to support our claims.

Chapter 1

From Handmaid to Goad of the Governing Elite? ICT Orientations of Broadcast Media Professionals in Metropolitan Lagos, Nigeria

Victor A. Aluma
University of Lagos, Akoka, Lagos, Nigeria

Abstract

The Nigerian broadcast media tends to play the role of handmaid to the governing elite. This role is supported by Nigeria's history of undemocratic colonial and military government and the hegemonic nature of the modern mass media. The entry of ICT promises a role change because of its post-modern, non-hegemonic character. But is this role change likely to occur? In line with the social shaping of technology perspective, this paper asserts that broadcast professionals' ICT comprehension and appropriation is significant for their political role change from handmaid to goad of the governing elite. The author argues that the role change is not likely to occur among broadcast professionals in metropolitan Lagos given the character of their ICT knowledge, usage, and attitudes.

INTRODUCTION

A survey of Nigerian media history shows up two broad patterns of relationship between media professionals and the governing elite. One pattern, which is mainly associated with the print media, sees the media as adversaries and goads of the ruling elite, while the other pattern, which is mainly associated with the broadcast media, sees the media as servants or handmaids of the governing elite. A possible explanation for this divergence is the fact that, in the Nigerian context, the print media originated in circumstances that were markedly different from those of the broadcast media. While the print media evolved as private sector organizations that were taken over by the nationalist movement prior to the attainment of national political independence, the broadcast media were public sector organizations instituted and controlled first by colonial administrations, then in turn by indigenous civil governments and military regimes (Obazele, 1996; Sotunmbi, 1996). Indeed, private sector participation in ownership and management of the broadcast media did not take off until 1992 when the enabling law was passed.

Another explanation for the difference is the undemocratic nature of government both in the colonial era and in large parts of the postcolonial era. The undemocratic character of colonial administrations was reflected in a move toward establishing its hegemony (the so-called pax Britannica) over the Nigerian people. The same drive of the governing elite to establish its hegemony is shown by postcolonial Nigerian governments, in particular the military administrations. The drive to hegemony and the presence or absence of media resistance accounts for the conflictual relationship between the governing elite and the independent, private sector media as well as the master-servant relationship between the governing elite and the dependent, public sector media. What is apparent, therefore, is that the conjuncture of undemocratic governing elite and different fragments of the modern mass media in Nigeria resulted either in an independent and antagonistic relationship or in a dependent and submissive relationship (Mohammed, 2003; Agbaje, 1992; Altschull, 1984). The dependent status of the broadcast media may be seen, therefore, as a result of the interaction between the undemocratic nature of the governing elite and the tendency of the modern mass media, being centralized and capital intensive, to be instruments of hegemony or dominance in the hands of the elite[1].

In the last decade or so, information and communication technologies (ICTs) have been rapidly adopted in the Nigerian media landscape. From the ubiquitous mobile phone to the less widely dispersed personal computer, ICTs are being used by the Nigerian media. Analysts (Dijk, 1999; Croteau & Hoynes, 2000) have pointed out the fundamental difference in the nature of ICTs as compared with the mass media. Unlike modern mass media, which foster largely one-way, asymmetrical relationships between media institutions and their audiences, ICTs permit high levels of interactivity between communicators. This facilitation of interactivity implies a move away from the scenario of domination of the receiver by the sender which obtains in mass media to a more egalitarian scenario of conversation among interlocutors in the public sphere. Thus, ICTs lend themselves to a post-modern non-hegemonic relationship between participants in communication interactions.

Given this scenario, it is legitimate to wonder if the use of ICTs in Nigerian broadcast media is capable of bringing about a change in the relationship between the broadcast media and the governing elite from the current relationship of handmaid to that of goad. The same question may be put thus: given the fact that the print media have generally operated as goads of the governing elite, what are the chances that ICTs, because of their non-hegemonic character, may serve as the drivers of change in the nature of the relationship between the broadcast media and the governing elite?

The argument of the current chapter is that a role change of the broadcast media will depend on its professionals' comprehension and appropriation of ICTs. The basis for such an argument is founded on the social shaping of technology perspective. This perspective has also been referred to as the social construction of technology perspective or, more simply, as technological constructivism.

Social Shaping of Technology Perspective

It is necessary to explain the background of technological constructivism in order to better appreciate its main proposition. Technological constructivism may be understood as a historical reaction to technological determinism. Briefly put, technological determinism proposes that technology causes social change; or to be more specific, that changes in technology effect changes in society (Croteau & Hoynes, 2000).

In technological determinism, the view is that changes in technology precede and largely account for social changes; and technology is uncritically conceived as a sort of "black box." But in its reaction, technological constructivism argues that technological changes are driven by social demands; thus, the effect of technology on society is, in the first place, caused by social needs and demands for technology. Another rendition is that society determines the shape of technology (Edge, 2000; Lyon, 2000; Mackay, 2000; Williams & Edge, 1996; Woolgar, 1996). It is the view of this chapter that, in analyzing the effect of technology on society, it is important to describe the interaction of social groups with technology, since such interaction has the potential to select those aspects of a technology that could change society.

With reference to relationships between the broadcast media and the governing elite, the argument of technological constructivism is diagrammed below. In order to clarify important distinctions, the change path predicted by technological determinism is first presented, then that suggested by technological constructivism is discussed. Figure 1 below represents the change path predicted by technological determinism.

Figure 1. Path through which technological change effects social change, according to technological determinism

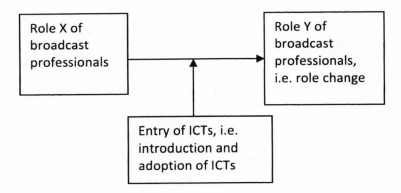

According to this logic, the entry and adoption of ICTs should lead to a change in the political role of broadcast media professionals from X (i.e. handmaid) to Y (i.e. goad).

A different path is suggested by technological constructivism. This path takes into account the influence of the nature of the technological comprehension and appropriation of specific social groups. Figure 2 displays the path of change predicted by technological constructivism.

Figure 2. Path through which technological change effects social change, according to technological constructivism

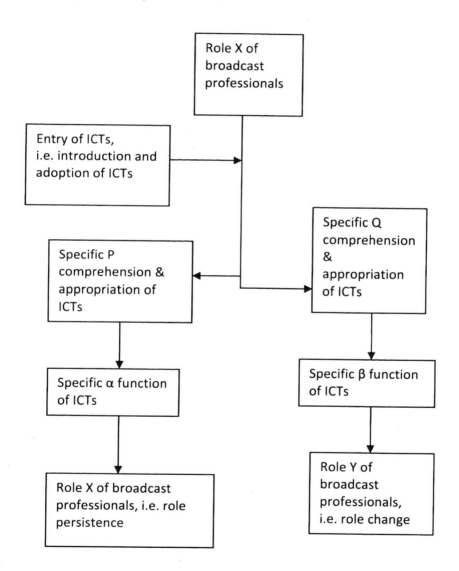

In this elaboration of the technological constructivist logic of social change, it is seen that the nature of the comprehension and appropriation of technology by a social group is vital since only a certain type of comprehension and appropriation is likely to lead to the specific kind of functions that can result in a role change. In other words, not all kinds of ICT functions result in role change. It is the argument of this chapter that the specific nature of ICT comprehension and appropriation among broadcast media professionals in metropolitan Lagos in Nigeria as such is unlikely to bring about a role change of broadcast media professionals from handmaid to goad of the governing elite.

Problem and Method

In line with the logic of technological constructivism (or the social shaping of technology perspective), this study sought to describe and analyze the ICT comprehension and appropriation of broadcast media professionals in the Lagos metropolis in Nigeria. Specifically, it surveyed the ICT knowledge, usage, and attitudes of broadcast media professionals. A 32-item, self-administered questionnaire was served on 190 broadcast professionals in Lagos. The questionnaire items comprised 20 close-ended, 10 Likert scale, and two open-ended questions. Items sought to measure, among other factors, the sampled professionals' ICT knowledge levels (or comprehension), ICT usage patterns (or appropriation), and attitudes toward ICTs in relation to broadcasting. (A copy of the questionnaire is provided as an appendix to this chapter.)

The broadcast professionals were purposively sampled from the ranks of senior and junior staffers of news and current affairs, as well as program departments of all the full-fledged radio and television stations[2] in Lagos. One hundred and ninety copies of the questionnaire were distributed to 19 radio and television stations at the rate of 10 copies per station, which meant five copies each to the program and the news and current affairs departments of each station. Out of the 190 copies distributed, 178 were duly completed and returned; thus, a return rate of 93.7 percent was attained.

In all, nine radio stations and 10 television stations were selected. The radio stations were: Brila 88.9FM, Cool 96.9FM, Eko FM, Metro 97.6FM, RayPower 100.5FM, Rhyhm 93.7FM, Star 101.5FM, Radio Lagos 107.5FM, and Radio Nigeria Ikoyi. And the television stations sampled were: Africa Independent Television (AIT), Channels Television, DBN, Galaxy Television, Minaj Broadcast International, Murhi International Television, NTA Lagos, NTA 2, and Superscreen.

The research questions addressed were as follows:

RQ1:   How may the ICT comprehension, appropriation and attitudes of broadcast media professionals in Lagos metropolis be characterized?

RQ2:   Which implications does such characterization have for a change in the political role of the broadcast media from handmaid to goad of the governing elite?

ICT Comprehension, Appropriation and Attitudes

It was found that 44.7 percent of the sampled broadcast professionals had inaccurate knowledge (or comprehension) of ICTs; while 40.4 percent and 14.9 percent had fair and accurate knowledge, respectively. Details are presented in Table 1.

Table 1. ICT Comprehension and Appropriation of Broadcast Professionals in Lagos, Nigeria

Variable	Attribute	Score
ICT Comprehension	Accurate knowledge of ICTs	14.9 %
	Fair knowledge of ICTs	40.4 %
	Inaccurate knowledge of ICTs	44.7 %
	N	94
ICT Usage at Work	Usage of ICT (especially PCs) for work	50.6 %
	Non-usage of ICT (especially PCs) for work	49.4 %
	N	174
Regularity of ICT Usage at Work	Regular ICT usage at work	60.6 %
	Fairly regular ICT usage at work	14.1 %
	Occasional ICT usage at work	25.3 %
	N	99
Areas of ICT Usage at Work	Data processing (including editing and graphics)	36.2 %
	Data storage and retrieval	36.6 %
	Data communications	9.4 %
	Database management	3.8 %
	N	265

ICT Communications Services Helpful at Work	Email	24.6 %
	World Wide Web	22.2 %
	Newsgroups	21.0 %
	GSM phone	15.1 %
	Teleconferencing, Chat groups	13.9 %
	Mailing lists	2.4 %
	FTP, Telnet	0.8 %
	N	252
Problems in ICT Usage	Hardware problems	31.9 %
	User problems	18.7 %
	Software problems	17.6 %
	Access problems	16.5 %
	Infrastructure problems	15.4 %
	N	91

Note: Variations in N are due to missing, invalid and, where applicable, multiple responses.

Regarding usage patterns (or appropriation), 50.6 percent of the professionals reported usage of ICTs in their work, while 49.4 percent reported non-usage of ICTs in their work. Further, among reported ICT users in work settings, 60.6 percent were regular users, while 14.1 percent and 25.3 percent were fairly regular and occasional users respectively.

Regarding areas of usage, 9.4 percent of the sampled professionals reported ICT (in particular, personal computer) usage for data communication, while 36.2 percent, 36.6 percent and 3.8 percent reported ICT usage for data processing, data storage and retrieval, and database management respectively. When asked to indicate the ICT communications services they considered most helpful in their work, the top four choices were: email (24.6 percent), the World Wide Web (22.2 percent), newsgroups (21 percent), and the GSM phone (15.1 percent). And when asked about the kinds of problems they faced in using ICTs, the top two picks were: hardware (31.9 percent) and other users (18.7 percent).

Finally, regarding attitudes toward ICTs, the sample was questioned on three groups of variables. The first group dealt with attitudes about ICTs' probable influence on the professional excellence of broadcasters. The second group had to do with attitudes about the desirable ICT policy directions of key institutions such as government, broadcasting companies, and associations of broadcast media professionals. And the third group centered on attitudes about the probable dysfunctional influence of ICTs in Nigerian society.

With respect to the group of variables dealing with the issue of ICTs and professional excellence, the broadcast professionals had a favorable view of the positive influence and salience of ICTs in the promotion of professional excellence among broadcasters. Three items constituted the first group. The items were: broadcast professionals' use of ICT will make them more responsible to the needs of people at the grassroots level; broadcasters who are competent in ICT will make better professionals than those who are not competent; and ICT use will revolutionize broadcasting. A majority (at least 60 percent) of the sampled broadcast professionals were favorably disposed to all three statements.

The second group of variables, which dealt with the issue of desirable ICT policy directions of key institutions, had three constituents. They were: governments should promote ICT skills acquisition by broadcasters; broadcasting firms should promote ICT competence among broadcasters by linking such competence to employment and advancement; and professional broadcast associations should take steps to promote ICT competence among its members. Again, a majority (at least 70 percent) of the sampled professionals were favorably disposed to all three statements of this theme.

The third group, dwelling on the probable social dysfunctionality of ICT in the Nigerian setting, also had three elements. They were: ICT dependence will make broadcasters less meticulous and painstaking; ICTs are a source of health hazards to broadcasters; and ICTs will promote foreign cultures to the detriment of indigenous Nigerian cultures. A slight majority (between 46 and 52 percent) were not favorably disposed to all three statements. Details are presented in Table 2.

At this point it is useful to highlight the emerging character of ICT orientations of the broadcast professionals in metropolitan Lagos. In this study, the operational definition of ICT orientation comprises ICT comprehension, ICT appropriation and ICT attitudes. With respect to ICT comprehension, it is observable that a minority, less than two in 10, of the broadcast professionals have an accurate knowledge of ICTs. And, applying less than strict standards, we may say that slightly more than five in 10 have a fair (and better than fair) knowledge of ICTs. In other words, only a slight majority have a fair (and better than fair) knowledge of ICTs.

Regarding the factor of ICT appropriation, it may be observed that users of ICT in work settings make up only half of the sample. These users employ ICTs mainly in data processing, storage and retrieval (as opposed to data communications). And their favorite ICT communication services are email, the web, newsgroups, and the GSM phone.

Concerning ICT attitudes, it is obvious that, among the sampled broadcast media professionals, ICTs are regarded in a favorable light. In relation to broadcasting, ICT competences and utilization are seen as non-dysfunctional, worthy of institutional support and promoting professional excellence.

Table 2. Attitudes toward ICTs among Broadcast Professionals in Lagos, Nigeria

Item	Attitude			N
	Favorable	Unfavorable	Neutral	
THEME 1. ICT USAGE & PROFESSIONAL EXCELLENCE OF BROADCASTERS				
1. ICT usage will make broadcasting more responsive to needs at the grassroots	59.9 %	18.0 %	22.2 %	167
2. ICT competent broadcasters will be better professionals than ICT non-competent broadcasters	67.8 %	19.3 %	12.9 %	171
3. ICT usage will revolutionize Nigerian broadcasting	86.8 %	9.0 %	4.2 %	167
THEME 2. DESIRABLE ICT POLICY DIRECTIONS OF KEY INSTITUTIONS				
4. Government should assist broadcast professionals to acquire ICT competence & resources	76.4 %	11.2 %	12.4 %	169
5. Broadcasting companies should make broadcast professionals' ICT competence a requirement for their employment and advancement	73.1 %	19.3 %	7.6 %	171

6. Professional associations of broadcasters should participate in enhancing members' ICT competence	82.1 %	8.8 %	8.9 %	168
THEME 3. DYSFUNCTIONS OF ICT IN SOCIETY				
7. ICT usage makes broadcasters less meticulous and painstaking	41.5 %	45.8 %	12.8 %	164
8. ICT usage has health hazards for broadcasters	22.0 %	52.6 %	25.6 %	164
9. ICT usage promotes foreign cultures to the detriment of indigenous cultures	30.9 %	51.8 %	17.3 %	168

Note: Variations in N are due to missing, invalid and, where applicable, multiple responses.

Implications for Role Change

The rationale of this chapter is that the character of ICT orientations has implications for political role change of the broadcast media. In this section, therefore, the focus will be on the implications that the character of ICT orientation of broadcast media professionals in metropolitan Lagos may have for their political role change. It should be stressed that the chances of ICTs catalyzing a role change will depend on the extent to which users' ICT comprehension, appropriation, and attitudes allow the free play of the change-inducing features of ICTs. As was noted earlier, these features are the non-hegemonic, interactive, many-to-many character of ICTs. The question, then, is: to what extent is the character of ICT orientation of the sampled broadcast media professionals conducive to the free play of ICT features? The character of ICT orientation indicated may be summarized as follows: one, a relatively low or poor level of ICT comprehension; two, a medium or average level of ICT appropriation, emphasizing data processing rather than data communications; three, a generally highly favorable disposition toward ICT as a vehicle for attaining professional excellence, as a target worthy of encouragement through policy, and as a non-dysfunctional influence in society.

While the ICT attitudes may be said to favor the free play or optimum influence of ICTs as a catalyst of broadcast professionals' role change, the comprehension and appropriation levels are not likely to function in a similar manner. The factor of poor ICT comprehension as well as of an average degree of ICT appropriation may be expected to hinder the capacity of ICTs to effect political role change of the broadcast media. Rather, what these factors predict is more of role persistence, since the factors that sustain the handmaid role will function with hardly any challenge and, possibly, hardly any displacement from the hampered influence of ICTs. It is only logical to expect that for ICTs to fully realize their potential to function as a vehicle for change, they must be fully adopted and deployed in a social-political context. But the character of ICT orientation of the sampled professionals does not permit this necessary condition.

The data presented above shows a disjunction between the direction of ICT attitudes and that of ICT comprehension and appropriation. While the ICT attitudes may be seen as enhancing the potential of ICTs to effect role change of the broadcast media, the observable ICT comprehension and appropriation of the broadcast professionals are inclined to hindering the potential of ICTs to effect role change. This disjuncture is rife with creative possibilities. The fact that ICT attitudes in the Nigerian setting being studied are so favorable suggests that there is indeed potential for ICTs to facilitate role change in the broadcast media provided ICT comprehension and appropriation are significantly improved.

Further scrutiny of the ICT comprehension and appropriation of the sampled professionals should yield useful insights. It is significant, for example, that roughly half of the sampled professionals were non-users. In other words, there is substantial capacity for appropriation of ICT that could be deployed, thus raising the power of ICTs to effect political role change of the broadcast media.

Also, the combination of poor ICT comprehension and an emphasis on data processing/storage usage pattern puts a question mark over the effectiveness of the products of data processing. If indeed the prevalent comprehension is poor, it may be expected that achievements of data processing will fall short of the potentialities of ICTs. In other words, the content being created may not be making full use of the communicative powers of ICTs. This line of thinking is reinforced by the observation that the direction of ICT appropriation among the professionals is only minimally inclined toward data communications. To render the situation in simple terms, perhaps it is the case that the broadcast media are producing political messages that do not make full or optimal use of the powers and possibilities of ICTs; and, worse, those messages are not being fully or optimally communicated to significant publics.

Yet another salient feature of ICT appropriation relates to the profile of problems associated with the use of ICTs. It was recorded that the predominant problems had to do with hardware and infrastructure. In other words, among the users of ICTs, infrastructural and hardware problems were the leading limiters of ICT effectiveness as promoters of role change.

Taking all of these issues together, it is clear that the character of ICT orientation of the sampled broadcasters, particularly regarding the critical factor of ICT appropriation, shows that ICTs can only function in a highly hampered way in the Nigerian setting. Thus, the ability of ICTs to drive a change in political role of broadcast media professionals is greatly limited.

Conclusion

The issue discussed in this chapter had to do with the unfolding social impacts attendant on the introduction and adoption of information and communication technologies in the Nigerian broadcast media. It was assumed that such impacts were indeed probable given the documented social changes being made through the implementation of technological innovations globally (Owhotu, 2006). The problem investigated was the likelihood that the deployment of ICTs would facilitate a change in the traditional political role of the broadcast media from operating as editorially dependent lapdogs or handmaids of the governing elite to being editorially independent watchdogs or goads of the political system[3]. Using the technological constructivist perspective, it was argued that the capacity of ICTs to transform the political role of the broadcast media would depend on the broadcast professionals' ICT orientation, that is, comprehension, appropriation and attitudes, toward these technologies. A purposive sample of broadcast media professionals based in metropolitan Lagos was then surveyed in order to measure and analyze their ICT orientation.

The disquieting highlights of the findings were that few professionals had a strong comprehension of ICTs or regularly used ICTs (particularly PCs) for work-related functions, including communications. The good news, however, was that most of the professionals held favorable views about the priceless value of ICTs to broadcasting. The inference made was that, given the current ICT orientation of broadcast professionals as exemplified in the sample studied, there was little likelihood that ICTs could facilitate the role change of broadcasters from handmaids to goads.

What steps need to be taken if the potentials of ICTs for liberating Nigerian broadcasting in the political sphere are to be realized? A three-pronged action is recommended in order to "upgrade" the ICT orientation of broadcast media professionals in metropolitan Lagos as well as in other similar settings. Firstly, a program of ICT education targeted at broadcast professionals should be promoted and facilitated by governments, broadcast companies, broadcast professionals' associations, ICT manufacturers and vendors, charities, and other concerned players. The aim should be to significantly improve the ICT comprehension of broadcast media professionals. Secondly, policy and program interventions targeted at deepening the ICT appropriation (and usage) of broadcast professionals should be promoted. The rationale for this lies in a cardinal lesson of technological constructivism which may be paraphrased as: a society gets the kind of change it desires through the kind of demands it makes on the technology it interacts with. Thirdly, research and project interventions should be implemented to define and reinforce (or discourage, as the case may be) the ICT attitudes of broadcast professionals. If attitudes predict and impel action, then the subjects and directions of ICT attitudes among broadcast professionals will be crucial for the outcome of any measures taken to upgrade their ICT comprehension and appropriation.

Notes

1 Quarmyne (quoted in Omu, 1997: 136) describes the phenomenon as "the 'Minister say' culture which has turned broadcasting into a public relations department of the government with the dissemination of government propaganda as its top priority." Akinwale (1990: 38) similarly asserts that "the best that can be said of professionals in Nigeria in government establishment, whether in broadcasting houses or in ministries ... is that they are professionals working as civil servants and being treated as one." And in Altschull's (1984: 157) rendition, "Whatever the specific rules at the particular time in the advancing world, the press acquiesced in – and promoted – the norms of the political and economic leadership."

2 The only radio station not sampled was Radio Unilag 103.1FM as it was basically a training facility of the University of Lagos, Nigeria, and not a full-fledged company.

3 The traditional vulnerability of the broadcast media to the hegemonic demands of the governing elite is acknowledged in Rønning's (2007: 15-16) statement that Broadcasters must be free from all forms of interference, and be independent of direct state, political and commercial influence in the programming. ... However, even countries that usually are regarded as beacons of freedom of expression do not totally adhere to these principles. ... In Norway it is the Ministry of Culture and Church Affairs that is the owner of the public service broadcaster. ... Furthermore, it is the Ministry which appoints its board of directors of NRK. ... The connection between a Ministry and the editorial leadership of the broadcaster is often complex, and does not always in principle conform with a strict separation of functions.

This vulnerability is usually rationalized on the grounds that governments need to regulate and license broadcasting as a user of the public airwaves.

REFERENCES

Agbaje, A.A.B. (1992). *The Nigerian Press, Hegemony and the Social Construction of Legitimacy* 1960-1983. New York: The Edwin Mellen Press.

Akinwale, A.O. (1990). The Nigerian broadcaster: A professional or a civil servant? *Media Nigeria – Dialectic Issues in Nigerian Journalism.* Akinfeleye, R.A. (ed). Lagos: Nelson Publishers.

Altschull, J.H. (1984). *Agents of Power: The Role of the Press in Human Affairs.* New York: Longman.

Croteau, D. and Hoynes, W. (2000). *Media/Society: Industries, Images and Audiences.* Thousand Oaks, CA: Pine Forge.

Dijk, J. van (1999). *The network society.* London: Sage.

Edge, D. (2000). The social shaping of technology. *Information Technology and Society: A Reader.* Heap, N., Thomas, R., Einon, G., Mason, R. and Mackay, H. (eds). London: Sage and Open University.

Lyon, D. (2000). The roots of the information society idea. *Information Technology and Society: A Reader.* Heap, N., Thomas, R., Einon, G., Mason, R. and Mackay, H. (eds). London: Sage and Open University.

Mackay, H. (2000). Theorizing the IT/society relationship. *Information Technology and Society: A Reader.* Heap, N., Thomas, R., Einon, G., Mason, R. and Mackay, H. (eds). London: Sage and Open University.

Mohammed, J.B. (2003). *The Nigerian Press and the Ibrahim Babangida Military Administration* 1985-1993. Ibadan: Book Builders.

Obazele, P. (1996). Beginning and growth of radio broadcasting in Nigeria. *Journalism in Nigeria: Issues and Perspectives.* Dare, O. and Uyo, A. (eds). Lagos: Nigeria Union of Journalists Lagos State Council.

Omu, F.I.A. (1997). Freedom and responsibility in broadcasting. *Deregulation of Broadcasting in Africa.* Lagos: National Broadcasting Commission.

Owhotu, V.B. (2006). The social dimensions of technological innovation and revolution. *An Introduction to Information Technologies in Education.* Owhotu, V.B. (ed). Lagos: Sibon Books.

Rønning, H. (2007). Broadcasting regulation versus freedom of expression and editorial independence - A contradictory relationship? *Nordicom Review,* Jubilee Issue 2007, pp. 9 – 19.

Sotunmbi, B. (1996). The challenges of television journalism. *Journalism in Nigeria: Issues and Perspectives.* Dare, O. and Uyo, A. (eds). Lagos: Nigeria Union of Journalists Lagos State Council.

Williams, R. and Edge, D. (1996). The social shaping of technology. *Information and Communication Technologies: Visions and Realities.* Dutton, W.H. (ed). Oxford: Oxford University Press.

Woods, B. (1993). *Communication, Technology and the Development of People.* London: Routledge.

Woolgar, S. (1996). Technologies as cultural artifacts. *Information and Communication Technologies: Visions and Realities.* Dutton, W.H. (ed). Oxford: Oxford University Press.

Appendix: Questionnaire

Hello! My name is Victor Ayedun-Aluma. I am at the Department of Mass Communication, University of Lagos, Akoka. I am carrying out a study on the attitudes of broadcast professionals to information technologies. It is an entirely self-sponsored research. Please, give frank answers to the questions. You will not be required to disclose your personal or corporate identity. Thank you very much.

Please, place an 'X' in the box next to your response.

1. Have you, in the last three years, attended any information technology (IT) training program(s)?
   - [ ] Yes   [If you chose this option, please go to Question 2]
   - [ ] No   [If you chose this option, please go to Question 6]

2. How many of such training program(s) have you attended?
   - [ ] One
   - [ ] Two or three
   - [ ] More than three

3. Who sponsored the training program(s)?
   - [ ] I (myself)
   - [ ] My organization
   - [ ] Other (specify):

4. Which of the following sets is made up of IT hardware only?
   - [ ] Television, Radio, VCR, CD-ROM
   - [ ] Cable, DVD, FTP, DSTV
   - [ ] Notebook, Desktop, Scanner, Tablet
   - [ ] Don't know

5. Which of the following sets is made up of IT software only?
   - [ ] Pentium, Celeron, OS/2, Dell
   - [ ] Windows, Unix, Gopher, Macintosh
   - [ ] Betamax, Umatic, Samsung, Philips
   - [ ] Don't know

6. Which of the following best describes your current duties as a broadcaster?
   - [ ] Reporting
   - [ ] Copy-editing
   - [ ] Tape-editing
   - [ ] Announcing

☐ Acting
☐ Directing
☐ Producing
☐ Lighting
☐ Set design
☐ Graphics
☐ Camera operation
☐ Console operation
☐ Administration
☐ Marketing
☐ Other (specify):

7. Do you personally use computers in your work?

☐ No   [If you chose this option, please go to Question 10]
☐ Yes   [If you chose this option, please go to Question 8]

8. How often do you use computers in your work?

☐ Regularly
☐ Fairly regularly
☐ Occasionally
☐ Never

9. Please mention **two** problems you have experienced in using computers at work:

10. Do other people who report to you use computers in the work they do for you?

☐ Yes   [If you chose this option, please go to Question 11]
☐ No   [If you chose this option, please go to Question 12]

11. How often do they use computers in the work they do for you?

☐ Regularly
☐ Fairly regularly
☐ Occasionally
☐ Never

12. In which of the following ways, if at all, have you found computers useful in your work?

☐ Graphics
☐ Editing
☐ Recording
☐ Playback
☐ Storage
☐ Communications

☐ Word-processing
☐ Spreadsheet Tasks (e.g. personnel/payroll tasks)
☐ Database Management (e.g. library)
☐ Other (specify):

13. In which of the following services, if at all, have you found IT helpful in your work?

☐ Newsgroup(s)
☐ Teleconference(s)
☐ E-mail
☐ World Wide Web
☐ GSM phone(s)
☐ Mailing List(s)
☐ Chat group(s)
☐ FTP
☐ Telnet

14. Which, if any, of the following benefits would you say you have derived from using

☐ IT in your work?
☐ Improved efficiency
☐ Automation of procedures
☐ Easing up of tasks
☐ Other (specify):

15. Which, if any, of the following would you attribute to the use of IT in broadcasting?

☐ Dominance of foreign programs
☐ Greater health risks (e.g. due to radiation)
☐ Openness to e-crimes (e.g. hacking, cracking)
☐ Other (specify):

16. Does your organization have its own website?

☐ Yes [If you chose this option, please answer the next question]
☐ No [If you chose this option, please skip the next question]

17. What is the address of your organization's website?

Please consider statements 18 to 27 below. And, in the appropriate box after each statement, put an 'X' to indicate whether you: Strongly Agree (SA); Agree (A); neither Agree nor Disagree (N); Disagree (D); or strongly Disagree (SD).

		SA	A	N	D	SD
18.	Broadcast organizations should make IT competence a requirement for employing and promoting broadcasters					
19.	Use of IT in broadcasting will promote foreign culture to the detriment of indigenous Nigerian culture.					
20.	Broadcasters who are competent in IT use will make better professionals than those who are not competent in IT use.					
21.	Government should assist broadcasters to acquire IT skills and equipment.					
22.	IT is an indispensable tool in broadcasting today.					
23.	Use of IT will make broadcasting more responsive to the needs of people at the grassroots.					
24.	IT is a source of stress and health					

	hazard to broadcasters.						
25.	(Broadcast professionals') associations have a vital role to play in promoting IT competence among broadcasters.						
26.	IT use will make broadcasters less meticulous and less painstaking than they could be without IT.						
27.	IT use will revolutionize broadcasting in Nigeria.						

28. What is your gender?
- [ ] Female
- [ ] Male

29. What is your age group?
- [ ] Less than 21 years of age
- [ ] 21—30 years
- [ ] 31—40 years
- [ ] 41—50 years
- [ ] 51—60 years
- [ ] More than 60 years of age

30. What is your highest educational attainment?
- [ ] No formal education
- [ ] Have some primary education
- [ ] Completed primary school
- [ ] Have some secondary education
- [ ] Completed secondary school
- [ ] Have some tertiary education
- [ ] Have a professional/technical certificate
- [ ] Have a professional/technical diploma

☐ Have a university degree
☐ Have a postgraduate degree
☐ Other (specify):

31. How long have you practiced as a broadcaster?
☐ About 1 year
☐ 2—4 years
☐ 5—7 years\
☐ 8—10 years
☐ 11—15 years
☐ More than 15 years

32. How would you describe the organization you currently work for?
☐ Public Radio station
☐ Public Radio network
☐ Public TV station
☐ Public TV network
☐ Private Radio station
☐ Private Radio network
☐ Private TV station
☐ Private TV network
☐ Other (specify):

Chapter 2

Media, Technology, and Democracy in Niger: What Did the Advent of ICTs Change?

Gado Alzouma
American University of Nigeria

Abstract

In this paper, I examine the relationships between the state and the media in Niger between 1960 and 2008, particularly the period after 1960, characterized by the state monopoly on media and framed by the ideology of nation-building, and the period after 1990 corresponding to the institutionalization of democracy and the advent of new information and communication technologies (ICTs). In contrast with arguments advanced by many authors (Grossman, 1995; Browning & Weitzner, 1996; Beacham, 1997; Ott, 1998; Norris, 2001; Clift, 2002), I challenge the idea that the use of ICTs is fostering democratic participation, weakening the state control over media and citizens, and expanding civic engagement. I argue that the preexisting social and political relations between groups and individuals are not suddenly erased by the use of ICTs. My paper takes place within the framework of the "structural constructivist" theory devised by Bourdieu (1977; 1991). I adopt a historical perspective and analyze the content of the political parties' websites, the

*differential use of ICTs by different social groups, and the activities of civil
society members in order to show how political competence is distributed
unequally and how this results in unequal possibilities for actors to reshape the
political landscape.*

INTRODUCTION

This work is a revised version of a paper presented at the Global Fusion
Conference in Athens, Ohio, from September 30 to October 2, 2005 (Alzouma
2005). It examines the relationships between the state and the media in Niger
between 1960 and 2008. Two important periods are distinguished: the period
after 1960, characterized by the state monopoly on media and framed by the
ideology of nation-building, and the period after 1990 corresponding to the
institutionalization of democracy, the advent of new information and
communication technologies (ICTs), and the diversification of media. In
contrast with the earlier period, many authors (Grossman, 1995; Browning and
Weitzner, 1996; Beacham, 1997; Ott, 1998; Norris, 2001; Clift, 2002) have
argued that the use of ICTs will foster democratic participation, weaken the state
control over media and citizens, and expand civic engagement, particularly in
African countries. This optimistic view is based on the idea that ICTs are
facilitating everybody's participation in the globalization process of the
information age because they are erasing traditional barriers and categories of
race, ethnicity, class, and culture. ICTs are said to be empowering individuals
and groups by giving them the possibility to challenge the state control and by
rendering meaningless physical constraints attached to face-to-face interaction
(O'Brien, 1999). It is believed that people denied information can have access to
it and thus are "empowered" as to the ways to pose and solve their problems.
The Internet also is said to be uniting communities in diaspora, helping them
create a new sense of identity. Online activism is a growing form of political
activism (Schwartz, 1996; Dartnell, 2006) and many scattered or persecuted
people throughout the world now are using the Internet to maintain and defend
their culture and community (Castells, 1997; Eriksen, 2007). In sum, the
Information Age is presented as an era of freedom, self-expression, and endless
possibilities, even for disadvantages communities that are marginalized and
denied political participation.

Journalists, political authorities, international aid agencies, civil society
activists, and human rights advocates all share this highly techno centrist
"ideology" centered around the "developmentalist," "participative," and
"transformational" role of new ICTs.

In this paper, I challenge this irenic and utopian view of technology. I argue
that the preexisting social and political relations between groups and individuals,
marked by inequality and differential access to power, are not suddenly erased

by the use of ICTs. Community participation is not fostered suddenly by access to ICTs and the political landscape does not change because people now are using computers and cell phones. Instead of expanding community participation and civic engagement, the use of new ICTs can mask new forms of state control and consolidate the positions of those who already control the power and economic resources.

Methodologically, I adopt a historical perspective that seeks to demonstrate how current use of ICTs by political leaders and authorities prolongs the previous forms of social control. I contrast the period between 1960 and 1990 and the period after 1990 by demonstrating how the political leaders adapted quickly to the new situation marked by the advent of democracy and new information and communication technologies. I analyze the content of the political parties' websites, the differential use of ICTs by different social groups, and the activities of civil society members in order to show how political competence is distributed unequally and how this results in unequal possibilities for actors to reshape the political landscape.

My paper takes place within the framework of the "structural constructivist" theory devised by Bourdieu (1977; 1991), in which the political field is one in which agents occupying different positions also are engaged in a struggle to change "the vision of social divisions" (Bourdieu, 1989) and therefore the social world itself. Those agents are endowed unequally with the capacity to use technology and therefore the capacity to reshape the political field. In this perspective, what is happening in the real social world helps explain the use and representations of ICTs (such as associated to democracy), not technological determinism.

I. Media in Niger

For more than 30 years, there were only a handful of media in Niger. These were the local broadcasting agency, ORTN (Office de Radio Diffusion et Télévision du Niger), the local television, Télé Sahel, and of course the local newspaper, Le Sahel formerly known as Le Temps du Niger under the regime of Diori Hamani (1960-1974). They all were properties of the state and "voices" of the government. No other private or independent media were allowed in the country, which, from 1960 to 1991, experienced three dictatorial regimes. Then, in July 1991, a National Conference was convened that marked the beginning of an era of democratization. The media landscape changed rapidly, and, in less than 10 years, a multitude of independent newspapers, private broadcasting companies, and televisions appeared, making freedom of expression and plurality of opinions an apparent reality.

However, although the media now enjoy an era of relative freedom, their relationships with the state remain very difficult and are marked by the historical legacy of dictatorship.

1.1. Media and Nation-building

From 1960 to 1990, the relationships between the state and media were framed by the ideology of nation-building. The notion of nation-building, in the context of francophone Africa, could be understood only in reference to the psychological and mental dispositions created by the French policy of "assimilation," which amounted to the amalgamation of diverse ethnic groups into one "nation," the rejection of all forms of expression of ethnicity, and the creation of a Jacobin state.[1] In this sense, the nation is a forged category into which natives were to be forced by the way of an amalgamation of the "ethnics" (French word for ethnic groups), which themselves were conceived on its model. For the nation to emerge in the place of the "ethnics," all differences were to be negated and "ethnics" were to disappear. Thus, "ethnics" became a kind of abnormal elements of the system, jeopardizing the move toward universal mixing and the birth of a citizen without particularistic ties.

Accordingly, constitutional laws banished any political use of ethnicity. Cultural expressions of group belonging were discouraged and any form of ethnic organization forbidden. The key concept was national unity, and differences were seen as threatening this unity. National identity was to replace the multiple ethnic identities, which had to be molded into one nation.

In this perspective, the media were conceived as the media of the state, and no independent press or radio were allowed. Along with nation-building, the notions of "development communication" and "development journalism" emerged as a framework for media activities. The press was co-opted and was to reflect only governmental positions and government activities. The journalists themselves were considered as civil servants, paid by the government to promote government policy and the mobilization and participation of citizens to the objectives of development. Radio and television were the main instruments of the state in this perspective (Charlick, 1991; Martin, 1991; Kimba, 2008).

1.2. Radio and Television

Since most people in Niger were illiterate or could not have access to print paper because of its cost, radio appeared to be the only medium within the reach of rural populations. It also was the only one that could reach them effectively because of its cheap cost, its user-friendly character, and its range, even in the remotest and most inaccessible areas. That is why, even today, one barely can find a family or a household without a radio, in the same way that one cannot imagine the daily existence of a European or American household without a refrigerator or a washing machine. Almost every home displays radios among other domestic objects. As soon as you enter one of those huts where the vast majority of Niger's population still lives today, you are likely to find a radio.

The first radio in Niger, Radio Niger, renamed La Voix du Sahel in 1974, was created in 1958. It has autonomous regional stations and many relays that cover all of Nigerien territory. Additionally, it broadcasts in French and in the eight other Nigerien languages. Formerly known as Radio Niger, La Voix du Sahel has played an important political and ideological role in Niger's history. It served primarily for dictatorial governments to maintain control under the guise of building a national identity and creating and reinforcing national unity in the multiethnic context of Niger. It also served to legitimize government's actions and to prepare Nigeriens' entry into what was called "the modern world." Because of the monopoly exercised by the government on access to radio, every program had to reflect its objectives and expectations. Thus, all aspects of the country's situation that could give an unfavorable image of the government to the outside world were carefully avoided in press and radio reports.

However, it also was an important source of entertainment, news, and information, and an indispensable tool for the emergence of a Nigerien identity. It was a door open to the outside world, providing the possibility to connect to distant foreign radios and international channels. Above all, it participated in the development of local cultures through various programs aired in local languages, as well as in the changing of attitudes and behaviors.

With the democratization era, although La Voix du Sahel, the national broadcasting company, continues to dominate the media landscape, broadcasting is expanding outside of governmental control.

Since 1994, there have existed many private broadcasting companies, almost all of them operating in Niamey. Some also have relays in the principal regional capitals of the country (Maradi, Zinder, Diffa, and Tahoua) and represent, at the local level, international stations such as BBC (British Broadcasting Corporation, through which Hausa programs are widely listened to among Nigerien populations), RFI (Radio France Internationale which too has now a Hausa service and programs), the Voice of America, and the Voice of Germany (which also has some programs in Hausa). In contrast with the deterioration of the written private press, private radio stations seem in full expansion.

As for television, the oldest and most-known operator remains the state-owned Télé Sahel, which covers most of the national territory, thanks to a network of 13 stations. Télé Sahel also has a complementary public initiative: an autonomous television production and diffusion that covers Niamey under the label of TAL-TV. Apart from these, there exist at least three other private television stations in Niger: Ténéré TV, TV Dounia, and Bonferey TV. They all broadcast successfully in the capital and its surroundings. Another private operator, Télé Star, gives access in and around the capital to a bouquet of many international chains of television, including TV5, Canal Horizon, CFI, RTL9,

CNN, or Euro News. It goes without saying that in Niger today, as in most countries, one easily can access any international channel through satellite television; this is a daily fact for many households.

Television was introduced to the public in Niger in 1978 (actually the first televisions date back to 1964 and were introduced as "educational television") and has become, for most urban households, a familiar domestic object. Until recently, its possession provided its owner a kind of prestige and indicated a somewhat high status. It also was a sign of modernity. This no longer is the case. Today, in urban areas, television participates in the notion of "home-building"; it is one of the first devices that recently married couples hastily acquire because each home is expected to display a television as one of the "indispensable" domestic objects. It is no exaggeration to say that television, as in developed countries, is infused with social meanings in a Nigerien context and participates in the creation, along with other familiar domestic objects, of a Nigerien urban sense of "feeling at home," in the way Lally (2002) understands this. It has gained an important place in families' projects, in the way they project themselves in the future and envisage their posterity.

The state's former monopoly on television is being challenged by opposition parties and civil society's demands for access to media, as well as by the creation of private stations and access to international channels through satellite.

1.3. The Independent Press

Like many francophone African countries, Niger formally declared freedom of press and independence of the media in the early 1990s. Many people saw in this formal declaration an era of gradual emancipation of the press, an era of a growing "autonomization" of the field of media.

Now, many years later, the situation appears more complex and one may wonder if the era of democracy corresponded to an actual freedom of the press for the following reasons. First, notwithstanding the existence of democracy, the state did not waive its intent to exert its hegemony over the media sector (Panapress, 2008; Committee to Protect Journalists, 2008). Secondly, with the liberalization of the media, the job market soon was fueled with journalists who were not salaried by the state, whose working conditions were precarious, and who depended – to provide for their means of livelihood – on subsidies related to advertising or the patronage of politicians.

This precarious condition of the press can be seen in the ephemeral character of numerous newspaper titles that have been created during this period. Just between 1991 and 2001, fifty newspaper titles became available in Nigerien kiosks (Boluvi, 2001). However, some of them did not last longer than one or a few months, essentially because running an independent press is difficult in a country where readers are only a few thousands and often do not have enough money to buy a newspaper. Because of that, fewer than twenty newspapers manage to publish regular editions. The most-known and most-read of them, are Le Canard Déchaîné, Le Républicain, or La Roue de l'Histoire. They have 2,000 to 3,000 readers, but probably far more than that because newspaper readership here is mostly collective. They usually are run by former young students who find in the creation of a newspaper a way to escape unemployment, or freelance journalists equipped only with their university training, sometimes in disciplines that have nothing to do with communication (Boluvi, 2001). They are not well-paid (half of them earn less than 180 euros (less than US$180) a month, according to Boluvi's study, and must have recourse to "supplemental work" outside journalism to make their living. This usually involves offering their services and "voices" to some local politician who finances them to have his political interests defended in the journal. Boluvi states: "The enemy of private publishers is the generalized financial crisis within the country and poor management, not to say absence of management or refusal to manage. Except for Le Républicain and Le Démocrate, rare are the newspaper owners who make it their duty to pay journalists salaries. In Niger, when politicians call journalists 'food journalists' and their press organizations 'food press,' it is not an empty accusation" (Boluvi, 2001, p.4).

In Niger journalists essentially are freelance journalists, paid informally, irregularly, with sums that vary according to the journals and what directors of publication want to pay. Most of them, therefore, are ready to "sell their pens" or to become "praise singers," all expressions used by common Nigeriens to describe them.

No newspaper owner can rely on sales alone to keep his publications afloat because only a tiny part of the population can read: according to the United Nations Development Program Report for 2007/2008 (p. 226), the literacy rate (the percentage of people aged 15–24 who can, with understanding, both read and write a short, simple statement related to their everyday life) in Niger is among the four lowest in the world. It stood at 28.7 percent in 2005; thus, an estimation of an overall illiteracy rate of 71.3 percent. Therefore, newspapers cannot count on their readership to survive and advertising, when it exists, becomes the only recourse. Only the government's daily Le Sahel and its weekly Le Sahel Hebdo are well-financed, being fueled by the state, but their quality is very mediocre and for many readers not worthy of attention.

As discussed by Accardo et al. (2007), this growing "precarization" of journalists' condition has: a significant impact on the production of the information because it installs more than ever journalists in a mercantile state of mind set which induces a commercial view of their activity and largely determines their survival in this profession (2007, p. 489).

It also induces an atmosphere of a "war of the trenches" between journalists or supporters and opponents of the state or corrupt politicians who seek to destroy the image of those of the "other side" by the permanent use of a language of shame and fabricated scandals. This is what Thompson (2000) called the "opprobrious language." The opprobrious language creates a context of distrust for the state and the rulers of the country. That is why the government regularly accuses private journalists of undermining Nigerien unity and essentially working for the opposition parties. The accusations are not entirely false. As stated by Nyamnjoh (2005): If private press and private radio stations of Africa are often independent and critical of government, they have not always succeeded in displaying a similar attitude vis-à-vis the opposition or other pressure groups and lobbies (ethnic, religious, and regional). Thus, instead of seeking to curb intolerance, fanaticism and extremism of all kinds in accordance with the logic of liberal democracy, some of the media have actually fueled them. Examples abound of newspapers...that have served as mouthpieces for divisive forces, often reproducing calls to murder (Radio des Mille Collines), destruction and hatred, and generally keeping everyone fearful of a Rwanda-type situation (Nyamnjoh, 2005, p. 56).

However, some attempts have been made to foster a peaceful cohabitation of media and political authorities. In 1992, all interested parties convened a conference with the aim to devise new legislation in favor of freedom of the press. Freedom of the press and freedom of expression were legalized and a superior communication council, whose role was to act as a regulatory organ between the state and the media, was created. However, the existence of the Superior Communication Council did not result in the end of the conflictual relationship between the state and the media. To the contrary, the CSC (Conseil Supérieur de la Communication) often has been accused of siding with the government and many reworking of the laws have been called for by the opposition parties as well as journalists. As stated by Boluvi, "The new legal code on information that arose from the reworking of the 1993 texts not only installed new relations of suspicion and distrust between the authorities and the press, it also created new offenses and alterations in the status of media businesses and their staff and introduced new mechanisms of repression for press misdemeanors" (Boluvi, 2001, p.5). The main complaint of the press today is that the slightest investigation or inquiry about any suspicious activity of any member of the government or otherwise powerful politician or businessman usually results in journalists being sued, newspapers suspended, and heavy penalties and long prison terms inflicted (Panapress, 2008; Committee to Protect Journalists, 2008).

In this perspective, many journalists, activists, exiled political opponents, and communities in diaspora are increasingly hailing and using the new information and communication technologies to escape the state repression and political control. Along with the press, private radios, and televisions, ICTs are viewed as the new panacea for the exercise of political freedom and empowering tools for civic engagement and democratic changes.

II. ICTs and the Expansion of Civic Engagement

As in all countries worldwide, the use of information and communication technologies is growing rapidly in Africa and Niger (ITU, 2004; 2007; INS and PNUD 2009). Seemingly, political actors are using the Internet and cell phones more and more to display their programs, or to fight their opponents. For example, since the beginning of 2007, two rebel movements led by Tuareg insurgents have been fighting the government on both the military front and the virtual front. They are active on existing virtual networks such as discussion forums and online media web sites, and have created their own web sites and chat rooms. In the name of national unity and peaceful development, they are being countered by the state, as well as other citizens of the diaspora. (Alzouma 2009). In the same way, civil society organizations and international NGOs are promoting the use of ICTs to foster development, good governance, democracy, and political participation. Human rights advocacy groups in particular found in the ICTs a way to expand their campaigns in order to redefine the relations between the state and citizens (notably through the Nigerien Réseau des Journalistes pour les Droits de l'Homme (RJDH)-Network of Journalists for Human Rights). Some groups of media activists, such as Alternative group members, have placed the ICTs at the center of their efforts to foster democratic governance in Niger. The main goal is to promote the "democratization of access to the Internet" (RJDH web site: www.rjdh-Niger.org), and to help the greatest possible number of people have access to the Internet through training and also through the implementation of a cybercafé they call "point d'accès communautaire" (community access point). Alternative also has created an audiovisual production unit that aims to produce "documentaries for the campaigns of mobilization and advocacy of the civil society" (Alternative web site: www.alternativeniger.org).

Besides, various Nigerien newspapers have seized the opportunity to expand their readership beyond the national borders by making themselves accessible online. On the web sites of Tamtaminfo.com and Baobabinfo.com, it is possible to read most of the Nigerien newspapers online, as well as have access to various private radios and televisions. This corresponds not only to a diversification of the forms under which information is made accessible, but also to a diversification of the readership. More importantly, spatial and temporal constraints, coupled with financial obstacles that always have kept the African press in a marginal locus of the international media, now can be overcome.

Also, many political parties have set up web sites to make themselves known by their citizens and to spread their programs and ideologies. This is the case for the PNDS, (Parti Nigérien pour la Démocractie et le Socialisme-Nigerien Party for Democracy and Socialism: http://pnds-tarayya.net), the CDS Rahama, (Convention Démocratique et Sociale-Democractic and Social Convention: www.cdsrahama.org), the MNSD (Mouvement National pour la Société de Développement-Nigerien Movement for the Development Society:

www.mnsd-nassara.org), or the new-born Mouvement des Patriotes Nigériens–
Matassa (http://partidesjeunes.unblog.fr), etc. These web sites also fulfill another
function: they help present these political parties as engaged in "modernity" and
modern, technological solutions to development problems. Thus, on the web site
of the PNDS, the main information presented includes news concerning the
activities of the party; speeches of the leader; lists of national representatives,
mayors, and other elected officials members of the party; foundational texts of
the party; leaders of the diverse organizations affiliated to the party, etc.
Seemingly, the Convention Démocratique et Sociale, the third most important
political party in Niger after the governmental MNSD-Nassara and the opposing
PNDS-Tarraya, has set up an almost identical web site on which the main links
are related to the "life of the party," the party constitution texts, the composition
of the political bureau, and a "tribune" where militants can express their ideas.
On all of the above-mentioned web sites, a disproportionate place has been
reserved, in the texts and the news, for the party leadership, which appears to be
the central point from which everything is organized.

For its part, the government, in 2003, drafted a "National Plan for the
Development of Information and Communication Infrastructures" or Plan
National pour le Développement des Infrastructures en matière de Technologies
de l'Information et de la Communication (NICI). The NICI plan, designed with
the collaboration of the United Nations Economic Commission for Africa
(UNECA), was launched in 2002. It has been conceived as part of a wider
national policy for the fight against poverty and efforts aimed at giving access to
basic social services to low-income populations. NICI proceeds from the
following vision: "The appropriation and generalization of ICTs in Niger will
contribute, around 2008, to reduce poverty significantly. All social classes will
have access to information and the knowledge necessary to take part in the
democratic process and to develop their cultural and economic heritage" (my
translation) (Haut Commissariat a l'Informatique et aux Nouvelles Technologies
de l'Information et de la Communication, 2003; p.12). The development of
contents, empowerment through the use of ICTs, and e-government are the main
aspects of this policy.

As it appears above, journalists, civil society activists, and the government
all share the idea that ICTs are tools for democratic participation and
empowerment. This is part of a highly technocentrist "ideology" centered on the
"developmentalist" and "transformational" role of new ICTs that is strongly
endorsed by international development agencies. These views tend to associate
the Internet, computers, and cell phones with development, "modernity," and
futurity. In this perspective, being connected becomes an idealized model of life.
It is proof that the society is "integrated' into the "global" modern world. Of
course, one of the perceived features of that "global world" is technological
democracy, or the promotion and use of technology in the public interest.

However, the extent to which the full significance of e-government, as linked to good governance, is understood by the Nigerien political authorities is questionable. For example "open government," one of the major goals new technologies are supposed to achieve in democracies, still is far from being realized in Niger. "Open government" is defined as follows by the Center for Democracy and Technology, an influential organization that "works to promote democratic values and constitutional liberties in the digital age": "The public has the right to know about information collected, disseminated, and maintained by the government in order to increase accountability and public awareness." (CDT web site, www.cdt.org). It is well known that secrecy and lack of accountability are the major characteristics of most African dictatorial governments. Over the course of the last 10 years, Amnesty International, various human rights advocacy groups and NGOs, as well as the civil society and the media in the country, all have constantly denounced the various abuse, corruption, and lack of accountability in Niger (Committee to Protect Journalists, 2008).

It does not seem that the government has done anything to improve this situation based on the use of ICTs. Although the government has implemented its own web site (http://www.presidence.ne/) it does not give access to any official document and no interactive tool has been created that would help citizens act as interpellators of the government and to receive useful responses in return. What we are offered is the usual top-down approach: official news such as it emanates from the government; official receptions of ambassadors; the president's speeches; the various development projects carried out by the government, as well as the activities carried out by...the First Ladies! Therefore, the irenic view of ICTs as tools for liberation that can help cross over not only the physical and natural constraints, but also the political constraints (particularly authoritarian control) is far from true.

Seemingly, to evaluate the effect of technology on democracy in Niger, we can calibrate the content of the various political parties' web sites against the three main benefits that ICTs are supposed to bring to democratic life: rapid access to information, increased political participation, and more direct interaction between the governed and the rulers (Rodota, 1999). Of these three functions, it appears clear that only the first one is being pursued by the Nigerien political parties on their web sites in a rather biased and misleading top-down approach. None of those parties indicates, for example, an e-mail address that may help citizens convey their preoccupations to the parties' leadership and to receive responses. None of them installed an online forum in which the militants and other citizens can freely discuss political issues and other issues of public interest. People who visit those web sites cannot make any kind of suggestion or offer new ideas to the parties in order to enrich political debates. The parties, in turn, cannot have any indication of how public opinion is judging their positions on various issues of national interest because no survey tool (even informal) exists on the web sites that can evaluate public reception of the parties' ideas.

Traditional media have been criticized for the unilateral and unidirectional aspect of the messages they deliver, and the Internet has been hailed for making possible the participation of users. However, Nigerien political parties and political authorities are using the Internet with the same mindset they had in the era of radio and television: The party "informs" and citizens have no way to influence or control the political leaders' ideas or actions. We can show this through an analysis of the Nigerien Government's website (http://www.presidence.ne) and the presidential political party's website (www.mnsd-nassara.org):

The upper part of the Nigerien government's website is composed of three lines reading: Présidence de la République du Niger (Niger Republic Presidency), the country's motto, Fraternité, Travail, Progrès (Brotherhood, Work, and Progress), and the country's flag. Under this we find three columns: the left side column highlights the presidential activities, the government's important projects and programmes, the news, and the activities of the First Ladies. We also find links for past elections, some publications such as the Constitution of the country or a report from the National Committee of Human Rights, and various links and archives. The middle column is entirely devoted to the news related to the presidential activities, which are updated as they unfold. The right side column presents from top down, a map of the country, the symbols of the Niger Republic, the different institutions of the country, the main texts such as the constitution, the political parties' charter, the electoral code, etc. and a list of the former presidents of the country. As for the MNSD Nassara's website, the upper part presents the name and the logo of the party. Under this line we find three columns presenting, from the left side to the right side, news related to the party's activities, and links to speeches, political texts, etc. The middle column is completely empty and the left column highlights the photographs of the two main leaders of the party: the president and the secretary general.

As can be seen, the parties' leadership conceived the ICTs as "informative" and completely played down their interactive character. With regard to the use of ICTs, no difference exists between the MNSD and the opposition parties which websites appear to be almost interchangeable with each other. More importantly, the reality on the social ground appears even more disenchanting and, for the people of Niger, the obstacles hindering the path toward e-governance are numerous. They range from problems related to literacy to political competence. These the issues are mostly related to access.

2.1. The Access Issue

The first issue Nigerien people are facing in their use of ICTs is unequal access to information technologies. Cost and illiteracy are obvious obstacles to the use of ICTs, in particular computers. According to the ITU (2007), in 2007, Niger had only 0.03 Internet subscribers for 100 inhabitants and 0.28 users per 100 inhabitants. Of course, most of users are concentrated in urban settings. Things are quite different when it comes to cell phones. The spread of cell phones has been very rapid because of their relatively low cost as compared to computers, but also because they do not require literacy. A recent study of the INS (Institut National de la Statistique-National Institute of Statistics) and the PNUD (Programme des Nations Unies pour le Développement-UNDP-United Nations Program for Development) (2009), indicates that, out of fifteen million Nigeriens, more than 1.3 million aged 15 or more (or 20 percent of the entire population) use cell phones. In 2005, the percentage of users was only 4.6 percent. For a country that is said to be one of the poorest, if not the poorest, in the world, the pace of adoption of the mobile phone obviously is impressive. However, important disparities exist between the different regions of the country. Niamey, the capital city with 57.8 percent of users, and Agadez, a notorious tourist destination, with 54.1 percent, are the regions where the use of cell phone is the most important. Regions such as Maradi and Zinder count only for 11 percent of users. There also are disparities between sexes, since women account for only 12.8 percent of users who "frequently" use cell phones while men account for 28.2 percent. Besides, 52.2 percent of people living in urban settings use cell phones while this figure is only 13 percent for those living in rural areas (INS and PNUD 2009).

Therefore, with regard to democratic participation, it appears that those who have limited access to the new information and communication technologies also are limited in their political activities. They can be increasingly marginalized as large parts of political activities are being progressively undertaken through ICTs. As stated by Papacharissi (2002), "Moving political discussion to a virtual space excludes those with no access to this space" (2002, p. 13). This exclusion is aggravated by the unequal ability to read, understand, and process information using digital means, namely literacy and digital literacy in particular.

2.2. Illiteracy and Digital Illiteracy in Particular

In a country such as Niger, where more than 70 percent of the population is illiterate, the limited effects of computers appear obvious, particularly when it comes to empowering citizens to "take matters in their hands." For example, only the most active and educated of them can participate in text message campaigns, online social networks, or citizen media networks. Not only do citizens have a differential access to ICTs but there also appears to be a differential use of ICTs, a split in the modalities of use. Beyond the digital divide, the gap between the haves and the have-nots that characterized the early years of the information age, we now have a gap in the capacity to use ICTs coupled with a differential level of political competence. People who lack the skills to use computers can be said to be digital illiterates whose capacity "to develop new social and economic opportunities for themselves, their families, and their communities" (Microsoft Digital Literacy Home website, www.microsoft.com) is seriously limited. The gap in digital literacy introduces a split in the society between those who are able to use computers for their own benefits and those who find themselves diminished, incapacitated, and paralyzed by the new socio-technological landscape. I will illustrate this situation through the case of the Nigerian diaspora, one of the most active users of ICTs as compared to other groups of citizens.

2.3. ICTs and the Nigerien Diaspora

A large part of the Nigerian diaspora comprises people who migrate seasonally from Niger to other African countries, particularly Nigeria, Cote d'Ivoire, Ghana, Togo, and Benin. These migrants mostly are rural and illiterate peasants. Instead of computers, they mostly use cell phones and almost solely for communication purposes. The other component of the Nigerian diaspora is urban educated young people, most of them students but also workers who migrate in Europe, particularly France and Belgium and recently in the USA and Canada. There is a clear distinction in the ways these two categories of Nigerian migrants use ICTs. Students and young workers in Europe and the USA not only use the cell phone but they use it differently, in a more diverse and sophisticated manner: for example to enjoy music, to send text messages, or to surf on the Internet (Alzouma, 2008). They also are involved heavily in online activities such as Nigerian online forums, particularly Tamtaminfo.com, Agadez Niger.com, and other international francophone African and black diaspora forums such as Grioo.com or Africamaat.com. They use chatting groups and read online newspapers (on the web site of Nigerdiaspora.com, more than 35 Nigerian newspapers are accessible online). Some of them have set up blogs and carry out online political activities (the MNJ, a Tuareg-led rebellion, in Niger has set up, since its inception, a web site that disseminates its propaganda: m-n-j.blogspot.com).

These students and Diaspora workers have played an important role in the promotion and the diffusion of information and communication technologies in Niger. In this perspective, they have set up many active online groups, such as the Group Internet-Niger, the RJDH, the Internet Society-Niger, the *Association Nigérienne des Professionnels de l'Informatique,* the *Association Nigéerienne pour Linux et Logiciels Libres,* etc. The members of those groups are mostly young, educated, and working in international development organizations,

NGOs, or the government. They share a set of dispositions and worldviews that are highly "modernist" and "technocentrist." Their cultural backgrounds, as well as their social capital, lead to their propensity to act in favour of technological solutions to development problems, including democracy and governance problems.

2.4. ICTs and Political Competence

The above-mentioned fraction of the Nigerien diaspora not only is digitally literate, but it also is politically competent. Therefore, it can use digital technology to foster its social or political agendas. On the contrary, the other components of the Nigerien diaspora – those who are mostly illiterate, mostly use cell phones, and have very limited digital skills – also appear to be less politically competent. They share this lack of political competence with the largest part of other citizens. It follows that the determining factor in civic engagement and democratic participation does not reside in the availability, access, or use of digital technologies; rather, it is the already acquired political competence that determines the use of technology.

Therefore, the idea that it would suffice to equip people with cell phones and computers to boost civic engagement and democratic participation minimizes the importance of the preexisting social conditions and the different political aptitudes with which diverse groups of people, occupying diverse positions in the social and political landscape, are endowed with. People are not "naturally," "spontaneously" politically competent in such a way that we could say technology would help expand an already existing political capacity. In the case of countries such as Niger, not only are most people illiterate, but they also lack the level of information and knowledge that can make them citizens capable of making responsible political decisions in their own interests and in the interest of the community. The political impediments of African citizens have been abundantly documented and analyzed: exclusion of women from the political sphere; ethnic or "tribal" vote; clientelism and the heavy influence of traditional rulers all are obstacles to true democratic participation. This means that the way technology is going to be used is not to be found in the possibilities offered by the technological devices themselves but rather in the preexisting social and political conditions that determine the technological behavior of the agents.

Thus, against the presupposed idea of a rational choice, we should oppose Bourdieu's idea of political competence (1991) that determines participation as well as nonparticipation in the public sphere. Indeed, the ability to play in the field of politics, as well as the ability to make political choices compatible with one's interests in the field, is related closely to the ability to convey a specific form of cultural capital. In this perspective, the dispositions "cultivated" in individuals and groups, their habitus (which, in the boudieusian language refers to the set of dispositions and habits that determine an individual's behaviors and attitudes), along with the opportunities offered to them in the social world, determine the degree of civic engagement and political participation they can perform. Technology does not guarantee their use of devices because ICTs have a double facet: they can help segregate as well disaggregate the foundations of existing societies. That is the issue we address in the following section.

2.5. The Two Facets of Technology

In their work about how technology affected Kenyan elections in 2007, Goldstein and Rotich conclude: "While digital tools can help promote transparency and keep perpetrators from facing impunity, they can also increase the ease of promoting hate speech and ethnic divisions" (2008, p.1). Also, as shown above by Nyamjoh, in most African countries, the tendency to serve ethnic and regional interests is pervasive in the private press. It is even more so on the Internet for diverse reasons. Because ICTs can help escape governmental censorship, they make possible the present expression of long-repressed tendencies in the context of French-inherited Jacobin states, particularly ethnic hatred. With the Internet and online forums, it becomes possible to disguise the origin of the messages as well as the identity of the person sending them. This creates a situation in which hate discourse easily can thrive. Abusive language and ethnocentric expressions are not uncommon on Nigerien online forums, particularly in discussions between the Tuareg diaspora and other Nigeriens on the Agadez-Niger.com forum.

Their impact, particularly on national politics, can be felt in the way contemporary national and identity issues are discussed in Niger. For example, in the case of the online activities of the Tuareg-led rebellions, it is obvious that the Tuareg diaspora is feeding Tuareg ethnonationalism in Niger and therefore heavily influencing the orientation of national debates and shaping identity issues and identity views through ICTs (Alzouma 2009). Indeed, ICTs have helped them expand their reach and their ties abroad, threatening the notion of "national unity" such as it always has been understood in Niger. For this reason, one can wonder if ICTs are "tools for integration or tools for segregation" (Kalathil, 2002) in the African democratic context.

Conclusion

The period between 1960, the era of independence, and 1990, the era of democratization processes, has been viewed and characterized as the period of nation-building ideologies and control over media and opinions in Niger. By the late 1990s and early 2000s, the advent of new information and communication technologies has generated the hope that it can become possible for African citizens who usually have been marginalized and kept away from the political arena to participate in decisions that affect them. However, evidence suggests

Media, Technology, and Democracy in Niger:
What Did the Advent of ICTs Change?

39

that civic engagement and political participation only have improved in a very limited way. Even in a seemingly democratic environment, state power and clientelism have persisted, coupled with social impediments such as illiteracy and differential use of technology. These, in turn, have had an effect on political competence and the degree to which Nigerien citizens can use ICTs to change political conditions.

Notes

1 The Jacobin state is the excessively centralized state inherited from the French Revolution and transposed in the French African colonial territories. It is based on universalistic and assimilationist principles (one nation, one language, one culture) and the indivisibility of the Republic.

REFERENCES

Accardo, A., Abou, G., Balbastre, G., Dabitch, C., & Puerto, A. (2007). *Journalistes précaires, Journalistes au quotidien.* Marseille : Agone.

Alzouma, G. (2005). The State and Media in Niger: 1960-2005. *Global Fusion Conference*, Athens, Ohio, September 30-October 2, 2005.

Alzouma, G. (2008). Téléphone Portable, Internet et Développement en Afrique: L'Afrique dans la Société de l'Information? *Revue TIC et Société*, 2 (2), 35-58.

Alzouma, G. (Forthcoming 2009). The State and the Rebel: Online Nationalisms in Niger. Journal of Contemporary African Studies, September 2009.

Beacham, F. (1997). *The Internet: Will it Become the Next Mass Media?* In: Media and Democracy: A Collection of Readings and Resources. Retrieved on January 15, 2008 from http://www.igc.apc.org/an/book/beacham7.html

Boluvi, G.M. (2001). *Media Status Report: Niger.* Retrieved on July 25, 2005 from http://www.gret.org/mediapartner/uk2/ressource/edm/pdf/ niger.pdf.

Bourdieu, P. (1977). *Outline of a Theory of Practice.* Cambridge and New York: Cambridge University Press.

Bourdieu, P. (1989). Social Space and Symbolic Power. *Sociological Theory* 7(1), 14-25.

Bourdieu, P. (1991). Political Representation: Elements for a Theory of the Political Field. In J.B. Thompson (Ed.). *Language and Symbolic Power* (pp. 171-202). Cambridge: Harvard University Press.

Browning, G. & Weitzner, D.J. (1996). *Electronic Democracy : Using the Internet to Influence American Politics.* Wilton: Pemberton Press.

Castells, M. (1997). *The Power of Identity, The Information Age: Economy, Society and Culture.* Vol II. Cambridge, MA; Oxford: Blackwell.

Charlick, R.B. (1991). *Niger: Personal Rule and Survival in the Sahel.* Boulder and San Francisco: Westview Press.

Clift, S. (2002). *The Future of E-Democracy-The 50 year Plan.* International World Futurist Society Conference. Retrieved on March 3, 2008 from http:// www.publicus.net/articles/future.html.

Committee to Protect Journalists. (2008). *Attacks on the Press in 2008 : Niger.* Retrieved on March 3, 2005 from http://cpj.org/2009/02/attacks-on-the-press-in-2008-niger.php

Dartnell, M. (2006). *Insurgency Online: Web Activism and Global Conflict.* University of Toronto Press.

Eriksen, T.H. (2007). Nationalism and the Internet. *Nations and Nationalism.* 13 (1). pp. 1-17.

Fleming, S. (2002). Information and Communication Technologies and Democracy Development in the South: Potential and Current Reality. *The Electronic Journal on Information Systems in Developing Countries,* 10(3):1-10. Retrieved on March 15, 2008 from http://www.ejisdc.org/ojs2/index.php/ejisdc/article/viewFile/56/56

Goldstein, J. & Rotich, J. (2008). Digitally Networked Technology in Kenya's 2007–2008 Post-Election Crisis. *Internet & Democracy Case Study Series at Harvard University.* Berkman Center Research Publication No. 2008-09.

Grossman, L.K. (1995). *The Electronic Republic: Reshaping Democracy in the Information Age.* New York: Viking.

Haut Commissariat à l'Informatique et aux Nouvelles Technologies de l'Information et de la Communication. (2005). *Plan NICI Niger.* Niamey : Bureau du Premier Ministre.

Institut National de la Statistique & Programme des Nations Unies pour le Développement. (2009). *Impact de la Téléphonie Mobile sur les conditions de vie des utilisateurs et des intervenants du marché : Rapport final.* Niamey : INS.

International Telecommunication Union (ITU). (2004). *African Telecommunication Indicators 2004.* Geneva: ITU

International Telecommunication Union (ITU). (2007). *Measuring the Information Society 2007: ICT Opportunity Index and World Telecommunication/ICT Indicators.* Geneva: ITU.

Kimba, I (Ed.). (2008). *Armée et Politique au Niger.* Dakar: Conseil pour le Développement de la Recherche en Sciences Sociales.

Kalathil, S. (2002). Community and Communalism in the Information Age. *Brown Journal of World Affairs.* Volume IX (1), 347-354. Retrieved on February 6, 2008 from http://www.watsoninstitute.org/bjwa/archive/9.1/Essays/Kalathil.pdf

Lally, E. (2002). *At Home with Computers.* Oxford: Berg.

Martin, F. (1991). *Le Niger du Président Diori : 1960-1974.* Paris : Harmattan.

Munoz, C. (2006). Internet et les partis politiques: quelle place réelle pour les citoyens?' *Les Enjeux de l'information et de la communication.* Retrieved on February 8, 2008 from http://www.u-grenoble3.fr/les_enjeux | 2005.

Norris, P. (2001). *Digital Divide: Civic Engagement, Information Poverty, and the Internet Worldwide.* Cambridge: Cambridge University Press.

Nyamnjoh, F.B. (2005). *Africa's Media: Democracy and the Politics of Belonging.* London and New York: Zed Books.

O'Brien, J. (1999). Writing in the body: Gender (re)production in online interaction. In Smith, M.A. & Kollock, P. (Eds.), *Communities in Cyberspace.* London and New York: Routledge.

Ott, D. (1998). Power to the People: The Role of Electronic Media in Promoting Democracy in Africa. *First Monday*, 3 (4 – 6). Retrieved on June 25, 2005 from   http://firstmonday.org/htbin/cgiwrap/bin/ojs/index.php/ fm/article/view/588/509

Panapress. (2008). Les médias privés dénoncent le muselage de la presse au Niger. Retrieved on January 8, 2008 from   http://www.afrik.com/ article15043.html

Rodotà S. (1999). *La Démocratie électronique. De nouveaux Concepts et expériences politiques*, Rennes : Apogée.

Schwartz, E. (1996). *NetActivism : How Citizens Use the Internet*. Cambridge, MA: O'Reilly Media.

Thompson, J.B. (2000). *Political Scandal: Power and Visibility in the Media Age*. Cambridge: Polity Press.

Chapter 3

Role of ICT in Election Coverage by the Nigerian Print Media: A Study of the 2007 General Elections

Solomon O. Akinboye and Ibitayo S. Popoola
University of Lagos, Nigeria

Abstract

Information Communication Technology (ICT) has emerged as the greatest human inventory of our time, exerting tremendous impact on news production and dissemination across the world. In Nigeria of yesteryear, messages were transmitted across the length and breadth of the community through interpersonal channels, such as the gong, folktales, festivals, mirrors, gunshots, town criers, wooden flutes, horns, drums etc.

These early communication technologies were deficient in a number of areas. According to Schramm (1972:28) "some factual news might be spread very rapidly while more complete information might be disseminated at a much slower pace and with great variety in repetition."

This paper therefore takes a look at the impact of ICT in election coverage in Nigeria with specific reference to the 2007 general elections.

The paper used the survey method in gathering information from senior journalists in the Nigerian print media. It arrives at the conclusion that ICT has assisted the Nigerian print media in reporting timely information to their audience.

INTRODUCTION

A renowned political thinker and statesman, Thomas Jefferson, once declared that were it left for him to decide whether "we should have a government without newspapers or newspapers without a government, we should not hesitate to prefer the latter" (Koch& Paden 1944:1 cited in Popoola 2003:45).

Jefferson made the declaration in a bid to stress the role of the media in any political community. There is no doubt that the relationship between the press and government is an interesting one. The government needs the media to get the people informed and the political parties equally require the media to sell their candidates and programmes to the electorate.

A fundamental driving force of the globalization phenomenon of the 21st century is Information Communication Technology (ICT). The revolution in computer technology has significantly led to the advancement of information transmission across the global system (Akinboye, 2007). Information and Communication Technology, within the context of our analysis, is simply a technological device which strengthened the ability of the media to efficiently and effectively carry out their professional and statutory duties.

This chapter provides an insight into the impact of ICT in reporting with special reference to election coverage in Nigeria. It demonstrates the impact of ICT in the discharge of the statutory and professional duties of the Nigerian print media, especially during elections.

Methodology

The study adopted the survey method in eliciting responses from senior editorial members of staff of reputable newspapers and magazines establishments in metropolitan Lagos. The choice of Lagos was informed by the fact that two-thirds of Nigerian media are located in the state (see Akinfeleye, 2003: 57).

Simple, open-ended questions were drawn up and administered on the respondents on their perception of the impact of ICT in election coverage. The study used an open-ended questionnaire of manageable size of the interviewees coupled with the need to provide them greater latitude to express themselves. Furthermore, the sampling frame was a size that could conveniently be handled through unstructured questions. The questionnaires were administered on 11 newspapers and five magazine establishments which have maximally explored ICT technology in reaching their target audience.

Research Questions

1. How has ICT redefined political reporting especially at election periods in Nigeria?

2. How has ICT affected the quality of photographs used by the print media?

3. Does ICT exert any impact on gathering and disseminating political stories?

4. What are the available ICT facilities for reporting in your medium?

5. Does ICT enhance the professional and statutory duties of the press with regards to painstaking dissemination of information of election results?

6. Does ICT portray a brighter or glooming future for the Nigerian print media?

7. Does the so-called Nigerian factor have any role to play in the sustenance of the current state of the art technological equipment being used in reporting?

Conceptual Clarifications

ROLE: This has to do with what members of the public expect from the Nigerian print media, especially with regard to dissemination of information about the various subterranean moves on the political terrain during election periods. Election times are critical periods when most people are always anxious to have the latest information about developments in the polity. It is generally assumed that any medium of mass communication which avails itself of the opportunities offered by ICT would always be ahead of its competitors when it comes to releasing timely or breaking news to the public.

ICT: One of the concepts which have attracted commentaries from academics in recent times is that of Information Communication Technology (ICT). While some abbreviate it as IT, others would rather prefer to call it Info Tech (Evans 1990: 77).

> *The term information Technology was first widely
> employed in 1981 to describe the equipment and
> system which were being introduced in both private and public
> sectors to create, store and distribute information.*

Talking about any device which could create, store, and distribute information, what readily comes to mind is computer. In the words of Mohammed (1990:9), "computer is the most pervasive of all the new communication technologies." Besides satellite, he states, "it is about the only device that has a hand in all the pies of communication: print, radio, television, telephone, fibre optic, film, photography, cinema, etc."

Scholars disagreed on the exact time when the computer started. Parker cited in Pool and Schramm (eds) (1973:620) and Popoola (2003:45) that it traced its origin to 3,500 BC when it was used as a simple adding machine. Pelton (1981:25) says the "oldest one that springs to mind is a Babylonian computer that dates from 1921 BC." Yet, Hofbaver (1990:22) asserts that "the history of computers can be traced roughly from the year 1812, when the English Mathematician, Charles Babbage, designed what he called a different machine which could automatically work out trigonometric and logarithmic function."

Newspaper: A newspaper is a periodic publication containing timely reports. According to Newson and Wollert(1988:74):

> *The newspaper is the medium 'of record.' It's what
> you consult to find out the most information about
> everything that happened on a certain date in that
> community and surrounding area. They provide
> clues that a reporter can investigate to find a story
> that was missed.*

In other words, just as a newspaper offers information on happenings in a political community, the medium also provides the lead, which reporters could pursue for publication. Tracing the origin of the name, Uyo (1987:6) says:

> *There is a French word, **nowelles**, which, through imitation in
> Middle English, became newes. The French also have a word
> papier, derived from the Latin word **papyrus**, the material on
> which people could write and print. Newes and papier
> together make up newspaper. More than 40 words you block.*

Based on frequency of publications, the following are types of newspapers in Nigeria; namely: Daily (published Monday–Friday i.e. weekdays), Weekend (published on Saturdays) and weekly (Published only on Sundays).

Magazine: Unlike newspapers, magazines are collection of various editorial materials, which are judged to be of interest to the reading public. Attempting a distinction between newspaper and magazine, DeFleur and Dennis (1981:148) say magazine "shows less concern for information on the immediate day's events and more for interpreting and correlating topics in a broader context." For this reason, Uyo (1987:10) says, "Magazines are a cross between books and newspapers"; on its origin, Uyo avers: "The word 'magazine' comes from the French word 'magasin' which in turn comes from the Arabic word 'mahkzan' meaning a general storehouse." Magazines could be published weekly, fortnightly, monthly, quarterly, and annually. However, the study focused on the weekly news magazines. In journalism or Mass Communication parlance, newspapers and magazines are known as print media because they involve the pressing of ink on paper.

Literature Review

The basic goal of "Political Reporting," especially at election periods, can be deduced from Article 22 of the 1999 Constitution of the Federal Republic of Nigeria, which stresses the obligation of mass media as that of upholding the "Fundamental Objectives" contained in Chapter II of the Constitution, as well as upholding the responsibility and accountability of the Government to the people. The "Fundamental Objectives," which are found on pages A 882 – 887 of the Constitution concerned among others, the Economic, Social, Educational, as well as Directive on Nigerian cultures.

Of special interest to this paper is the need for every media establishment in the country to identify with the political objectives of the state as contained in Article 15 (ii) of the Constitution which states that "accordingly, national integration shall be actively engaged whilst discrimination on the grounds of place of origin, sex, religion, status, ethnic or linguistic association or ties shall be prohibited."

A major way of the media demonstrating their unalloyed support to the realization of the political objective is by way of educating and enlightening the citizenry about what goes on in or around the government. This is what Sobowale (1986:111) calls "surveying the environment" or which Lasswell refers to as "correlating parts of the environment and transmitting culture."

The Nigerian media began to play these roles in 1859 when the first newspaper began courtesy of the pioneering efforts of British Missionary, Rev. Henry Townsend.

While newspapering began in 1859, election coverage by the print media could not start until 1922. According to Ezera (1960:30) the birth of electioneering politicking began following the adoption of Sir Hugh Clifford's 1922 Constitution. "The development led to an unprecedented political awakening. Political parties sprang up overnight and several newspapers commenced publication." The papers emerged in order to propagate the objectives of political parties vis-à-vis that of their founding fathers.

Leading nationalist leaders in Nigeria then, in a bid to propagate their visions established their own newspapers. Examples are Herbert Macaulay, who bought over Lagos Weekly Record from Thomas Horatio Jackson in 1891. He also took over the ownership of Lagos Daily News from Victor Bababunmi in 1926. The two papers supported fully his political party, the Nigerian National Democratic Party (NNDP).

There was also Eko Akete, owned by Deoye Deniga, which also supported the NNDP. Others are The Daily Telegraph and African Messenger owned by Ernest Ikoli which supported the political aspirations of the Union of Young Democrats. Late Dr Nnamdi Azikiwe and Chief Obafemi Awolowo were not left behind. They established the West African Pilot and Nigerian Tribune respectively.

This trend remains to date and has been identified as a major problem of partisanship by the media when it comes to reportage of political stories. Since 1954 when Nigeria began to conduct federal elections, election 2007 was the ninth in the series.

According to Popoola (2007:5) to date, federal elections have been conducted in Nigeria in the following years: 1954, 1959, 1964, 1979, 1983, 1993, 1999, 2003 and 2007.

The first election to be covered by the Nigerian Press after 1960 independence took place in 1964. However, assessing the performance of the media after independence Omu (1996:25) says:

> *The first few years of independence saw little change in the political style of the newspapers. Indeed, the struggle for power among the politicians assumed a new fury and the competing party newspapers advertised their fanaticism. The Action Group crisis of 1962, the census crisis of 1963-64and the Federal Elections of 1964 and its aftermath — the newspaper press provided a remarkable example of overzealous and irresponsible partisanship and recklessness.*

Events after the election confirmed Omu's assertion. According to Oyediran (1976:17):

The 1964/5 elections have often been referred to as a classic
case of the politics of brinkmanship. It was during the election
that the first plot for a military coup d'etat was planned.

Prior to the election, there was realignment of political forces, leading to the emergence of two major alliances, which contested the election. They are the Nigerian National Alliance (NNA) comprising the Northern Peoples Congress (NPC), Nigerian National Democratic Party (NNDP), Dynamic Party of Prof Chike Obi, and Mid-West Democratic Front. The second alliance was the United Progressive Grand Alliance (UPGA), which made up of the NCNC, AG, NEPU and UMBC. The result of the election was stalemated as a result of inability of allying parties to pull enough seats required to form government. During the election, the flash point of violence in the country was the Western Region; hence, Mackintosh (1966) cited by Popoola (2003:60) referred to the region as "the cockpit of the Nigerian Politics," particularly between 1962 and the time Military took over the reigns of government in 1966.

At the time of independence, politicians who were freedom fighters during the colonial days owned 98 percent of newspapers in the country.

The nationalist leaders established the newspapers to advance the struggle for political independence. Thus, at any slight disagreement between the political leaders, such disagreement would become top story on the pages of their newspapers. For instance, during the disagreement between the leader of the defunct Action Group (AG), late Chief Obafemi Awolowo and his deputy, late Chief Ladoke Akintola.

The Nigerian Tribune pitched its tent with its proprietor, Chief Awolowo. Stories concerning Chief Akintola would not only be a calculated attempt to ridicule him, but also to portray him in bad light to the public. For instance, Oyediran (1976:21) quoted one of the election speeches of Akintola as published by the Tribune, which for several years made alliance between the East and West difficult.

According to him, Akintola in an attempt to justify his preference for an alliance between the North and West told his supporters:

While the Northerners have a good exchange of commodities
in kolanuts and cows with the Yoruba, the Igbo have nothing
to offer the Yoruba except second hand clothing.

The Daily Sketch, a newspaper founded by Akintola while he was Premier of the region equally launched an offensive against royal fathers in the region who were perceived to be sympathizers of the AG. According to Popoola (2003:60):

> *About a month to the election, the government owned*
> *newspaper, The Daily Sketch warned, when an Oba takes it*
> *upon himself to oppose the Government, he has shown himself*
> *as an enemy of his people…*

Thus, Nigeria's first attempt at democratizing was short-lived due to overzealous, recklessness, unethical and irresponsible partisanship of the media as well as dissemination of poisonous campaign speeches.

PRESS COVERAGE OF THE 1979 SECOND REPUBLIC ELECTIONS

Following the collapse of the First Republic on January 15, 1966, the military held on to power until October 1, 1979 when Nigerians had another opportunity at democratic governance.

Five political parties contested the elections, namely: The National Party of Nigeria (NPN), Unity Party of Nigeria (UPN), Nigerian Peoples Party (NPP), Great Nigeria Peoples Party (GNPP) and Peoples Redemption Party (PRP).

At the conclusion of the election, NPN candidate Alhaji Shehu Shagari was declared the winner after serious controversy had trailed the results of the election as a result of what constituted two-thirds of 19 states. To Chief Awolowo, the UPN presidential candidate alleged that the defunct Federal Military Government under Gen. Olusegun Obasanjo (rtd) and the defunct Federal Electoral Commission (FEDECO) betrayed a historic assignment freely undertaken by them in favour of Alhaji Shehu Shagari. According to Ojo (1985:57):

> *Chief Awolowo in a detailed reply to General Obasanjo's*
> *letter showed that the Federal Military Government favoured*
> *Alhaji Shagari during the elections and also did all it could to*
> *see him win…*

While the crisis lasted, Awolowo mobilized his supporters through The Daily Sketch and Tribune to the extent that his supporters held the notion that Shagari "stole" the presidency.

Press Coverage of the 1983 General Elections

Notwithstanding DeFleur's 1970's modification of the Bullet or Hypodermic theory of the mass media, in which he punctuated the direct effect of media message with personality, attitude, intelligence, interests, etc., available evidence suggests that the violence which characterized the conduct of the 1983 polls can be best explained by the Bullet Theory and the Contagion effect. While the Bullet Theory assumes that people get information directly from the mass media and not through an intermediary and that reaction is individual, not based on how other people might influence them, the Contagion effect, according to Singer (1970) quoted by Popoola (2003:61) says:

> *The media variously can provoke a riot, create a culture of rioting, and provide lessons on how to riot, spread a disturbance from place to place... There is some evidence, even so, that the media can contribute by simply signalling the occurrence and location of a riot event.*

Electoral fraud, otherwise known as "rigging" was the main cause of the violence. According to Adamolekun (1985:74):

> *Judging by the violence and alleged electoral frauds that had characterized the preliminary electoral contests, there was widespread fear that serious violence and extensive rigging could mar the August/September elections. These fears became fulfilled prophecies. Law and order broke down completely in several states, with Ondo and Oyo states as the star cases that attracted international attention.*

According to him, "the official figure of 100 persons killed is widely believed to be less than in quarter of those who actually died in each of Ondo and Oyo states. This means that the total number of persons who lost their lives through electoral violence was close to 1,000; with wanton destruction of human lives and the extensive destruction of property in several states."

Particularly, mention must be made of the role played by the defunct FRCN, Akure and the state owned radio, Ondo State Broadcasting Corporation (OSBC).

While the FRCN was overtly drumming up support for Chief Akin Omoboriowo, the NPN gubernatorial candidate who was initially declared by FEDECO as winner of the governorship election with intermittent and regular playing of the record of Christy Essien's elpee titled "Give Peace A Chance," the Ondo State radio obviously supporting another candidate, late Chief Micheal Ajasin was also simultaneously playing the record of late Bob Marley titled "Get Up, Stand Up, Stand Up for Right."

As Singer (1970) earlier posited, the people decoded the message and instantly, took to the streets, attacking every identified members and leaders of the NPN. They did not spare their property as well. Some of the houses that were razed during the fracas are yet to be rebuilt to date.

The violence, which occasioned the conduct of the election, was therefore, one of the major reasons identified by the military for taken over the reign of government again on December 31, 1983.

Press Coverage of the Aborted June 12, 1993 Third Republic Elections

If there is any date that will remain evergreen in Nigerian political history, that date was June 12, 1993 – the day Nigerians from all walks of life defied ethnicity, religion, north-south dichotomy as well as other vices, which had seen Nigerians voting ethnic or religious lines in the past. It would be recalled that both the presidential candidate of the defunct Social Democratic Party (SDP), who was widely believed to have won the election, late Chief MKO Abiola, and his running mate, Ambassador Babagana Kingibe, were Muslims.

The election was not only peaceful, but also orderly throughout the federation. It is also on record that June 12 was the first election since independence in which a Nigerian party would win by a landslide in all the geo-political zones in the country.

However, the result of the election was annulled by self-styled Military President Gen. Ibrahim Babangida (rtd) on June 23, 1993, without any convincing logical reason. Following the annulment, sporadic riots and protests took place all over the country. The international community was not left out. Apart from expressing dismay, they also imposed wide-range sanctions on the country in protest.

The media kept on fighting for the de-annulment of the election until its presumed winner, late Bashorun MKO Abiola, died in detention in 1998.

Press Coverage of 1999 Fourth Republic Elections

During the 1999 elections, stakeholders were cautious based on the experiences of the past. That is however not to say that all the politicians demonstrated political maturity. Quoting a news report from TNT newspaper, an evening tabloid which circulated in Lagos, Ogun, Oyo and Osun states, Popoola (2004:196) picked on the choice of words of Chief Olusegun Obasanjo, then PDP Presidential candidate while addressing a political rally in Lagos where he told his supporters "to exchange fire for fire" if attacked by members of the AD." Such a story should have been watered down by the TNT newspaper, instead of going to town with its explosive headline – "Its fire for fire – Obasanjo."

However, controversy trailed the conduct of the elections as it became the object of litigation. The Alliance for Democracy (AD) and All Peoples Party

(APP) joint presidential candidate, Chief Olu Falae, challenged the result of the election, which gave victory to Chief Olusegun Obasanjo. He alleged, among other allegations, that the election was riddled by wide range electoral malpractices. However, the court dismissed his petition. The media helped significantly in persuading him through editorials and feature articles (among others) not to pursue the matter to the Supreme Court in order not to give the military any excuse not to handover power again on May 29, 1999 as scheduled.

The Media and the 2003 Elections

Wright, quoted by Uyo (1987:2) identified surveillance of the environment as one of the primary duties of the mass media, stressing that "it refers to the collection and distribution of information concerning events in the environment, both outside and within any particular society."

Thus, based on the professional mandate of the media, all activities leading to the conduct of the 2003 elections were adequately covered by the media. There were lots of violence reports across the country prior to the election, which took place between April 29 and May 3. In a special news report entitled "more violence, less campaign." The Punch newspaper notes.

> *One of the very prominent features of this campaign is electoral violence. The gubernatorial race is more notorious for this. From Kwara state to Delta state, Benue to Ogun and Enugu state to Bayelsa state, Political violence has become a recurring decimal* (Punch, March 2, 2003 cover story).

Press Coverage of the 2007 Elections

It is instructive to note that of all the nine general elections so far held in Nigeria, the 2007 was the only election in which ICT was optimally used at all the stages of election process, i.e., reporting built up stories to the elections, reporting campaign by the political parties and dissemination of stories about election results. Details are in the subsequent section of this paper.

Theoretical Framework

This study is anchored on the Libertarian Media Theory, otherwise known as the Free Press Theory. According to McQuail, "This relabelled version of Siebert et al's Libertarian Theory has its origin in the emergence of the printing press from official control in the seventeenth century and is now widely regarded as the main legitimating principle for print media in liberal democracies" (McQuail, 1987:112).

The main gist of the theory is that "the press functions to uncover and present truth to the people, operating chiefly as a private enterprise, and without government control" (Blake and Haroldsen, 1975:95). The philosophy of the theory is situated within the context of the ideas of renowned writer Milton, and philosopher, John Locke (among others) that man has the right to pursue truth and that truth is best advanced when there is an open marketplace of ideas. Quoting Milton, Folarin says, "Central to this theory was Milton's idea of the self-rightening process of the free market-place of ideas that good would drive out bad ones if all ideas were guaranteed free expression" (Folarin, 1998:26).

Of special interest to this paper are five of the eight-point principles of free press listed by Wintour (1973) quoted by McQuail (1987:115-116) that:

- Publication should be free from any prior censorship by any third party

- There should be no compulsion to publish anything.

- No restriction should be placed on the collection, by legal means, of information for publishing.

- There should be no restriction on export or import or sending or receiving "messages" across national frontiers.

- Journalists should be able to claim a considerable degree of professional autonomy within their organization.

Aside from these principles, McQuail further contends that "free press theory would seem to need no elaboration beyond such a simple statement as contained in the First Amendment to the American Constitution, which states that congress shall make no law... abridging the freedom of speech or of the press."

Unarguably, the free press theory exists to check excesses of government; however, the truth of the matter is that freedom to publish is not a license to defame, indulge in unbridled obscenity, invade privacy of individuals, or publish seditious stories. As a matter of fact, the free press theory does not advocate press immunity to the rule of law and cannons of civilized social conduct (Ibid., 114). A semblance of this could be found in Article 22 of the Nigerian 1999 Constitution which states that: The press, radio, television and other agencies of the mass media shall at all times be free to uphold the fundamental objectives contained in this chapter and uphold the responsibility and accountability of the government to the people.

In line with the spirit of this theory, the current civilian government in Nigeria has been rigorously pursuing a policy of divestment of government shares from businesses where hitherto it had either 100 percent or 60 percent shareholding. In pursuant of this policy, the oldest newspaper in the country, the Daily Times was out rightly sold to a local investor in 2003.

With the withdrawal of government funding or other financial support to the media, it was thus incumbent on management of such media establishments to evolve various survival strategies, one of which included the idea of gathering additional juicy stories through the Internet, as well as foreign news agencies, to ensure that newspaper and magazine audiences got stories that were really worth the value of their money.

Data Analysis

As earlier stated under sample size, this study was carried out on all the newspaper and magazine establishments in metropolitan Lagos. It is instructive to note that over 2/3^{rds} of Nigerian print media establishments are based in Lagos. The study focuses on all the 16 print media establishments in Lagos which represent 64 percent of the existing 25 print media in circulation in the country. The questionnaire administered on the respondents had the objective of providing answer to the research questions.

TABLE 1

	Options	Frequency	Percentage
Does ICT exert any impact on election coverage by Newspapers and Magazines in Nigeria?	Yes No	16 -	100 -
	Total	16	100

All the respondents, as could be seen from Table 1 above, agreed that ICT has made a lot of impact on political reporting by newspapers and magazines in Nigeria. Mr. Gbenga Omotosho, editor of The Nation newspaper, described one of the products of ICT, the Internet, as "One of the wonderful developments of the 21st century," pointing out that "when it comes to sourcing political news, the Internet facilitates quick sourcing; as a matter of fact, it's information in seconds."

John Awe, Head, Communications Desk of the Nigerian Tribune, a newspaper established by the late sage Chief Obafemi Awolowo in 1949, on his part equally expressed similar view. He said the Internet has positively shaped the news contents of the newspaper adding that "We send stories and photographs to our head office in Ibadan via Internet. In addition, we source several other political stories from Independent National Electoral Commission (INEC) offices online."

The editor, Metro Desk of Guardian newspaper, Mr. Nnamdi Inyama, on his part equally acceded to claims that the Internet provides wider source of stories. He pointed out that, just as it provides quick sourcing of stories, the technology also enhances what he called "precise editing." He, however, pointed out that a major problem associated with sourcing stories through the Internet is the credibility of sources.

A similar view was expressed by the editor of the oldest newspaper in Nigeria today, Mr. Akeem Bello of the Daily Times, who argued that the Internet has enhanced the production of the newspaper as it provides easy sourcing and sending of stories and photographs.

The editor of one of the newly-established tabloids in the country, Daily Independent, which was established in 2001, revealed that the secret of colourful political pages of the newspaper was as a result of the fact that a lot of the scintillating foreign stories, which made the newspaper thick, were sourced through the Internet and foreign news agencies such as the BBC, VOA, and CNN. Mr. Gbenga Adefaye, the editor of Vanguard newspaper expressed a similar view.

The Editorial Page Editor (EPED) of Thisday newspaper, Mr. Godwin Agbroko, equally alluded to the fact that the Internet and foreign news agencies, especially, CNN, facilitate communication by providing what he called "instantaneous information."

The business editor of Champion newspaper, Mr. Chinedu Dike, in his contribution, stated that the Internet was very vital to modern newsgathering and news dissemination. He was, however, quick to add that technical problem with Internet Service Providers (ISPs) and the Nigerian Telecommunication Plc (NITEL) were two major problems which could frustrate newspapers' aspirations to avail themselves of the enormous benefits on Internet in newspaper production.

A deputy editor of Sunday Punch, Mr. Kunle Oderemi, in similar fashion avers that the Internet provides for "faster communication, greater access to information, and currency of information." Like other editors, he equally remarked that a lot of funds are required to constantly enjoy the Internet facilities for newspaper and magazine production.

A senior editorial staff member of one of the country's oldest news magazines, Newswatch, Mr. George Oche, in his view also said, "The Internet helps in quick exchange of information, thereby making newsgathering more convenient and at a reduced cost."

While trying to compare the Internet with fax machine, a technology popularly used by the Nigerian media prior to the emergence of the Internet, Mr. Oche said, "Internet makes newsgathering so efficient that Fax machines will look like the 'talking drum.' It makes newsgathering quick and cheap because it delivers the information about the world without delay, thereby helping in the free flow of information." It would be recalled that "talking drum" was one of the traditional means of communication in the Southwestern part of Nigeria prior to the emergence of the modern means of mass communication.

The head of the Business Desk of The Week News Magazine, Mr. Adedeji Ademigbuji, on his part says the Internet helps the reporter and the medium in meeting production deadlines, stressing that "it's faster than any other communication technology when it comes to sending information from one point to another. Above all, it's less stressful and easy to use."

Mr. Victor Ogene, the Associate Editor of The Source magazine said, "The Internet is a great reliever for every medium of mass communication when sourcing for foreign news is the issue at hand." He cited the American-led war against Iraq in 2003 as an example of a foreign story requiring minute-by-minute updates, which can only be best handled through information from the Internet and CNN.

TABLE 2

	Options	Frequency	Percentage
Are there visible gains of ICT in political reporting in Nigeria?	Yes	12	75
	No	4	25
	Total	16	100

From Table 2 above, 12 of the 16 respondents, that is, 75 percent, agreed there are visible gains of ICT in reporting politics or elections in Nigeria. They contended that ICT has strengthened local and foreign news agencies such as News Agency of Nigeria (NAN), Agence France Presse (AFP), and Reuters, among others, in a way that stories or photographs of major political events which are not captured by local reporters are made available by these agencies.

Other deducible gains of ICT observable from the study include:

1. Elimination of production tension: For many reasons, election coverage is usually a tension-soaked exercise in Nigeria. First, the politicians usually organized their campaigns in a way that would clash with production deadlines. These are times when rallies are organized until 7:00 p.m. In such a circumstance, political reporters are usually under tension to get their stories across to their editors. The tension is further heightened by the fact that most of the rallies are covered live by the Nigerian Television Authority (NTA), a medium that has the largest broadcast network in Africa.

In times past, stories were sent to the newsroom through telex, radio message, and telephone. However, with ICT, minutes after the event reporters only need to look at 10 to 15 minutes of airtime through a nearby cyber café to send their stories. This is a tension-relieving exercise because in the past, the reporters would have to either dictate the story word-for-word through the telephone or radio.

2. Public Participation: Another deducible impact of ICT on election coverage observable through the study covered public participation in the newsgathering process. The entire scenario has really enhanced public participation in SMS through the GSM network or E-mail any information at their disposal to the media houses. Furthermore, it was discovered that political parties no longer send press invitations through the surface mail, but rather send them via the Internet.

3. Elimination of Channel Noise: Another gain of ICT in election coverage discovered through the study is that of elimination of channel noise.

Some are of the opinion that developing nations will catch up with the nations already fluent with ICT the soonest; however, those who disagree with this are of the view that it's only a matter of time before developing African countries catch up with the already developed countries— if they are directed by sincere and purposeful leadership with a clear sense of direction. They cited the examples of India and Pakistan as examples of what developing nations could do when there is leadership with focus and sense of direction. It should be recalled that India and Pakistan have joined the league of countries of the world with nuclear technology; while Indonesia, another developing nation, only recently developed a home-grown satellite.

Discussion and Conclusion

This chapter has critically examined the impact of ICT on election coverage in Nigeria. The paper observes that ICT has revolutionized the process of news gathering and reporting generally in Nigeria. With ICT, tremendous changes have taken place in news gathering, editing, and reporting. In the past, the appearance of Nigerian newspapers and magazines was dull and unattractive. However, as this study has revealed, ICT has changed all that. Newspapers and magazines are now colourful and fascinating. The layouts, typography, type-setting and printing are now more audience friendly. With timely dissemination of news through the ICT, the young Nigerian democracy has a great hope of survival. Unlike the previous elections in Nigeria, the 2007 elections were the fastest in history. Results of elections were collated fast as a result of optimal usage of ICT. Thus, the outcome of the study provided positive answer to Research Question 1, which is "How has ICT redefined political reporting, especially at election period in Nigeria?"

RQ2 centred on how ICT affected the quality of photographs used by the print media. The answer is also in the affirmative. All the sampled media establishments used digital cameras and publish in colour

RQ3 asked if ICT exerts any impact on gathering and disseminating political stories. The answer is also positive. Many of the results that were released before 12 noon were top stories in the evening newspapers.

RQ4 asked for the available ICT facilities which the editors freely listed as: digital camera, modern telephony system, i.e., GSM, Internet facilities, and scanners, among others.

RQ5 asks whether ICT enhanced the professional and statutory duties of the press with regard to timely dissemination of information at election periods. The answer is also positive. The major role of the press, as further advocated by the theoretical framework of the paper, is to inform the citizenry about timely events in the society which ICT has made very easy.

RQ6 asked if ICT portrays a bright or gloomy future for the Nigerian print media. The answer is equally positive. With ICT, the Nigerian media would continue to be relevant by exerting positive influence on the people.

RQ7 asked if the Nigerian factor has any role to play in the sustenance of the current state-of-the-art technology available for political reporting. The answer for now is yes, but could change as nobody can predict the direction of government policy at any point in time.

However, to strengthen the 10-year-old new democratic governance in the country, the chapter makes the following recommendations.

1. That media owners should step up immediate action in the direction of strengthening the existing ICT facilities in order that the media could effectively carry out their statutory and professional duties.

2. That the various media establishments should be strengthened via regular training and retraining of media men for effective operational performance.

3. That more funds be allocated for the acquisition and maintenance of the existing ICT facilities in order that at all times the media would not be found wanting in the discharge of their sacred duties to the public.

4. That the Nigerian government should stop paying lip service to the issue of technological advancement. The technological drive by India, Pakistan, and Indonesia is worthy of emulation. While India and Pakistan had developed nuclear technology, Indonesia recently developed a homemade satellite. It is high time Nigeria also began to produce most of the ICT facilities required in news reporting.

5. That the National Assembly should pass without further delay the Freedom of Information Bill (FOIB) that has been sent to the House for consideration and approval since 2007. The passage will greatly help the media in sourcing and reporting accurate and timely information to the people.

REFERENCES

Adamolekun, Ladipo (1985) *The fall of the Second Republic* Ibadan; Spectrum Books Ltd.

Akinboye, S.O. (2007), "Globalization and the Challenge for Nigeria's Development in the 21stCentury" in *Globalization*, Cited in http://globalization.icaap.org/content/special/ Akinboye.html

Akinfeleye, R.A. (2003), *Fourth Estate of the Realm or Fourth Estate of the Wreck: Imperative of Social Responsibility of the Press.* Lagos, University of Lagos Press.

Baskakor, Edward (1987) "The Culture Bomb", in *Information and Nuclear Free World*, New York, Allied Publishers. *Constitution of the Federal Republic of Nigeria (1999)* Lagos; Federal Government Press.

Daramola, Dayo (2001), *Introduction to Mass Communication*, Lagos , Rothan Press Limited

DeFleur, Melvin L & Dennis, Everette E. (1981), *Understanding Mass Communication,* Boston, Huguton Mifflin.

Evans, Desmond et al (1990), *People, Communication and Organization* (Second Edition) London: Pitman Publishing

Hotbarer, Michael (1990), "Information Technology: Hardware and Systems" in Desmond, Evans (ed), *People, Communication and Organization*, London: Pitman Publishing.

McQuail, D (1987), *Mass Communication Theory* (Third Edition), London, SAGE Publication.

Mohammed, M (1990), "Traditional Forms of Communication in Borno State." An unpublished paper presented at international communication conference, University of Maiduguri.

Newsom, Dong and Wollert. A. James (1988), *Media Writing*, California: Wadsworth Publishing Company.

Ojo J.D. (1985) *The Development of the Executive under the Nigerian Constitutions, 1960-1981*, Ibadan: University Press Ltd.

Omu, I.A. Fred (1996) "Journalism in Nigeria: A Historical overview" in *Journalism in Nigeria Issues and perspectives* Olatuji Dare and Adidi Uyo (eds) Lagos: NUJ Lagos State council.

Oyeleye, Oyediran (1976) "Background to Military Rule" in *Nigerian Government and Politics Under Military Rule 1976-1979* London: Macmillan Publishers.

Peden William & Adrienne Koch (eds) (1944), "The Life and Standard of Thomas Jefferson" cited in Popoola's "UBE and the Mass Media: Striking a Golden Accord," in the *Journal of Nigerian Languages and Culture*, Vol.5, March 2003, Owerri, Imo State University.

Popoola Tayo (2003), *GSM as a tool for news reporting in Nigeria*, Lagos: NUJ and Corporate Lifters International.

Popoola Tayo, (2003) "Mass Media Communication practitioners and mobilisation of Nigerians for political participation" in *POLIMEDIA Media and Politics in Nigeria*. Ikechukwu Nwosu (ed) Enugu: ACCE Nigeria chapter.

Popoola Tayo, (2007) "2007: Mass Media and the quest for peaceful electioneering" paper presented at the faculty of social science workshop on "Road Map to peaceful elections in 2007" held at Lagos Airport Hotel, Ikeja.

Schramm, Wilbur (1972) "Models of Traditional, Transitional and Modern Communication System" in *Communications and Political Development* Lucian W. Pye (ed) Princeton University press.

Sobowale, Idowu (1986) "Influence of ownership on Nigerian newspaper coverage of National Issues" in *Mass Communication in Nigeria: A Book of Reading* Onuora E. Nwuneli (eds) Enugu: Fourth Dimension Publishers.

Uyo, Adidi O (1987), *Mass Communication Media: Classification and Characteristics*, New York: Civiletis International.

Press reports

"100 Feared dead in PDP, ANPP clash." *New Age* newspaper March 31, 2003.

"Violence Trail election 2003 campaign." *Punch* newspaper March 2, 2003.

"It's fire for fire says Obasanjo." *TNT* newspaper, Feb. 24, 1999.

APPENDIX

A SURVEY QUESTIONNAIRE ON THE IMPACT OF ICT IN POLITICAL REPORTING AND ELECTION COVERAGE IN NIGERIA

1.   Name of Newspaper:

2.   Year of Establishment:

3.   Mission Statement:

4.   Name of Editor:

5.   Since establishment of your newspaper, how many elections have you covered in Nigeria?

6.   Briefly state the nature of the elections i.e. (whether state Assembly, National Assembly Local Government or General electrons):

7.   Briefly list the available ICT facilities for the coverage of elections:

8.   In comparison which previous elections in Nigeria, what difference would you say ICT has made in your coverage of 2007 elections in Nigeria?

9.   An issue that usually raise tension in the polity concerned the issue of delay in announcing election results. In some cases, it takes between 3 or 4 days to announce results of gubernatorial and presidential elections especially during the first and second republics. With ICT, would you say the trend has changed? Yes/No

10.   Briefly justify your response to question 9:

Chapter 4

The Role of Online Media Technology and Democratic Discourse in Cameroon: A Case Study of *The Post* and *Cameroon Tribune*

Kehbuma Langmia
Bowie State University

Abstract

The Cameroonian online newspaper has equally made its presence felt in the cyberspace. Apart from publishing articles to be read by those at home and abroad, it is also being used as a new public sphere where socio-political and cultural issues about Cameroon can be discussed and debated. The birth of ICTs (Information Communication Technologies) has altered dissemination, consumption, and the content format of some Cameroon newspapers. The presence of multiparty politics in Cameroon in the early 90s made most media outlets yearn for quick and easy means to reach greater numbers of Cameroonian citizens at home and abroad. With the economic hardships plaguing the nation, newspapers have decided to go online so as to invite debates from all the corners of the globe. This paper, therefore, intends to examine two online newspapers with opposing views on how their contents have been able to reflect the influence of technology in shaping the way people discuss their country's pressing political needs. A critical analysis of the constitutional amendments' theme of these papers during the month of March 2008 has been used. This is the period when Cameroon was rocked with incessant violence with the purpose of stopping President Paul Biya from amending the constitution to enable him rule for life.

INTRODUCTION

New media technologies have ushered in another form of dissemination and consumption of news and entertainment. Media practitioners and audiences alike are fashioning ways to adjust to the ever-changing landscape of the media world. This new wave of information dissemination has dramatically altered people's way of life and thinking in Africa. The issue of democracy is central to Africa, and the prominent avenue to discuss some of the tenets of democratic ideals is none other than the media. The media are used as a tool to send messages about the growth and functioning of democratic institutions. If the media are dynamic in their approach (by dynamic I mean the ability to involve both proposing and opposing views) then the users are subtly influencing discourse that can shape government policies. On the other hand, if the media are the extended arm of a ruling government or being controlled and censored by the government (Eko, 2003; Eribo & Tanjong, 2002, Nyanmjoh, 2005), as is the case in Cameroon, then contrary views and opinions maybe hard to come by.

Since the era of multiparty politics in Cameroon, there have been a significant number of newspapers, radio stations, and television stations that have mushroomed in the country. The question is whether these media outlets with new technological inputs are able to help foster the democratic principles needed to improve the lives and hopes of Cameroonians. Noted for its poor telecommunication infrastructure (Muluh & Ndoh, 2002; Nyamnjoh, 2005; Ndangam, 2008; Langmia, 2007) and a plethora of illiterate rural population mass with no knowledge and skill of the computer, Cameroon, like many other African countries, is facing a daunting task of accommodating new forms of technology to disseminate information to its citizens. This paper intends to examine the role of online news content in Cameroon with particular emphasis on two print media, *Cameroon Tribune Online* and *The Post News Online,* and how they are shaping the way Cameroonians at home and abroad are reacting to this new form of communication. The reason for choosing these two papers is to find out the approach they used to report about the national strike that was remotely sparked by the news about constitutional amendments. It should be recalled that the month of March 2008 will go down in history as one of the bloodiest months in Cameroon, as many civilians were killed on the streets protesting President Paul Biya's intention to unilaterally change the constitution and make himself a life president with immunity from persecution.

A significant number of Cameroonians live abroad; the only other means for them to get acquainted with and contribute to the growth of democracy at home is through the online medium. There are a couple of other newspapers in the country that have web pages with online news contents and weblogs. They include: *The Entrepreneur, L'effort Camerounais, the Eden newspaper, The Sun,* and *The Frontiere Telegraph.* The reason for selecting *Cameroon Tribune* and *The Post* is for comparative reasons based primarily on their opposing philosophies of news presentation in the offline editions. *The Post* is primarily an English newspaper, while the *Cameroon Tribune* uses both French and English. In addition, the *Cameroon Tribune* is a government-sponsored newspaper, while *The Post* is an independently-owned newspaper.

Brief Background Information

To understand the media in Cameroon is to understand the political climate in Cameroon from pre-colonial to post-colonial. Before the colonization of Cameroon by Germany, France, and Britain in the early 18th Century, the inhabitants were a group of homogenous indigenes speaking various indigenous Bantu languages, but united in purpose. They were governed by hereditary chiefdoms. With colonization, they were forced to follow new ways of governance where power was concentrated in the hands of the colonial representatives. To make matters worse, after the First World War when Germany was defeated, Britain and France succeeded to chase them from Cameroon and divided the country into two entities: Anglophone and Francophone. The media in the country have been categorized into two camps: French or English. This has gone on since the country had its independence in 1960.

The state of the Cameroonian newspaper has been a cause for concern both before and after the introduction of multiparty politics in the country since the early 1990s. The government on its part has monopolized certain arms of the print and audio visual media for propaganda purposes (Gros & Mentan, 2003). The other privately-owned and managed media outlets have tended to act freely, but not without censorship from the government (Eko, 2003). Furthermore, the prominent private newspapers in the country, as outlined by Akwa (2004), were *Le Messenger, Challenge Hebdo, Le Front Indé pendant, La Nouvelle Expression,* and *Le Mutation,* all published in the French language. But two prominent private newspapers were published in English to cater to Anglophone Cameroonian interests. They were the *Cameroon Outlook* and the *Cameroon Times* (Eko, 2003). There were also magazines like *Fako Magazine* and *Cameroon Life.* During the 1990s when Cameroon was debating whether or not to welcome or reject multiparty politics in the country, having been ruled for over 30 years using a one-party system, the main English newspapers were *The*

Post and *The Herald*. When multiparty politics became a reality in Cameroon, both privately-owned French and English newspapers became critical of the regime. The result was that some of the issues of those papers were seized and some journalists actually went to jail. This is how Eko (2003) sums it up: "Ahidjo's successor, French-educated Paul Biya, maintained the harsh regime of pre-publication censorship, seizure of newspapers, and intimidation of journalists" (p. 86). Tanjong & Ngwa (2002), citing from a previous study, confirm that "between 1991 and 1993 the government of Cameroon seized 146 issues of 16 different newspapers in the country" (p. 21). This has happened only to the privately-owned newspapers and not the government-sponsored newspaper like the *Cameroon Tribune*. The reason to compare and contrast the privately-owned and the government-owned newspapers in this study is to ascertain whether by going online, where freedom is relatively assured, these papers have adopted new approaches to political discourse in the country, or have they still maintained their differing stances. The discussion of these two online newspapers has been examined using critical qualitative content analysis to answer the following research question: What are the similarities and dissimilarities between the government newspaper, *Cameroon Tribune*, and the independent newspaper, *The Post* in their online content of constitutional amendment discussion during the March 2008 political turmoil in Cameroon?

Review of Related Literature

The shift to embrace online media as the new form of news dissemination has been embraced all over the world. Boundaries have been narrowed as people are now able to get news quicker and easier from newspaper websites. This has brought in the question of the future of the traditional media. In a study published by "The state of the news media 2006: an annual report on American journalism" released on www.stateofthemedia.org, the general future of both the traditional and online media is in doubt. For the online newspaper to thrive, lots of capital is needed. Since it is cheaper for the consumer to get news online, newspapers are not going to make money, except those that are financially backed by the government. Traditional media, on the other hand, will have their audience diminished as they gravitate to the less expensive form of news consumption. But the article again argues that since radio and television news are also expanding their reach on the Internet, it will become very difficult for lesser known news outlets to compete with big names like BBC, CNN, and Al Jazeera, for example, that receive some form of funding from their government or corporations. In fact, Tim Curran in this same article predicts the doom of traditional media if they fail to adapt to the changing times.

However, in a Pew Research Center project published in 2007 under the title "World public welcome global trade — but not immigration," the findings were surprising. In a survey conducted on people's attitudes on media and technology, published by the Pew Research Center website (pewglobal.org), it was discovered that newspaper readership is declining because more and more people are turning toward television for their primary news medium. The lone exception in the world was in Africa. People in some African countries rely mostly on the radio as their primary source, but they found out that online news was attracting only a small group of people. They also noted in this study that cell phones all over the world were becoming one of the most important means of communication.

The Internet continues to be the most reliable source of news in the global economy. The Pew research study in 2008, and most recently 2009, titled "Internet overtakes newspaper as news outlet" and "Virus Goes Viral Online" respectively, the Internet continues to top the list on the source for news information when people were asked which media they preferred. This goes to underscore the importance as well as the inevitability of Internet news delivery as a medium that is here to stay.

The contribution of the Internet in nation building cannot be overstated. Eriksen (2007) study on " Nationalism and the Internet" captures the overriding theme of this study on the role of online news in nation building. His study examines the creation of "virtual community" (p. 1) on the Internet. This virtual community, he contends, has deterritorialised nation states, making them share commonalities that would have been difficult with the presence of physical boundaries. He goes on to emphasize the point that not only are online newspapers playing a crucial role in making readers far and near to be informed about happenings in their states and countries, but immigrant and interest groups are using the weblogs on some of their nations online newspapers to contribute to the political and economic debates. Some of the diasporan groups are also using discussion groups to advance political courses in their home countries. "Some of the nationalist groups that appear to be most active on the Internet are Sri Lankan Tamils, Kurds, Palestinians, Sikhs and diasporan Iranians" (Eriksen, 2007, p. 8).

Olorunnisola (2000) discusses another sensitive issue with respect to the role of African website content providers. Since most African diasporans get their news from home on the Internet, it is necessary that the content providers make those sites efficient. But what this author has noticed is that most of the websites are void of originality. Apart from South Africa, which has a domain name (see http://www.mg.co.za), a majority of the websites are hosted by third parties. These third parties, mostly in the West, now advertise their products and businesses on the website content. There are no advertisements for local businesses in the home country or facilities. There are equally no advertisements for opportunities and other amenities for those Africans living, studying and working in the diaspora. This situation can only right itself if African governments invest in digital technologies. "The reluctance of many to invest in domain ownership maybe indicative of late adoption of the full capabilities of the Internet than lack of interest" (Olorunnisola, 2000, p. 5).

Another study worthy of note that has equally contributed to the ongoing debate about the role of Internet news and the contribution of the diasporan has been carried out by Dana Ott, titled, "Power to the People: The role of electronic media in promoting democracy in Africa." This article is published on native.org. It examines the meaningful contribution of pro-democratic groups in the West who are influencing decision-making processes in their home country. This paper argues that since new communication forms have burgeoned all over the world, the nature of political communication is going to experience a dramatic shift. Citizens, especially at home, are going to have direct impact on decision-making with their home governments. This therefore entails a shift in political communication from the home country itself. "The electronic media has given a larger percentage of constituents than ever before the ability to easily and quickly transmit their opinions policy issues to their representatives" (Ott, 1998, see www.native.org). Ott goes on to argue that even though this electronic revolution has transformed our polity by increasing the number of citizen's participation, there are going to be some disadvantages as well as advantages. One of the setbacks is the influence of the "tyranny of the majority." Since most African countries are being ruled by what is called "factionalism," it will be difficult to uproot them from their old practices. In fact, one of the challenging issues that this article underscores is that "at present, there is no empirical evidence that electronic media have thus far contributed to 'democracy' in Africa." One of the reasons, the author states, is that only a relative few Africans still have access to the new media.

On the contrary, Bernal (2006) sees the crucial role the Internet has played in African democracy almost 10 years after the publication of Anthony Olorunnisola's article. In the views of Victoria Bernal, the Internet has increasingly become the new public sphere for diasporans to contribute their own quota to advancing democratic ideals in Africa. They do this, she writes, by actively debating on the net, resolving ideological conflicts, advancing new ways to political representations, and best of all, raising money and mobilizing themselves to further the cause of meaningful democracy in their various countries. Her article focus more on the role diasporan Eritreans have played in helping their country financially to fight war with their neighboring Ethiopia and contribute their own ideas in the formation of the country's constitution, among others. She goes further to say that the role the diasporans play is very significant because they are operating in a relatively free terrain as opposed to their counterparts at home who are handicapped by stringent laws that limit free speech or access to the Internet.

This literature review has, in a nutshell, laid a framework for the role of online news especially for the diasporan Cameroonians and how they have helped in their own way to contribute to advancing democracy in Cameroon. The commentary column created by *The Post News Online* has been that arena where Cameroonians, especially those in the diaspora, are making their voices heard. Since they too, like most other diasporans, are operating in a relatively free context to say what they feel and think, their contributions have helped in advancing the ideals of free speech in Cameroon, which is an essential component of democracy. It should be noted that contributors to these two newspapers are conscious of the fact that their submissions are being read on the Internet by the vast majority of Cameroonians outside the country. Cameroonians inside the country have to pay certain sums of money to use the cyber cafés that are found mostly in the urban city centers of Douala and Yaounde. Those in the diaspora have Internet facilities at work, in school, and at home, with relatively less financial access than their counterparts at home. The appropriate method chosen to study the two online newspapers in Cameroon is qualitative content analysis.

Qualitative Content Analysis

The inductive qualitative content analysis is being used to code and categorize the data from the two newspapers under study. Elo and Kyngas (2007) distinguish between inductive and deductive qualitative content analysis. The process that the researcher can use for inductive analysis is to begin with coding the data, followed by creating the various categories on which the data can be classified on the bases of similarities and dissimilarities. The last step will be the abstraction, which involves a general description of the underlying data. These are the "themes" that will generate the entire discussion of the research topic. The deductive approach, according to these researchers, involves testing the categories or hypotheses. For the purpose of this research, the inductive approach is used in combination with critical analysis. The critical aspect constitutes a holistic examination of the context of the concepts used in the newspapers. A comparative analysis of how the categories have come to be in these newspapers and the socio-political and cultural knowledge of Cameroon has played a leading role in deciphering the ways in which these papers differed in their coverage of the February, 2008 political riots.

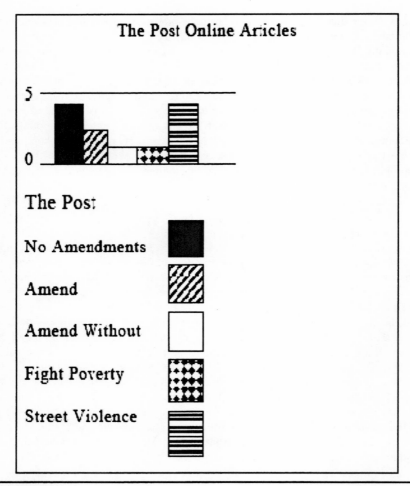

Figure 1

As seen on the bar chart above, there were 11 postings in March 2008 on *The Post* online newspaper that were directly discussing the February unrest. Four out of 11, representing 44 percent, discussed the theme of no constitutional amendments. It was followed by articles that were tailored on analyzing the street violence that occurred as a result of the anger over the President's decision to amend the constitution. These articles represented 30 percent of submissions. Only few articles were in favor of amendments. They were 18 percent of the articles that were in favor of constitutional amendments.

The Post (Weblog) Comments

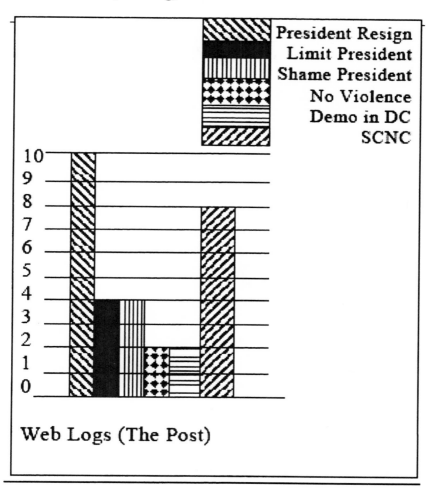

Figure 1.1

Cameroon Tribune Online Articles

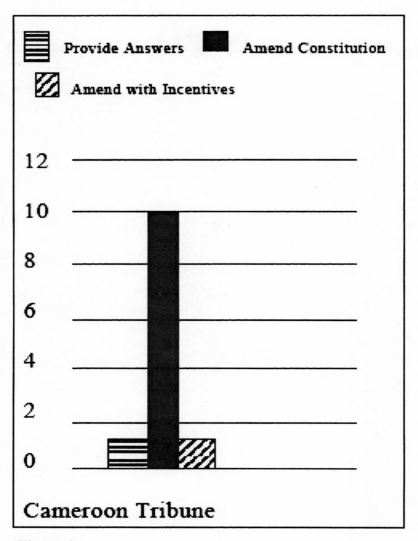

Figure 2

Here in figure 2, the Cameroon newspaper online had a majority of its
articles of the March 2008 edition discussing the amendment of the constitution
in the affirmative. A total of 11 articles had as their theme "Amend the
constitution" representing 85 percent of all the submissions. As seen on the chart

above on figure 2, the rest of the other themes, like providing answers to the
meaning of constitutional amendment to citizens who were unfamiliar with the
term, or providing jobs and other incentives to the people before amending the
constitution to run for office again after serving over 25 years in office by
President Biya, got minimal attention in the papers.

Online Newspaper and Weblog Themes and Classification

The Post: 11 articles	Cameroon Tribune: 13 articles	Weblogs: (The Post): 43 comments
No Amendments: **4**	Provide answers to socio-political affairs: **1**	The President should resign: **16**
Amend constitution 6(2)= **2**	Amend the constitution: **11**	Limit presidential mandate: **4**
amend constitution without change to article 6(2)= **1**	Amend and give incentives: **1**	Shame to supporters of the President: **11**
fight poverty instead: **1**		Violence is not the answer: **2**
Street Violence: **3**		Demonstration at Cameroon Embassy in DC: **2**
		SCNC is to blame for violence: **8**

The Classification of the two online newspapers (*The Post* and *Cameroon
Tribune*) yielded similarities as well as dissimilarities with regards to the themes

that were ascertained from the archival documents. One glaring dissimilarity was that *The Post* had a comment section (weblog) on its site while *Cameroon Tribune* did not. The major themes that were gleaned from *The Post* were: "No Amendments to the constitution," "Amend the constitution," "Amend the constitution but no change to article 6 (2)," "Fight poverty instead" and "Street violence." In all, the one that drew the most response was "No amendment to the constitution." As an oppositional newspaper, most of the articles were very critical of the decision to amend the constitution. They sought to challenge the incumbent head of State, Paul Biya, not to amend the constitution that would give him the opportunity to continuously seek reelection. This is what a group of authors of a combined article titled "Act before it's too late: An appeal to CPDM parliamentarians" stated:

> *For once, show some courage; steer clear of infamy! Our future is priceless; do not gamble with it! Most importantly, do not play with fire! Amending article 6 of the Constitution of the Republic of Cameroon would weaken the institutions that protect Cameroonian citizens* (postnewsonline.com, March, 2008).

This direct appeal by a group of concerned patriots was a clarion call to rally support from the parliamentarians of the governing party, the Cameroon People Democratic Movement (CPDM) to block the President from amending the constitution. In another subsequent article published in the same month, the same tone was struck, but this one was in favor of amending a constitution for the benefit of the entire population and not for the sole purpose of satisfying the personal political appetite of the President:

> *Why must the constitution of this nation be amended at any one time for the benefit of one person? If Biya says we should amend the constitution and states categorically and publicly that he would not be a candidate beyond 2011, then I would support the amendment. Cameroonians should not be taken for a ride* (postnewsonline.com, March, 2008).

It can be deduced from this argument that the writer will in fact favor an amendment if only the Head of State withdraws his candidacy for 2011. But that is not the purpose for the amendment. The constitution already limits him from running after 2011, but he still wishes to run. That is why the whole debate about constitutional amendment is even being discussed at this time. Thus, there is no question that the contributor does not favor constitutional amendment.

On the other hand, those who wrote in favor of the amendment were seen in both newspapers. The difference was that, of all the 13 articles about the constitutional debacle in Cameroon during this period as discussed in *Cameroon Tribune*, 11 of them were in support of the amendments representing 98 percent. Only two articles in the total of eleven in *The Post* argued in favor of the amendment. So 98 percent of the articles were in one way or the other against the amendment. One argument from *The Post* about amending the constitution was from. the former Prime Minister of Cameroon, Achidi Achu. This is what he said in support of the amendment: "We have already taken our firm stand on this issue that the constitution be changed and Biya is OK with our proposals and we will proceed to Yaounde to amend it for the good of all Cameroonians" (*postnewsline.com*, March, 2008). In fact, this is contrary to the above-mentioned article on the same theme from another author who said the amendment of the constitution had no benefits for the Cameroonian citizens. It was a single-handed political motive by the incumbent President to run for reelection in 2011. But here we have the former Prime Minister of the country defending the thesis that indeed the amendment of the constitution will benefit the country. He meant that if Biya runs again in 2011, there will be sustainable peace and development in Cameroon.

In *Cameroon Tribune* online, the majority of the points advanced by mostly the government ministers touring the country was in favor of constitutional amendments. In fact, in one of the articles, one of the militants of the CPDM made this remark about amending the constitution for Biya to rule as long as he wishes. The argument posited was that Cameroon had seen more prosperity and that now Cameroon enjoyed "a shining liberal democracy with a prudent economic management, political stability, and efficient welfare system to help meet economic and social challenges" (*Cameroon Tribune Online*, March, 2008). This very article cites another militant of the government party from the Anglophone part of the country saying "… the majority of countries in the free world today have constitutions that do not limit the mandate of the president" (*Cameroon Tribune* Online, March, 2008). This militant, the papers maintains, was saying this to a group of grassroots militants in the Northwest part of Cameroon. It should be borne in mind that these followers of the President had to use all tools at their disposal to make a compelling case for the incumbent President to have another mandate to run. They stand to gain much if he runs. During municipal, parliamentary, and presidential election campaigns in Cameroon, party leaders and their militants go out around the country making stump speeches. They do not have a town hall format like in the United States, where citizens have the opportunity to question the candidate. If the latter were to take place, then more questions could have cropped up for much more evidence to be presented to back up the claim that in some countries there were constitutions that did not limit the mandate of the President.

In its attempt to convince the people of Cameroon that constitutional amendment was perfectly right to extend the mandate of the president, his supporters spared no efforts to dissuade the population. In the same edition of

March 2008, CPDM militants went as far as telling the Cameroonian people that "in old democracies, like France and Britain, the mandate of the president is not limited" (*Cameroon Tribune* Online, March, 2008). This is an attempt to use every means to make the people see the rationale of constitutional change. Cameroon should look at France as a role model for future democracies and not back at the past. By the way, Britain and France had had dictatorial regimes dating back hundred of centuries. When democracy actually got a stronghold in these countries around the 19th century, they all had limited terms for their presidents, in the case of France, and Prime Minister, in the case of Britain. So, for militants of the ruling party to use deception in order to have their way to win over the people is rather unfortunate. To make matters worse, the paper even dared to make a point that "limitation of the presidential mandate is undemocratic" (*Cameroon Tribune*, March, 2008). Again this is downright fallacy. If democracy is government of the people, for the people, and by the people, then it is very legitimate for the people's voice to be heard on matters related to governance. There has not been a referendum organized to sample the views and position of the people on whether they will welcome a limited presidency or not. Instead, they have been arrested and brutalized for daring to go out in the street and demonstrate for what they see as a rape of the country's constitution. And the supporters of the regime in place are always quick to blame mass mobilization of the people on the diabolic efforts of the opposition party to seize power as clearly seen in these statements from *The Post News Online*. This is what Paul Atanga, speaking on behalf of the CPDM party, said to the Anglophone people about the strike action to protest President Biya's decision:

> *You have to be as strong as the military, because it beats my imagination how a nonentity or a riff-raff would order you to close your shop and you quickly obey. Why did you not shy away and could not defend the state institutions* (postnewsonline.com, March, 2008).

To put this in context, Cameroonians from all parts of the country went on the street destroying property and burning tires to protest price hikes, poverty, and worse of all, President Biya's decision to unilaterally change article (6) 2 to be able to stand for reelection. With the mounting of tension over his long serving terms as Head of State since 1982, the Cameroonian people were angry and frustrated by the tyranny of a privileged few. This speech by Paul Atanga in Bamenda, the stronghold of the Anglophone Cameroon opposition party SDF, was aimed at ridiculing its party chair Ni John Fru Ndi who, he believes is the architect of mobilizing young people to go out for demonstrations. It should be noted that in this same venue he distributed millions to people as a way to dissuade them from further demonstrations.

Another prominent theme in these newspapers was fighting crime and poverty. In the *Cameroon Tribune* online, their approach to fighting crime and poverty was to tell the citizens to rally support for the incumbent head of state. In *The Post News Online*, it was to make the case that the dictatorship of Biya is responsible for continued poverty, crimes, and street protests. Shey Peter Mabu, writing on the editorial page of *Cameroon Tribune* online, presented in a nutshell the message of the head of state:

> *Measures have been taken to defend our purchasing power. These measures ... would include strategies aimed at combating price hikes, fighting speculation, removing of taxes on essential goods and liberalizing the importation of some goods direly needed by* Cameroonians (*Cameroon Tribune* Online, March, 2008).

These are the issues that the government wants to use to resolve the tension about, fighting crime and poverty in Cameroon. But this is what *The Post News Online* stated in its commentary section:

> *Speaking to the nation on February 11, 2008, just two weeks earlier, Paul Biya pretended that the future was rosy for the youth of Cameroon. Now, barely two weeks later, his helicopter gunships and machine guns slaughter these very youth, letting the world know that by "rosy" he actually meant bloody future for you. And your offense? Asking for employment and fair prices for basic needs. No family head butchers a hungry child for crying. If Biya were serving you and your country, he would never call you "apprentice sorcerers"...* (*The Post News Online*, March, 2008).

As earlier noted, the issue of constitutional amendment was among many grievances that the people had. The term "apprentice sorcerers" used by the head of state infuriated the young people more to go out into the streets, because they thought their head of state was not acting in a fatherly manner; rather, he was dismissive of their plight. The immediate pain that the people were facing was poverty, rising prices, and increased crime waves. As clearly noted above, the way the two papers covered the issue of poverty and crime was radically different. While the *Cameroon Tribune* online was seeking to appease the people using incentives from the president about a rosy future, *The Post* characterized all the lofty speeches of the president as hogwash aimed at disguising his real plans at cracking down any opposition to this government.

As there were similarities in the themes that were ascertained in *The Post* and *Cameroon Tribune*, there were also differences. *The Post* had a weblog column on its site while *Cameroon Tribune* did not have. These weblog sections created an opportunity for readers to place comments about the issues that were being discussed and debated on the main paper. This portion gave voice to many people who were either on the side of the government, or the opposition, to present their arguments online. On *The Post* weblog as described on the table in this chapter, there were 43 comments on wide ranging themes that surfaced on the paper. The major theme was that "Biya should resign," with 16 postings, and "Shame on the supporters of the President," with 11 postings. On the issue of Biya's resignation, there were a couple on interesting comments: "...we want Biya to go by 2011 so that Cameroonians sit down and make their constitution..." (Delors, March, 2008). It was also followed by another similar clarion call: "My people! This reminds me of Albert Hirshman's concept of Voice, Exit and Loyalty. Cameroonians have been too loyal to the regime to fault..." (Mimboman, March, 2008). This writer is implying that if Biya doesn't exit, they should use force to push him out, because they've been too loyal to a fault. "Mr. Biya, can you not see that it is you who is the demon? If you cared anything at all about your country and its people you would step down" (Lawrence, March, 2008). It should be borne in mind that the writers are using pseudonyms so as to disguise their true identity for fear of repercussions. The use of the word "demon" is in direct reference to the fact of Biya calling the demonstrators "apprentice sorcerers" at his address to the nation when the strike began. Since most of the surrogates of President Paul Biya were the ones going around the country singing his praises, a lot of the commentaries on the blog were also directed at them under the theme "Shame to the supporters of the President." In those postings, they singled out various campaign ministers and former ministers, and lashed out at them for being traitors, blind loyalists, and greedy thugs who only catered for their private wellbeing instead of the general good of the country.

Conclusion

This paper set out to answer one research question: What are the similarities and dissimilarities between the government newspaper, *Cameroon Tribune* and the independent newspaper, *The Post,* in their online content of political news coverage during the March 2008 political turmoil in Cameroon? It can be deduced from the analysis of the data presented on the online sites of these newspapers that there were more dissimilarities than similarities. On the main issue of the constitutional amendments, the opposition newspaper, *The Post* sought to demonstrate the rationale behind the huge disapproval for the incumbent Head of State's decision to maneuver the parliament to make provisions in the constitution for him to stand for reelection. For someone who has been in power since 1982, it was just but normal in any given democracy for the columnists in *The Post News Online* to call for his resignation simply because the country's law did not give allowance for any incumbent to rule after a certain term. It is worthy to note that later in the months that followed, President Biya made cosmetic economic amenities to the people, like lowering the price of gas, reducing taxes, and promising to increase the salaries of government workers. With that said, the parliament then went ahead to amend article (6) 2 of the constitution, putting an end to presidential term limit.

With respect to *Cameroon Tribune* online, the discussion was to push for the amendments. All the articles that were published on this site had strong endorsement from the government ministers to rally support for the changes. Since in the final analysis the parliament yielded to the call for amendments, it can be concluded that the *Cameroon Tribune* achieved its objective of convincing the citizens. It should also be noted that *The Post* had all kinds of writers making the case against amendments, and even had the weblog section where people contributed to convince Cameroonian not to fall prey to the diabolical plans of the Head of State. On the other hand, it can be argued that the law to amend the constitution was not done through a referendum; rather, it was done in the parliament that has the representatives of each section of the country. Nonetheless, people had the opportunity to express their opinion freely which had no possible room for any censorship.

REFERENCES

Akwa, C.D. (2004). The feedback phenomenon in the Cameroonian press, 1990-1993. *Africa Today, 51,* 85-97.

Bernal, V. (2006). Diaspora, cyberspace and political imagination: the Eritrean diaspora online. *Global networks, 6,* 161-179.

Eko, L. (2003). The English language press and the "Anglophone problem" in Cameroon: group identity, culture, and the politics of nostalgia. *Journal of Third World Studies,10,* 79-102.

Elo, S. & Kyngas, H. (2007). The qualitative content analysis. *Journal of Advanced Nursing, 62,* 107-115.

Eribo, F. & Tanjong, E.(Eds). (2002). *Journalism and Mass Communication in Africa.* Lanham, MD: The Rowman and Littlefield publishing group.

Eriksen, T. H. (2007). Nationalism and the Internet. *Nations and Nationalism,13,* 1-17.

Gros, J. & Mentan, T. (2003). Elections and democratization in Cameroon: problems and prospects. In J. Gros (Ed.) *Cameroon: politics and society in critical perspectives* (pp.131-167). Lanham, MD: University Press of America.

Langmia, K. (2007). *The Internet and the construction of the immigrant public sphere: the case of the Cameroonian diaspora.* Lanham, MD: University Press of America.

Muluh, H. Ndoh, B. (2002). Evolution of the media in Cameroon. In F. Eribo and E. Tanjong (Eds.), *Journalism and Mass Communication in Africa* (pp. 3-17). Lanham, MD, Rowman & Littlefield publishing group.

Ndangam, L. N. (2008). Free lunch? Cameroon's diaspora and online news publishing. *NewMedia Society, 10,* 585-604.

Olorunnisola, A. A. (2000). African media, information providers and emigrants as collaborative nodes in virtual social networks. *African Sociological Review, 4,* 46-71.

Ott, D. (1998). Power to the people: the role of electronic media in promoting democracy in Africa. Retrieved May 26, 2009 from http://www.nativeweb.org/info/zumthema/articles/Ott1.rtf

Pew Research Center. (2008, Dec. 23). Internet overtakes newspapers as news outlet. Retrieved May 26, 2009, from *http://pewresearch.org/pubs/ 1066/internet-overtakes-newspapers-as-news-source.*

Pew Research Center. (2009, May 6). Virus goes viral online. Retrieved May 26, 2009, from *http://pewresearch.org/pubs/1216/swine-flu-internet-information-most-useful.*

Pew Research Center. (2007, Oct. 4). World politics welcome global trade-But not immigration. Retrieved May 26, 2009, from *http://pewglobal.org/reports/display.php?ReportID=258*

Tanjong, E. & Ngwa, G. (2002). Public perception of Cameroonian journalists. In F. Eribo and E. Tanjong (Eds.), *Journalism and Mass Communication in Africa* (pp. 17-25). Lanham, MD, Rowman & Littlefield publishing group.

The State of the News Media 2006. (n.d.). Retrieved May 26, 2009, from http://www.stateofthemedia.org/2006/narrative_radio-roundtable.asp?cat=9&media=9

Chapter 5

Localism in the South African Media Context: A Comparison of the South African Local Content and Canadian Content Rules

Adele M. Mda

Abstract

This paper examines and analyzes the localism principle in international contexts, particularly from a communications policy standpoint. Special reference is made to the South African and Canadian content rules for radio and television. The paper looks at the underlying rationales for localism and their relevance across a wide range of contexts to provide a foundation for developing a broader perspective on the localism principle. Content policies in SA and Canada are about the citizenship of the people who make TV programs, or those who compose or perform music. Comparisons are made between Canada and South Africa because South Africa is a young democracy that is trying to protect the interests of South Africans and the local culture. Canada has, to a certain extent, successfully implemented the local content rules. Comparisons are done between the progress of the Canadian regulation under this legislation and the South African media regulation. Similarities and differences between these two countries provide insights into their efforts toward stimulating the production of local content and their effectiveness.

INTRODUCTION

Although localism is one of the core principles that exists in media regulation and policymaking around the world, it is the least understood and definitely a topic that needs further research. As will be shown later, empirical literature on localism is scant. Few researchers have defined it and fewer still have studied it. Inspired and perhaps motivated by positive conclusions by other researchers, that continued demand among media audiences for locally-owned news, information, and entertainment will compel the continuance of the localism principle. This paper will explore the specific definition of this concept and how it is applied in other countries. This paper will look at the underlying rationales for localism and their relevance across a wide range of contexts to provide a foundation for developing a broader perspective on the localism principle and attempts to define it as informed by literature. Various definitions, interpretations, and the relevance of the localism principle in contexts other than broadcasting will be explored to help us understand the meaning of this principle. The paper will also examine and analyze the localism principle in international contexts, particularly from a communications policy standpoint. Special reference will be made to the South African (SA) and Canadian content rules for radio and television and their definitions of localism. This context may be useful to inform the United States (U.S.) content providers and government policy-makers with a broader perspective on how localism is being conceptualized and applied in other nations.

This study evaluates to what extent SA and Canada have benefited from the requirements of the cultural policy to broadcast in these countries' airwaves and movie theatres. The study also determines whether the legislation's goal of encouraging the use of local talent and expertise has really improved the lives of the locals or preserved the cultural values that are distinct for these nationalities. Comparisons are made between Canada and South Africa because South Africa is a young democracy that is trying to protect the interests of South Africans and the local culture. Canada has to a certain extent, successfully implemented the local content rules. Comparisons are done between the progress of the Canadian regulation under this legislation and the South African media regulation. Similarities and differences between these two countries provide insights into their efforts toward stimulating the production of local content and their effectiveness.

The analysis of the regulation of the content rules in these countries is significant to other countries, who must maintain required levels of locally-produced content in their own countries. Producing and broadcasting local programs is important to the nation since the native communities need to utilize the expertise that is available in their own communities and know what is going on in their backyards.

Empirical studies show that broadcast media are extremely influential, and invasive, and therefore, consider it vital to maintain strong regulation on local media content. As the Federal Communications Commission (FCC) Commissioner Adelstein noted in 2004:

> *Localism is an integral part of serving the public interest. It requires stations to be responsive to the particular needs and interests of their communities. Every community has local news, local elections, local government, local weather, local culture, and local talent. Localism means providing opportunities for local self-expression. It means reaching out, developing and promoting local performing artists, musicians and other talent. It means dedicating resources to discover and address the unique needs of every segment of the community (p.25)*

This definition is critical as a core broadcast policy goal to be discussed in this chapter, and is the foundation of local programming and services. It highlights the sustained significance of localism in broadcast media. Some developing nations have in recent years introduced strict content rules for radio and television. South Africa is one of them. They have adopted and introduced local content quotas using both the Australian and Canadian content models which advocated for local content as an operational prerequisite, and also as a condition of getting access to resources. To stimulate production of local content, a number of countries have put into place a variety of incentives, such as subsidy programs and favorable tax treatment, to ease the financial burden, create employment, and to encourage entrepreneurship in the media industry. For example, according to Article 19: Tanzania's Broadcasting Services Act (1993) requires broadcasters to encourage the development of Tanzanian and African expression and culture; serve the interests and needs of Tanzanians; and to contribute through programming to shared national consciousness, identity and continuity. The Act further requires broadcasters to provide programming that caters for culture, arts, sports, and education pertaining to Tanzania and Africa (p.166).

Both the Canadian and the South African (SA) policies have been sharply criticized. Their critics argue that the local definitions of the two countries are not about content as such. Rather, they are about the citizenship of the people who make TV programs, or those who compose or perform music. In fact, it means that anything produced by a group of citizens is local content regardless of its quality or substance.

REVIEW OF LITERATURE
Localism and Rationales for this Principle

There are several approaches to defining, conceptualizing, and studying localism in the literature. Napoli (2001) argues that "localism has long been considered one of the central guiding principles in communications policymaking" (p.203) domestically in the U.S., meant to encourage the creation of communications services oriented around local communities. It is worthwhile to note that localism as a policy principle extends well beyond the realm of communication and media. It is clear from the literature that in the U.S., the concept of localism has never been sufficiently well-defined, probably due to the debates over the specific meaning and even the relevance of localism in communications policy circles (Napoli, 2000). There is compelling evidence that localism has both the political and the cultural rationales that emphasize decentralization in a democracy and preservation of the unique cultural character of the specific nations.

Political Rationales of Localism

From a political point of view, democratic governments usually emphasize the need for local governments to be granted greater autonomy to run their own affairs without a lot of interference from their central administration. According to Frug (1980), "This localization of political power was seen as promoting political participation and education among the citizenry" (cited by Napoli, 2001). Furthermore, individuals could learn democracy by participating in activities at the local level (Napoli, 2000).

Cultural Rationales for Localism Principle

There is increasingly consistent agreement among authors that the cultural dimension focuses on what others have called "protectionism," where localism is seen as essential to preserve and reflect the cultural values, languages, life experiences, and artistic expressions that are unique and distinct within particular nationalities. Seemingly, the communications policymakers borrowed and applied the localism principle in regulatory circles of the media industry, as well as emphasizing the preservation and promotion of local cultures.

Critical scholars noted the one-way flow of cultural products originating from Hollywood and other parts of the U.S. to the rest of the world (Schiller, 1981 & Hamelink, 1990). They were worried about the homogenizing effects of American culture on the indigenous ones. Similarly, policymakers were also concerned that all sorts of foreign content might inundate their information superhighways (Kim, 2004). As a result of such anxieties, local film producers in Korea called for continued governmental protection such as the screen quotas. In New Zealand (NZ) the Broadcasting Commission was directed to ensure the provision of programs reflecting NZ identity in prime time (Debrett, 2004).

Some communication researchers tend to see this as a new problem that started with the advent of electronic media and mass communications, while others, in fact, saw the electronic media as powerful means to promote the distinct norms of a society. It was concerns like those that intensified the application of local content and led to the regulation of the systems of electronic communication. Napoli (2000) noted that research indicates significant relationships between use of localized media and the strength of community ties, positive attitudes toward the community, the intensity of community commitment and level of knowledge of local political issues. These findings, therefore, strengthen a need for the preservation and promotion of localized means of self-expression that can enhance cultural objectives. The subsequent paragraph will look at the definitions of localism.

Definitions of Localism

Stavisky (1994) suggests that there is common agreement among researchers that there is an untested assumption, especially for broadcasting, that programming services based locally will be more effective in terms of producing content that addresses local interests and concerns. Some scholars advise that policy makers should place less emphasis on the geographical dimension of localism, and place more emphasis on servicing the needs and interests of the citizens within particular communities (Stavisky, 1994; Napoli 2000).

Some scholars have analyzed localism in international contexts with a broader perspective on how it is being conceptualized and applied in other nations. While their nations share both the political and the cultural rationales of the localism principle, their perspectives go beyond the geographic programming issues to include foreign productions, which are adapted to the local needs of the other nation. For instance, the version of "The Apprentice" (an NBC show in the U.S.) is produced by South Africans and broadcast on South African TV. "The Apprentice" concept appealed to the SA broadcaster, but it had to be localized to provide an outlet for local voices, cover local issues, and use local talent.

Unless the underlying motivations for the localism policymaking are clearly articulated in the policy, it is no surprise that policy analysts lament the ambiguous definition of this term. In Canada and SA, the purpose of the localism principle was clear from the onset. It was used in effort to promote and preserve cultural values and to protect their citizens from those cultural industries that had matured already by creating some barriers. These can be eradicated once the community achieves their targeted goals. There is evidence in literature that shows other assumptions of localism as protectionism, self-promotion, catering for certain minority interest audiences, or even building brand awareness, and this can be demonstrated in the flowing two areas: First, the economics of the international markets decidedly favor big commercial interests and countries with highly developed media and production industries. This partiality places severe threats to the survival of the local programming in countries with smaller sectors. Particularly, the United States programs, which are mass-produced for export, are cheaper than the cost of the local programs, and have the potential to displace local programming, hence the need for statutory regulation to protect local media producers. Second, local content media is highly likely to serve the needs and interests of the vulnerable within a particular society. Programs intended for international markets are unlikely to reflect the circumstances and aspirations of the locals. Some audiences are underserved by commercial media and their views are oftentimes neglected.

Public broadcasters are, therefore, required to prioritize and serve marginalized communities. For instance, the Canadian content rules state categorically that through their programming and employment opportunities, the broadcasters must serve the needs of interests of the Canadian men, women, and children, and reflect their circumstances and aspirations. Similarly, the Tanzanian Broadcasting Service Act of (1993) stresses that above all the broadcasters must encourage the development of the Tanzanian culture and African expression of culture, as well as serving the interests and needs of Tanzanians. This is the reflection of protectionism and promotion of these countries' cultures and guarding the interests of its citizens.

Although the local content quotas differ from country to country, several countries in Europe and Asia have local content rules that protect and promote local programming in broadcasting. For instance, European Union members required that a primary portion of the local content be sourced from the European Union countries. In France, the local content quotas for television are 40 percent French productions and 60 percent European production. In Spain, private television quotas are 40 percent their own productions, and 50 percent of film broadcasts must be European and in Spanish. Prior to 2000, in Malaysian television, 60 percent of programming was in national language, and it increased to 80 percent in 2000 for cable and satellite channels and free-to-air television (Toby Mendel, 2001; Nyman-Metcalf, K., Hills, J., Honeyman, R., Mbaine, A., Francis B. Nyamnjoh, F.B., Kariithi, N., & Kupe, T., 2003). Most proponents of localism argue that the local content rules are essential because economically, international markets favor countries with large broadcasting sectors and well-developed production houses. The disadvantage of such favoritism is that the programs of developed media production sectors can easily displace local programs in countries with less developed broadcasting industries.

With the advent of new technologies, which certainly threaten the traditional interpretation of the localism principle, the debate has gained momentum and a number of scholars question whether the principle can survive such changes that are taking place in the media environment (Sohn & Schwartzman, 1994).

The Purpose of Localism Principle in Other Nations

Countries around the world have expressed an increasing desire to protect their national identity, values, and beliefs through a range of policies on culture (Sauve & Steinfatt, 2003). Culture gives people a sense of themselves and their identity. Strong arguments have been raised against programs that originate from other nations, particularly in the U.S., as not educative, irrelevant to the realities of other societies, or even as pure cultural imperialism. Trachtman (1998) reminds us that as early as the 1920s, a number of European countries introduced quotas in order to protect their fledgling film industry from a sudden influx of films from the U.S. Canada shared a similar sentiment and introduced quotas in 1970 to try to keep their culture distinct from that of the U.S., and preserve that which they viewed as "Canadian." Pierre Juneau, the chair for the Canadian Radio-Television Commission (CRTC) in the 70s is quoted as saying that "Canadian broadcasting should be Canadian...[and] that Canadian broadcasters were behaving like mouthpieces for American entertainment factories" (Broadcast, 1970). Several other countries in Asia and Africa followed this example and did the same.

In SA, there has always been an argument made that international programs are less expensive and, therefore, it makes business sense to purchase them instead of local ones, which are much more expensive to produce. Feigenbaum (2004) agrees that "private networks, now the majority in most countries ... have evoked a strong preference for importing cheap American products over locally-owned TV shows..." (p. 7) The Freedom Expression Institute (FXI), however, strongly argues that reference to the cost of local programs as compared to international programs is disturbing. They forcefully argue that "...international programs (or at least most of them) have nothing to do with educating South Africans about other important realities that they need to know. Rather, most of them are entertainment programs that only serve to enhance the cultural imperialism of the developed countries" (Freedom of Expression Institute, n.d.). This view is shared by various groups in SA who argue that the international programs that are being shown on South African Broadcasting Corporation (SABC) are a very low quality and are lowly rated programs in the developed world (FXI and National Community Radio Forum, 2004).

Although the Independent Communications Authority of SA's (ICASA) 2002 position paper on local content said that "despite anxieties at the time of introducing SA content requirements, SA broadcasters have overwhelmingly exceeded their quotas," there are opposing views that note that the South African Broadcasting Corporation (SABC) also shows a significant number of imported programming. The South African Communist Party (SACP) became more vocal when they related their disappointment in their submission to ICASA that "nine years into democracy, the SABC is still dominated by cheap and low quality programs imported from the U.S. and Britain. Current SABC programs are still biased in favor of western knowledge at the expense of indigenous knowledge, developing world knowledge and alternative history" (South African Communist Party, 2003).

SOUTH AFRICA
Historical Background of Broadcasting Environment in South Africa

Prior to 1994, SA television broadcasting depended on cheap imported programming and little local content was seen, especially in genres such as soap operas, situation comedies, drama, films, and SA music. The electronic media were seen as crucial mechanisms for the dissemination of news and information before SA's first historic elections. As a result, in the 1990's media activists (trade unions, church groups, broad alliances of academics, youth organizations, and the government) negotiated for transparent control of the electronic media which were all controlled by the State at the time. These negotiations resulted in the re-regulation of broadcasting in the early 1990s (ICASA, 2004).

In 1993, the Independent Broadcasting Authority (IBA) was established and tasked to regulate the country's broadcasting industry. The IBA changed its name to the Independent Communications Authority of South Africa (ICASA) in 2000 after it merged with the then South African Telecommunications Regulating Authority (SATRA). One of IBA's first duties was to conduct a wide-ranging policy inquiry known as the *"Triple Inquiry"* into a) public broadcasting, b) cross-media ownership and c) local content. Like any other policy development, the *Triple Inquiry Report* followed a public inquiry process that received both written and oral submissions on the key areas identified. That is, the SA music regulations and local content rules for radio and television which became part of the Broadcasting Act of 1999.

The Broadcasting Act of 1999 required ICASA to prescribe specific broadcasting license conditions regarding local content and SA music. "For both domestic and international reasons, the Authority was obliged to seek ways to ensure that broadcasters do help develop the local culture and industry by broadcasting SA-made material" (ICASA, n.d). The ICASA Community TV Broadcasting Services Position paper (2004) indicated that the South African TV content was seen as vital to ensuring that South African TV reflected and developed SA's local, regional and national identities, cultures, and characters, and that content regulations were seen as a mechanism to assist in the promotion and development of the South African TV production industry.

ICASA continues to review the quotas every three years through the public hearing process to give all the interested parties the opportunity to contribute their views. It is through this process that various stakeholders make submissions to ICASA after they have looked at the discussion paper, which originates from ICASA. While film and satellite television also have specific quotas, they are not going to be part of the discussion in this paper.

South African Local Content Regulations

The rationale and goals for the SA content requirements are clearly articulated in the preamble of the Broadcasting Act of 1999 and all related statutes in public documents. Although the issue of quotas was received with mixed feelings by various stakeholders, a number of written submissions show that with the exception of the National Association of Broadcasters (NAB), the majority of them wanted them. The goals are social and economic in nature — such as empowerment, diversity of services, universal access and growth of local content to redress the imbalances that were created by the apartheid system in SA.

"You need[ed] someone to lay down fair and impartial rules and regulations as … the basis of fair competition between them [broadcasters] and appropriate local TV and music content regulations that will make sure our musicians and TV producers can compete with the deluge of US music and television that swamp South African audiences" (Mail & Guardian Online,1996).

The proponents and supporters of local content believed that the content quotas would facilitate economic opportunities for many South Africans, particularly those involved in the music, TV production and related industries. The NAB submitted during the ICASA public hearings in Johannesburg that it would be difficult to achieve such goals without a thriving and growing industry (NAB, 2003). The policy makers were hopeful that the regulations would also motivate and encourage broadcasters to invest in the development and improvement of a variety of SA music, TV programming, and the development of SA talent.

The Triple Inquiry's initial recommendations for local content rules for radio and TV in 1997 were: 20 percent SA music quota for all radio stations broadcasting in excess of 15 percent music and 20 per cent SA content quota for free-to air TV. However, the International Network on Cultural Policy (INCP) shows that these figures have actually gone up by almost 100 percent. For instance, SA Content Position Paper and Regulations 2002 local quota requirements are as follows and need to be implemented within 18 months of the issue of a license:

FIGURE 1

Radio			Television		
Public	Service	Stations	Public	Service	Broadcasting
40%			55%		
Community	Radio	Stations	Commercial	Free-to-Air	TV
40%			35%		
Commercial	Radio	Stations	Terrestrial	Subscription	Services
25%			8%		

Source: SA Content Position Paper & Regulations 2002

For television, ICASA also introduced quotas for various categories of local programming. They currently stand at:

FIGURE 2

	Public TV Service	Commercial TV	Subscription TV
Program Type	New Quotas	New Quotas	New Quotas
South African Drama	35%	20%	20%
Children's Programming	55%	30%	*
Documentary Programming	50%	30%	*
Informal Knowledge Building	50%	30%	*
Current Affairs Programming	80%	50%	*
Educational Programming	60%	N/A	*

*Subscription Television has to comply with a 15% SA content for its other programming

Source: SA Content Position Paper & Regulations 2002

It is crucial to note that the current quotas are a result of the reviews that assess the impact of quotas on the industry. The section that follows defines what is considered SA music and SA TV content.

Napoli (2001) lamented the inherent lack of definition of terms in the U.S.'s Telecommunication Act of 1996 which leads to multiple interpretations. Because of this perceived lack of a clear definition of localism, the *Mail & Guardian Online* argues that "The FCC in the U.S., ... spends much of its time in court and on Capitol Hill explaining decisions" (Mail and Guardian, 1996). Learning from experiences such of these, the SA Broadcasting Act of 1999, on the other hand, has a glossary section that defines all the relevant terms in the Act, including what they mean by local content, and is described in terms of where it originates. It must originate from SA, be produced by South Africans (producers, air talent, directors and actors must be South African), the cost of production must be incurred in SA, and in co-productions, SA citizens must at least have a 50 percent financial interest. All in all, the TV content covers programming that is produced in-house by the broadcasters and independent producers who are citizens and are in SA at the time of producing the program.

Definition of South African Music (Radio)

Section 53(1) (c) of the IBA Act (1993) defines SA music as a musical work that fulfills at least two of the following four requirements:

- *lyrics* (if any) be written by a SA citizen
- the *music* was written by a SA citizen
- the music and lyrics be principally performed by *musicians* who are SA citizens
- If it's live performance, the music must be recorded in SA or be broadcast live in SA (Production and place of origin should be SA).

These definitions were met with differing views from various media players. Those who did not support them argued that the definitions excluded citizens whose work may originate from outside SA.

Definition of South African Television Content

Section 53(1) (a) of the IBA Act (1993) defines SA TV content as television programming (excluding transmissions of sports events, advertisements, teletext and continuity announcements) which is produced:

- by a broadcasting licensee or
- by a person who is a citizen of and permanently resident in SA, or
- by a juristic person the majority of the directors, shareholders or members of whom are citizens of and permanently resident in SA
- in co-productions, SA citizens own at least a 50 percent financial interest

- producers must be SA citizens and residing in SA
- production costs must be incurred in SA

Various submissions were made to require broadcasters to include 10 percent of news from other parts of Africa (ICASA, 2004) and these recommendations have been accepted, but still have to go through parliament to be ratified at the time of writing this paper. Perhaps SA is in a better position to learn from the experiences of other countries (their successes and shortfalls) which have a history of independent regulation. SA can then judge what can best work in its context. The following section will discuss the Canadian Content (CanCon) regulations.

CANADA
Historical Background of the Canadian Content Regulations

As mentioned earlier in the paper, Canada's struggle to protect its identity dates as far back as the1920s when its government was challenged that "Canadians were folding to the unstoppable force of the American's social invasion" (Broadcast, 1976) and that Canada as a nation was threatened by the U.S. In 1970, the Canadian Radio-Television Commission (CRTC) introduced the Canadian Content (CanCon) rules which applied to film/video, the sound recording sector, and broadcasting. However, for the purpose of this paper, only radio and television content rules will be analyzed. According to the Canadian Broadcasting Service (CBS), "The 1970 Canadian content regulations for TV were phased in over two years ... CBS was [however], required to meet these requirements almost immediately" (Broadcast, 1970).

Canadian Content Rules

In their website the CTRC describes CanCon as:

It's about Canadian artists and Canadian stories having access to Canadian airwaves... culturally, Canadian programs and music give voice to Canadians, to their talent and their shared experiences... economically, the CanCon means jobs for thousands of Canadians – from creation to production and distribution on the airwaves (Broadcast, 1970).

These policies are aimed at Canadian ownership and control of the broadcasting system and, of course, how much content should be aired on radio and TV by prohibiting the importation of foreign programming. This intent is shared by the SA rules although Canada has been doing this for decades and they have been under enormous pressure from the Canadian Cable Telecommunication Association (CCTA) to allow American companies to distribute through cable systems. On November 2004, the CBC News reported that the CRTC approved an application for the Fox News Channel (an American channel) to broadcast in Canada (CBC, 2004) under their specialty or pay-TV services, and this was considered as a defeat by CCTA that had failed on a number of occasions to convince the CRTC to block Fox. Similar to SA, their broadcasting system is made of public, private, and community components.

Canadian Radio & Television

The definition of what makes a Canadian song is determined by the Music, Artist, Production and Lyrics (MAPL) system and must meet at least two of the following MAPL system requirements:

- Music is composed entirely by a Canadian
- Artist is Canadian
- Produced in Canada and
- Lyrics were written entirely by a Canadian.
-

The following is a snapshot of their radio and TV local content quotas:

FIGURE 3

Radio	Television
Commercial Radio	*Private Television*
All AM & FM air per week 35%	6.00am to midnight 50%
6.00am to 6.00pm weekdays 35%	*Public broadcaster* (CBC)
French-Language per week 65%	6.00 to midnight 60%
(vocal music)	*Pay TV or Specialty TV*
6.00am – 6.00pm vocal music 55%	Set by CRTC as condition of license
(weekly)	*Co-Productions*
Ethnic Radio Stations 7%	Canadian production company to retain at least 50% financial participation and 50% share of profit

Source: www.media-awareness.ca/english/issues/cultural_policies/
canadian_content_rules.cfm

Similar to the SA broadcasting environment, Canada has public, private, and ethnic TV stations as well as pay-TV, specialty, or pay-per-view services. SA policies use exactly the same system as the Canadian MAPL. It follows the same criteria of meeting two of the four components. Canada's MAPL's objectives can also be found almost word-for-word in the SA Act. The primary objective here has been described as encouraging increased exposure of Canadian musical performers, lyricists, and composers to Canadian audiences, and to strengthen the Canadian music industry, including both the creative and the production component (Broadcast, 1970). For a television program, it is

certified as Canadian only if it meets all of the three criteria, which stipulate that
a) the producer must be Canadian, b) the key creative personnel must be
Canadians and c) 75 percent of service costs and post-production lab costs must
be paid to Canadians. The figure is slightly less for SA because they require that
in any co-productions, S. Africans must have a 50 percent financial interest.

Methodology

This study explores the specific definition of localism and how it is applied
in other countries. The research design of this study is a textual analysis. It looks
at the fundamental rationales for localism and their relevance across a broad
range of contexts to present a base for developing a wider outlook on the
localism principle and attempts to define it as informed by literature. Several
authors recommend that social scientists use multiple sources of data where
possible. Babbie (2004) suggests that one must obtain data from a variety of
sources representing different points of view. He recommends that researchers
"examine the official documents, charters, policy statements, speeches by
leaders and so on" (p. 335). According to Patton (2001), "records, documents,
artifacts and archives ... constitute a particularly rich source of information ....
Organizations of all kinds produce mountains of records, both public and
private... that can be mined as part of fieldwork" (p. 293). Data for this project
were generated from a number of sources. Policy documents were the primary
source of data collected in both South Africa and Canada during the researchers'
visits. Most documents came from South Africa's ICT regulator, the
Independent Communications Authority of South Africa (ICASA), and South
Africa's government printers. I used publications as another source for this
research article, scholarly magazines and articles, some journalistic reports, and
trade press to provide an external view of regulatory practices in these countries.
Such publications revealed things that had taken place before the study under
review started. A degree of triangulation was provided in this study by means of
cross-referencing analysis. A variety of documents provided the researcher with
information about many things (such as public submissions to the regulator) that
the researcher accessed, and this range of tools assisted the researcher to
triangulate an array of views. The triangulation and cross-checking increased
confidence in research findings and provided trustworthiness of the present
study (Glesne, 1999, p. 31).

ANALYSIS AND COMPARISON OF THE CANADIAN AND
SOUTH AFRICAN CONTENT RULES
Analysis of Similarities

In both SA and Canada, the creation of programming is sensitive to local
interests and concerns of the local communities. However, it should be noted

that some international programming is allowed, though at a minimal rate. Napoli (2001) suggested that policymakers should move beyond the point of origin to include digital penetration as dictated by new technologies. He is quick to caution that local interest can originate from afar but this is definitely what Canada and SA are trying to control. In SA, genres such as international reality show concepts are also localized if they appeal to the SA public to fit the criteria set for TV local programming requirement. For instance, SA bought the concept of "Who Wants to be a Millionaire?", which originated from Britain, "Big Brother," which originated in the Netherlands, and "The Apprentice," which is the US concept. These are programs that originate from other countries but they are localized and produced in SA by South Africans so that they can be broadcast on SA TV under local content rules. Canada, on the other hand, is under sharp criticism from the media players that foreign ownership rules should be reviewed and we have seen earlier that they are slowly reviewing their policies.

Both the CanCon and SA local content rules focus on their citizens. Their philosophies are the same, though SA emphasizes that they have to redress the imbalances that were created by Apartheid (a policy of racial segregation formerly practiced in the Republic of South Africa, involving political, legal, and economic discrimination against nonwhites) system. Canada and SA are also focusing on the promotion of their own music, talent, and nurturing of respective creativity of media personnel in their home countries. There is also an issue of creating employment for local people, although this can be debated that it is only for a small group of people and not for all citizens. SA is being criticized that it has now created a "black middle class" and left a majority of people as poor and unemployed because of privatization policies.

In terms of the definition of terms, it is obvious SA's regulations are a carbon-copy of the Canadian rules. There are slight changes in terms of quotas, but still the majority of them are similar and SA continues to increase their quotas. This study discovered that SA has basically duplicated the Canadian content models. *The Mail & Guardian Online* confirms that "local content and programming regulations used by IBA counterparts in other Commonwealth countries, including Canada, Australia and Britain, were taken into account" (M&G, 1996).

In both Canada and SA there is evidence that there is an increased consumption of local programs. For instance, the Canadian Culture Working Group is cited as arguing that "the Canadian music industry has achieved international recognition over the past 20 years, thanks primarily to (Canadian Content) CanCon regulations in radio" (The Fraser Institute, 1998). However, in SA the viewers could argue that the choice of programs is limited. The public broadcaster is required to have very high levels of SA content, and if it is not your taste you have to resort to Direct Satellite Television (DStv) where viewers have to pay to view. In the *Mail & Guardian* editorial, the IBA was complimented when it licensed more than 80 community radio stations countrywide in 1996. "....the scale of this expansion and empowerment of local community broadcasters has never been achieved elsewhere in the world" (M&G, 1996). This means that the SA ownership and control of the broadcasting systems also increased.

The Canadian quotas are small compared to the SA ones considering that South Africa is such a young democracy. The writer feels that SA took such a giant leap from zero to content percentages that almost match those of countries that have been implementing local content rules for more than 30 years (a margin of 5-10 percent). For instance, the public TV broadcasters in Canada and SA need 60 percent and 55 percent of local content respectively, and 35 percent and 25 percent for commercial radio stations. The other differences are that in SA both public and community radio stations' quotas are the same (40 percent). In Canada, ethnic radio stations are only required to meet seven per cent of the CanCon rules except the French-language radio stations that are required to play 65 percent of the popular vocal music selections. Canadian quotas for TV are split according to the day parts (like morning, evening, and peak viewing hours) and can claim time credit of up to 150 percent of Canadian dramas when they are aired during prime time. This is different is SA because South Africa does not focus on day parts. Different types of programming are allocated quotas by ICASA.

Criticisms of Both the Canadian and the SA Content Rules

The aims of the local content in both SA and Canada have explicitly mentioned empowerment and creating economic opportunities for a number of people to enter the television production industry. However, the question is: Whose economic interests does localism serve...the public broadcasters or independent producers? Critics argue that only a few people benefit from content rules. In Canada, "artists, actors, executives, and politicians squared off... [in fact] one of the main factors in determining whether a work is 'Canadian' relates to the key creative personnel involved in its making: a minimum number of key creative positions (e.g. director, screenwriter, actor, performer, composer, etc.) must be filled by Canadians [and] points are ascribed for each of them" (Canadian Content Rules, 2001).

The SA Content Regulations Position Paper (2002), indicates that the economic opportunities of the TV production industry should be spread across the country (p. 17), but the media watchdogs like FXI have sharply criticized SA that the recently published UNDP Human Development Report indicated that "inequalities in the country are growing," (p. 19). Obviously, such policies only benefit a certain class of people (the cultural and political elites). In both SA and Canada, when the quotas were first introduced, radio stations were concerned that they would lose thousands of listeners and the broadcasters were anxious about the ability of the locals to create quality shows that would be watchable. Other critics challenged the localism assumption that "it seems like in accordance with the CanCon rules, whatever is produced by Canadians and broadcast over outlets owned by Canadians would touch the hearts of Canadian identity" (The Fraser Institute, 1998). This actually raises an interesting point of whether content defined largely in terms of citizenship guarantees any appeal to all the citizens or can make them patriotic (through any shared values, customs or interests/tastes) to their country. However, the Fraser Institute confirms that there is no question that the CanCon requirements have increased the supply of programs or musical selections on radio…which would not have been achieved in the absence of such legal requirements (The Fraser Institute, 1998).

Conclusion

It can be concluded from this study that both the political and cultural rationales for the localism principle are applicable and relevant in media/communications policy. They are meant to allow communities to participate at the local level, and also promote their own cultural values. Certainly, there is a possibility that local origination may lead to content that addresses local interests and concerns. It is extremely important to spell out the underlying motivations and context for local content from the beginning and providing specific definition is certainly necessary so that everyone understands why the rules exist and how they are going to be implemented. As with any clear goal, the time frames for the review of such rules are essential so that their impact can be evaluated. Some of the criticisms raised about local content rules are appropriate and challenge policymakers to think through the communication policy issues and get deeper into the root of the problems, such as whether the policy indeed serves what it was meant to do, or to reconsider the relevance of the policy when the technological or even the socio-economic factors around them change. As seen in the literature review, lack of definition and specific time-frames leave policy analysts, courts and other end-users confused and speculating about the meaning and context.

Content rules may be used to achieve specific goals that respective countries may want to achieve within a medium term. Lessons from Canada and other nations' experiences and the challenges they faced due to digitalization indicate that new technologies will definitely affect the way people view local content regulations. As we have seen in the paper, when the need arises, some local content rules were reviewed and changed in Canada to allow foreign outlets (Fox News Channel, for example) to penetrate their markets. They realized that a competitive broadcasting market creates the conditions for wider choice and quality programming which can then be sold on international TV markets. South Africa is still young in this process and they have made it very clear in documents that these policies have been written in such a way that they can be revised later on. Local origination is presumed to lead to local interest programming.

Clearly, it has been demonstrated in this study that localism may includes among other things, programming in local languages, use of local talent and available resources, appreciation of local cultures, and promotion of various ways of self-expression. As we have seen from some European, North American countries, and Tanzania in Africa, the practicality of localism included expanded programming which embraces shared values and interests of the EU member countries and the expression of African cultures through the continent in the case of Tanzania.

However, as Napoli (2001) and other scholars suggested, there is indeed a possibility that local origination is likely to lead to content that addresses local interests and concerns; however, this assumption has not been scientifically examined. Policy-makers, policy analysts and other scholars need to investigate a key research question of whether there is a causal relationship between local production and addressing the local issues or concerns. In agreement with Stavisky's (1994) recommendation, this area has been neglected from a policy analysis standpoint and can provide insightful findings if investigated.

There are even more reasons and possibilities for future research in this area: gathering similar information from other countries at various stages of development, more thoroughly analyzing the relationship between such policies and regulations and their actual empirical results and examining local market forces' impacts on accomplishment of the intended results. All can inform and affect the approaches taken by governments and private regulators, as well as media industries, in the global communications community.

REFERENCES

Adelstein, J.S. (2004). Statement of FCC Commissioner Jonathan S. Adelstein in Notice of Inquiry, *Broadcast Localism*, MB Docket No. 04-233 (July 1, 2004).

Broadcasting Act No.4 of 1999 [Assented to 23 April, 1999]. Government of South Africa.

Broadcast. (1970). CRTC issues new Canadian content rules. November 06, 1970. CBC Archives. Retrieved March 07, 2005, from www.media awareness.ca/english/issues/culturalpolicies/canadiancontentrules.cfm

Canadian Content in the 21st Century: Review of Canadian Content in film and
Television Productions. (n.d.) Retrieved on March 08, 2005, from
www.cbc.radiocanada.ca/submissions/pdf/CBC_Submission_May_%20200
2.pdf

Canadian Content Rules (2001). Introduction. Retrieved March 05, 2005 from
www.pch.gc.ca/progs/ac-ca/pubs/can-con/can_con.html

CanWest Global Communications Corp. (2003). Foreign investment restrictions
applicable to the telecommunications sector. A study by the House of
Commons Standing Committee on industry, science and technology.
Unpublished paper. February 24, 2003.

CBC News (2004). CRTC approves Fox News for Canada. Retrieved March,
10, 2005. 18 November, 2004
from www.cbc.ca/story/ canada/nationa/2004/11/18

Debrett, M. (2004). Branding Documentary: New Zealand's minimalist solution
to cultural subsidy. *Media, Culture and Society*, 26 (1), 5-23.

Feigenbaum, H.B. (2004). Smart Practice and Innovation in Cultural Policy:
Responses to Americanization. Paper presented at the Conference on
"Smart Practices Toward Innovation in Public Management," University of
British Columbia, Vancouver, Canada, June 15-17, 2004.

Freedom of Expression Institute (FXI). Submission on the South African
Broadcasting Corporation's Application for License Amendments.
Submitted to the Independent Communications Authority of South Africa
(ICASA). Unpublished Paper. June 9, 2004.

Hamelink, C. (1990). *Information imbalance: Core and periphery in questioning
the media: a critical introduction.* London, Newbury Park: Sage.

Huelster, P. A. (1995). Cybersex and Community Standards, *Boston University
Law Review*, 75, 18.

Independent Broadcasting Act (IBA). No. 153 of 1993. Government of South
Africa.

Independent Communications Authority of South Africa (ICASA). (2004).
Community Television Broadcasting Services. Position Paper, November
30, 2004.

ICASA, Appendix K – Summary of Submissions on Local Content.(n.d.)
Retrieved February 9, 2005
from www.icasa.org.za/ Default.aspx?page=1272&moduledata=578.

ICASA. (2004) South African Content on Television and Radio, Position Paper
and Regulations, 15 February, 2004. Unpublished paper.

Kim, E. (2004). Market competition and cultural tensions between Hollywood
and the Korean film industry. *The International Journal on Media
Management*, 6 (3&4) 207-216.

Mail & Guardian Online. (1996). Get ready for a new, free TV Channel. 08
November, 1996. Retrieved March, 05, 2005, from www.mg.co.za

Mail & Guardian Online. (1996). The brazen boss of Bop-TV. March 15, 1996.
Retrieved March 05, 2005, from www.mg.co.za

Mail & Guardian Online. (1996) Please don't kill the IBA. December 06, 1996.
Retrieved March 05, 2005 from www.mg.co.za

Media Awareness Network. Canadian Cultural Policies: Canadian Content,
(n.d.) *Media Issues*. Retrieved March 8, 2005, from www.media-
awareness.ca/english/issues/culturalpolicies/canadiancontentrules.cfm

Mendel, T. (2000). Public Service Broadcasting. A comparative Legal Survey.
Kuala Lumpur: UNESCO, Asia Pacific Institute for Broadcasting
Development, 2000.UNESCO WebWorld. Communication and
Information. Public Service Broadcasting. Retrieved on January 9, 2005
from www.unesco.org/webworld/publications/mendel/saf.html

NAB Submission on the ICASA Discussion Paper on Regional and Local
Television, (2003). Retrieved February 9, 2005, www.nab.org.za/
submissions.asp

Napoli, P. M. (2000). The Localism principle under stress. *The Journal of
Policy, Regulation and Strategy for Telecommunications Information and
Media*, 2 (6), 573 - 582.

Napoli, P.M. (2001). *Foundations of Communications Policy: Principles and
Process in the Regulation of Electronic Media*. Hampton Press INC. New
Jersey: Cresskill.

Napoli, P. M. (2001). The localism principle in communications policymaking and policy analysis: Ambiguity, inconsistency, and empirical neglect. *Policy Studies Journal, 29, 372–388.*

Nyman-Metcalf, K., Hills, J., Honeyman, R., Mbaine, A., Francis B. Nyamnjoh, F.B., Kariithi, N., and Kupe, T. (2003). Broadcasting policy and practice in Africa: Global campaign for free expression. *Article 19.* Retrieved September 10, 2009.
http://www.article19.org/pdfs/publications/africa-broadcasting-policy.pdf.

SABC Editorial Policies – Submission by the Freedom of Expression Institute, (n.d). Retrieved February 9, 2005,
www.fxi.org.za/comm_ regul/sabc_editorial_policies.doc.

Sauve, P. & Steinfatt, K. (2003). Towards multilateral rules on trade and culture: protective regulation or efficient protection? *Harvard University and Organization of American Press.* Retrieved March 05, 2005 from
www.cid.harvard.edu/cidtrade/paper/sauve/sauveculture/pdf.

Schiller, H. (1981). *Who knows: Information in the age of the fortune 500.* Norwood, NJ: Ablex.

Sohn, G.B & Schartzman, A. J. (1994). Broadcasting licensees and localism: At home in the communication revolution. *Federal Communications Law Journal,* 47, 384-390.

Stavisky, A. (1994) "The changing conception of localism in U.S. public radio," Journal of Broadcasting and Electronic Media, 38 (1): 19-33.

Submissions on the draft editorial policies of the South African Broadcasting Corporation, (2003). Local content and language policy. Retrieved February 9, 2005, ww.sacp.org.za/main.php?include=docs/subs/2003/sub130603.html

The Fraser Institute, Critique of Canadian content regulations. (1998) Retrieved March 7, 2005 from
www.oldfraser.lexi.net/publications/ forum/1998/auguat/critique.html

Trachtman, J.P. (1998). Trade and problems, cost-benefit analysis and subsidiary, *European Journal of International Law,* 9 (1): 5

Chapter 6

The New Public Sphere:
Radio and Democracy in Kenya

George W. Gathigi and Duncan H. Brown
Ohio University

Abstract

*The beginning of the 1990s marked the end of a period dubbed the Second
Liberation, a clamor for opening up of the democratic space in Kenya. One of
the results was media liberalization. Eighteen years later, the hitherto
government-controlled broadcast media have become a mix of public, private
and community players. The number of full-fledged radio stations has grown
from two stations in 1993 to about 110 stations in 2008. This chapter will
examine how radio in Kenya has functioned as a public sphere, thereby
allowing for political participation and the formation of diverse opinions by the
citizens. The chapter will also analyze various radio programs that have sought
to provide a forum for discussion, public political awareness, and contributed to
improving democratic processes in Kenya.*

INTRODUCTION

Radio in Kenya occupies an important place in people's lives as it remains
the most accessible communication technology (Odhiambo, 2002; Steadman

Group, 2008). Radio audiences in Kenya have a wide range of options to choose from. There are different radio stations that broadcast a variety of content in multiple languages, a phenomenon that has arisen from the liberalization of the airwaves starting in the early 1990s. Since its inception in 1927, radio has performed numerous and evolving functions in Kenya. The current radio broadcasting system is highly developed and serves roles that range from the traditional information, education and entertainment provisions to promoting African cultures and languages, responding to listeners' everyday challenges, and providing a public platform for the democratic process, a function that this chapter addresses. These activities which characterize the liberalized radio market in Kenya can be referred to as "the third wave of radio" in Kenya (Gathigi, 2009). This period starkly differs from the two earlier "waves" in Kenyan broadcasting history in terms of population coverage, programming depth and stations' interest in audiences.

The colonial period is the first wave of radio in Kenya. Broadcasting targeted both the settlers and the local population. Broadcasting that targeted the local population was used to promote the colonial government's policies. The second wave began after Kenya's independence in 1963 characterized by thirty years of government-controlled, so-called "public radio." During the formative years of independence, radio broadcasting was chiefly intended for social and economic development (Bourgault, 1995; Roberts, 1974). Toward the end of 1970s there was the consolidation of one-party rule on the political front. Radio became one of the strongest political machines. Although development-oriented content was still included in the medium, political content took center stage. An important feature of the first two waves from a scholarly standpoint is that we can conveniently track the developments that were happening in the radio industry. The broadcasting system was centralized and dominated by two main stations that used two national languages, English and Swahili. The broadcasting hours were few and content was limited. However, the current third wave of radio is more complex. There are a growing number of radio stations broadcasting wide-ranging content in different languages. There are also numerous forms of interaction in the radio industry between the broadcasters and the listeners as well as an increased involvement of audiences in programming. This chapter analyzes an important role of radio in Kenya today, how the medium provides a platform for public engagement in civic discourse thereby contributing to the overall democratic process in the country.

Method

Data used in this research was collected between June and August 2008 through interviews with radio listeners in Kieni West Division, Nyeri District in Central Kenya. From the listeners' data, follow-up interviews were conducted radio executives whose stations and executives were indentified. All the radio stations that were identified by listeners are located in the Kenyan capital,

Nairobi. We have also analyzed the political oriented output of several radio stations over the last five years and some current radio programs.

The choice of Kieni West was based on the need to capture a rural radio audience. We viewed the rural audience as a segment that would allow a cogent examination of the current status of radio in Kenya. A decade ago, people living in a rural area like Kieni West would have considered their lives simple, uneventful and unlikely to draw the attention of the media. Rural listeners' interaction with radio was chiefly one-way, acting as relatively passive recipients while contributing little in return whether in terms of feedback to the broadcasters or any ongoing public debate. Processes such as listening to radio news meant interacting with events happening far away, mainly in the cities where the news usually originated. But in today's radio industry, which is more robust and diverse, even the humble circumstances of many rural dwellers do not stop them from attracting significant attention among radio broadcasters. On stations, such as the vernacular broadcasters who use local languages, rural areas make news. The rural people are increasingly becoming a point of focus for radio programmers as they design content with this segment of the audience in mind and taking into account their tastes and preferences.

The remainder of this chapter is divided into six parts. In the first part, we examine broadcasting during the colonial and post-independence government-controlled eras in particular noting the profound presence of the government and lesser citizen involvement. The next section discusses broadcasting in the 1990s, a period of media liberalization and deregulation that accompanied the political democratization movement. Media liberalization has subsequently seen the emergence of several different types of radio stations. In particular we focus on the rise of vernacular radio broadcasting and increasing interest in rural audiences in Kenya. The next section discusses the concept of the public sphere as conceptualized by Jürgen Habermas and the consequent reformulation of the concept. We then use the work of Robert Dahlgren (2005) to explicate our conception of radio as a public sphere in Kenya. In the fifth section we provide examples of how radio in Kenya has successfully enhanced democratic conversation as well as instances where this function has failed to be realized. Finally, we conclude by discussing what we see as the opportunities of radio in Kenya, and other African contexts, in cementing democratic traditions and facing the inevitable challenges the future will bring.

The Colonial Era and State-Controlled Broadcasting

Radio development in Kenya has gone through three broad periods since its inception. The first period was the colonial era and was heavily influenced by political forces. It was during this period that radio broadcasting was started for the first time beginning with the British East African Company relaying services to the expatriate community in Kenya (Bourgault, 1995). Colonial era broadcasting was minimal and rarely targeted the local population. The beginning of the Second World War saw broadcasts start to target the local African population mainly to inform relatives of African soldiers, who were then fighting on the British side, what was happening on the war front. In 1953, African Broadcasting Services (ABC) was established carrying an inclusive broadcast service for the local Kenyan population. Major African languages were used to air programs. In 1954, the Kenya Broadcasting Services (KBS) was established with three regional stations in the Coast, Central and Western Kenya. The British Broadcasting Corporation (BBC) World Service started broadcasting in Kiswahili in 1957 (BBC, 2009).

During the colonial era, the print media established themselves as a vibrant sector. The earliest documented regular publication in Kenya was *Taveta Chronicle* first published in 1885 by the Church Missionary Society (Karanja, 2000). Through missionaries, a number of publications were launched before the First World War. By 1906, laws governing the publication of materials had been put in place. The Books and Newspapers Ordinance, viewed as a very liberal law, required that newspapers should be registered with the government within a month of publication and that annual returns should be sent to the Registrar (Gadsen, 1980). Print media continued to grow especially after the First World War and were used to openly question the colonial government. Like changes that occurred in the broadcasting media, immediately after World War II there was an unparalleled growth in Kenyan print media especially in the local language press in (Rosberg & Nottingham, 1966; Scotton, 1975).

With Kenya's attainment of self-rule in 1961, the Kenya Broadcasting Corporation (KBC) took over broadcasting services from the Kenya Broadcasting Services. In 1962, television was introduced for the first time with limited broadcasts around Nairobi. In 1964, the Kenya Broadcasting Corporation became a state corporation and was renamed the Voice of Kenya (VoK) through an Act of Parliament. VoK reverted back to KBC in 1989 through an Act of Parliament. Between 1961 and 1990, under the state media monopoly, radio served two main functions. In the early years of independence, radio broadcasting was widely employed for social and economic development. The medium was used to provide various types of development-oriented information in areas such as primary health, family planning, agriculture and education. During the same period, there was the consolidation of one-party rule. Radio was eventually turned into one of the strongest political machines propagating the ruling party's, Kenya African National Union (KANU), policies. The medium was also used to silence those who presented opposing views, both within and outside the party. While the medium continued to provide development-oriented content, political content took the center stage. In this period, VoK's and KBC's activities were very closely monitored and controlled by the machinery of government (Bourgault, 1995; Odhiambo, 2002). During the state broadcasting monopoly era, radio broadcast in two main languages, Kiswahili (the national language), and English (the official language), as well as a host of local vernacular languages through the Central

Station. Different languages were allocated hourly slots throughout the day in two-hour or four-hour sessions (Roberts, 1974; KBC, 2009). VoK/KBC television broadcasts on the other hand were exclusively in English and Kiswahili and remain so to date. With the VoK/ KBC monopoly in radio and television, the role of media in promoting democratic and civic participation processes was undertaken by the print media. In contrast to the broadcast media the print media in Kenya have enjoyed more independence throughout their history.

Democratization, Media Liberalization, and Deregulation

Changes in the broadcasting industry that began in the early 1990s saw Kenya move away from a dominant state-controlled public broadcasting model to a liberalized media market. In 1990, the first independent television station, the Kenya Television Network (KTN) was established paving the way for private ownership in broadcast media (Odhiambo, 2002). Radio ownership remained in government's hands for a few more years until 1995. Broadcasting was on AM until 1995 when FM frequencies were opened up. A KBC subsidiary, Metro FM, was the first commercial station to go on air followed by privately owned Capital FM in the same year and Nation FM in 1996. The new FM stations targeted the young urban population with music as the predominant content and broadcast in English. The emergence of FM stations was revolutionary, in part because it marked the first signs of media freedom in broadcast media (Odhiambo, 2002). FM broadcasting also presented an opportunity for diversification of content to match the pluralist Kenyan society. However, there was little change happening in the language used in broadcasting. The new FM stations were all in the English language, surpassing Kiswahili language broadcasting by far. Despite the new developments, the lack of diversity in the new radio broadcasting continued to provide many options to the educated segment of the population who are comfortable with English. A majority of the people, especially those living in the rural areas, were left out first because the language was not friendly and second because the new FM stations were located and had broadcasting frequencies in the urban centers. This urban centeredness can be termed elitist because these broadcasting services only carried content that targeted a youthful middle and middle/upper class urban population.

We should, however, note that deregulation in the first years of the 1990s was limited. This also reflects what was happening in the political system. Despite the advent of multiparty politics, the then ruling party, KANU, managed to win two consecutive elections in 1992 and 1997. Under the repealed election rules, the incumbent president Daniel Arap Moi became eligible for two more terms, which he contested and won. When the first multiparty elections were held in 1992, President Moi had been in power for 14 years. The first 10 years of multiparty Kenya (1992-2002) were more of a continuation of the old regime which retained its grip on vital sectors including broadcast regulation. Despite deregulation, radio frequencies were being offered in the urban areas. This emphasis on urban broadcasting has been viewed as a strategy by the KANU government to stay in power because it enjoyed large support from the rural masses and felt less of a need to use radio to reach them or open up for contending views. Both the 1992 and 1997 general elections were also won amid tight control of the national broadcaster KBC which was still by the far the leading broadcaster. A head of a leading Swahili private station revealed in an interview that the inception of his station was purely inspired by the KANU's control of radio during the run up to the 1992 elections. According to him, "Moi won the 1992 election because of effective use of the radio. Radio must have been a powerful tool otherwise he would not have stopped us (the opposition) from using it" (W. Mburu, communication, August 14, 2008).

The Beginnings of Vernacular Radio

After the initial period of controlled deregulation, the broadcasting industry loosened up in the late 1990s. Commercial radio also started to move toward capturing a huge untapped audience in the form of the rural population. Traditionally, the rural audience attracts little attention due to the low economic prospects. In Kenya however, although scattered over a huge area, the rural population commands attention because they constitute 80 percent of the total population. In 1998, a radio station that broadcast predominantly in a local vernacular language was started. Broadcasting in the Kikuyu language, Kameme FM signaled the birth of vernacular broadcasting using a language other than Swahili or English. Sensing the new competition, KBC started another commercial station, Coro FM in 1999 also broadcasting in Kikuyu language. By the year 2000, the vernacular broadcasting was made up of three Kikuyu and one Luo station. Soon, vernacular broadcasting would expand when languages such as Kalenjin, Luhya, Kamba, Meru, Embu and Kisii had their own station. With these developments, the radio industry in Kenya has become highly segmented. Many sections of the Kenyan population is represented with different types of radio station emerging (Gathigi, 2007; Strategic Research, 2008).

The main distinctions between different stations found in Kenya today are their broadcasting philosophy, the language they use, their reach and content (Gathigi, 2009). The mainstream stations continue to broadcast in English and Swahili. Vernacular stations on the other hand use local languages in their broadcasts. In terms of reach, a group of national stations, such as KBC English, KBC, and Radio Citizen, broadcast across the nation. These three are the only stations that have been allocated frequencies that allow them to broadcast nationwide. Other stations have assumed regional dimension broadcasting to limited populations in specific geographic areas. Radio stations also have varied content. The national stations and vernacular stations mainly try to balance between education, information and entertainment. Urban-based commercial stations are entertainment oriented with a small percentage of information content. Other stations are religious in nature.

In 1998, the Kenya Information and Communication Act (KICA) was enacted to regulate the information and communication industry. The KICA established a three-tier broadcasting structure made up of public service broadcasting stations, commercial stations, and community radio stations. The KBC Swahili and English services are the public broadcasters. The commercial stations are the most dominant stations and include the vernacular stations, urban English language FM stations and variety of other stations. Community radio is made up of small stations distributed across the country broadcasting to a small section of people and addressing local issues. A key development in the past 10 years has been the diminishing role of the public broadcaster, KBC. This can be attributed to factors such as the history of the station, excessive government involvement, inertia and competition from commercial and community radio stations (Gathigi, in Press). With the slow development of community broadcasting, commercial stations have been able to strengthen their operations in a context of limited competition. These commercial stations are highly segmented. The vernacular stations, for instance, tend to attract people who share a common ethnic identity and language. They are popular with people in the rural areas because they use people's everyday language. There are also a number of regional radio stations that are sensitive to the social, cultural and religious characteristics of that region. Indeed, part of Kenyan commercial radio's success can be attributed to its ability to respond to the varied needs of its audiences.

In the remainder of this chapter, we will focus on the ways commercial radio in Kenya is promoting civic engagement. Here, radio can be seen as functioning as a public sphere where different people can deliberate issues of interest.

Radio, Democracy, and the Public Sphere

The introduction of the concept of the public sphere into media studies can be traced back to the translation into English of Jürgen Habermas' book *The Structural Transformation of the Public Sphere* that had originally been published in German in 1962 (Habermas, 1969/1989). Since its introduction Habermas' original conceptualization of the public sphere has been critiqued in many ways and substantially reformulated even in more recent work by Habermas himself (Goode, 2005; Garnham, 2007). However, for our purposes in this chapter many of those critiques, and debates over such issues as how accurately Habermas portrayed the development of a public sphere in 18th century Britain, can be set aside. The definition of the public sphere we shall use here comes from Dahlgren (2005, p. 318).

. . . a functioning public sphere is understood as a constellation of institutionalized, communicative spaces that permits the circulation of information and ideas. These spaces, in which the mass media figure prominently, serve to foster the development and expression of political views among citizens as well as facilitating communicative links between citizens and the power holders of society.

In later parts of the chapter we will describe how the introduction of vernacular radio in Kenya, linked with the growing use of cellar telephones, has facilitated those links and allowed individuals and groups previously excluded by language to participate in the democratic conversation about political topics and other social issues. But first we must explain a little more about the conceptualization of the public sphere we are using here.

First, it is important to note that there are multiple public spheres that include mainstream media, alternative media, and in some contexts community media (Ndlela, 2007, p. 328). Radio can play a significant role in many of these public spheres because in many areas it is more widely available than newspapers or television. This leads to a second characteristic of the public sphere that is important here. "At bottom, the public sphere rests upon the idea of universality, the norm that it must be accessible to all citizens of society" (Dahlgren, 2005, pp. 321-22). Again, radio, can serve this purpose well since relatively low production costs create the potential for multiple providers serving many groups other media might neglect. And the relatively low cost of reception makes it possible for virtually all to participate. A final characteristic of this conceptualization of the public sphere that we would want to emphasize here is its ability to enhance the democratic process by creating engaged citizens through active participation. In Kenya this has happened by combining vernacular radio with cellular telephones. Listeners are encouraged to call in to various types of programs with their views on issues and their questions for those who hold political power. As an individual, that citizen's question would probably be ignored by a politician. However, by creating this particular public sphere, a radio station can make it potentially costly for politicians and administrators who fail to respond or try to dodge the issue.

Dahlgren suggests that, rather than looking to Habermas, we should turn to the much earlier work of Thomas Dewey in the United States to think about the process by which "...people become engaged citizens, how they learn to participate" (Dahlgren, 2005, p. 319). Dewey's emphasis on active participation becomes clear in the work of James Carey when he describes Dewey's critique of Walter Lippman's book *Public Opinion* (Lippman, 1922). Carey explains that: "In Lippman's view, an effective public opinion exists when the individual minds that make up the public possess correct representations of the world" (Carey, 1989, p. 81). Those correct representations would be presented to the public by newspapers and, when those newspapers failed to provide the information because of limitations in the way news is created and disseminated, groups of independent social scientists would produce the correct representations and transmit them to the public. Here the public is a rather passive spectator receiving these correct representations. By contrast Dewey argued that:

Public opinion is not formed when individuals possess correct representations of the environment, even if correct representations were possible. It is formed only in discussion, when it is made active in community life. (Carey, 1989, p. 81)

It is when citizens can become participants, rather than spectators, that they can contribute to the political process and help create the world in which they live (Carey, 1989, p. 82). Commercial stations broadcasting in multiple languages make it possible for those discussions to occur and they open them up to individuals and groups previously excluded because they were not proficient either English or Swahili or were not provided with a platform where they can participate.

How Radio is Enhancing the Democratic Conversation in Kenya

The Kieni West area is a rural area in Central Kenya, sparsely populated and for the most part dry. People depend on their farms for their economic wellbeing. Radio is the most popular communication medium. Listeners can continue with their daily activities, such as tending the farms, taking animals to the grazing field or selling wares but the radio set is always near. Listeners here are very interested in politics. People are interested in what is happening in their immediate environment and beyond. Constantly, they question their leaders, both elected and appointed. They question the way the government works. This is based on an understanding that the performance of the government, and local leadership, directly affects their lives. For example, Mr. John Muchangi, a 33-year-old small trader in Mweiga town in Kieni West, said that "a government that is working is one that is aware of people's needs while effective leaders provide a link between the citizens and the government" (J. Muchangi, personal communication, July 25, 2008).

In the Kenyan political scheme, Kieni West is in a complicated position. It is a part of the larger Nyeri District, an area that is considered relatively developed compared to other areas of the country. In the national outlook, people in Kieni West are considered to be well off, after all Nyeri District has relatively good roads, is agriculturally productive, and has one of the best developed educational infrastructures. However, residents of Kieni West view their association with the larger Nyeri District as detrimental to their interests. This association masks special needs in most parts of the area. Due to these and similar challenges the people are vocal. For many people, only a functioning political system can change the prevailing conditions. During interviews residents constantly criticized the current president, despite the fact that he is also a member of their Kikuyu community and comes from Nyeri. In fact, the president owns a ranch in the area. Given the nature of Kenyan politics, people of the same ethnic groups are usually likely to support a president unanimously. However, the people of Kieni West are critical in their views based on their perception that the government has responded inadequately to their needs.

A Successful Program Format is Developed

The political discourse is not just negotiated in the daily conversation. Residents have taken it to the radio stations that have programs that give the people a chance to contribute and deliberate political discourses. To illustrate this we can take the case of Radio Citizen, the only national, private, commercial radio in Kenya. It is the favorite station for many listeners. Its popularity emanates from the political nature of its content. These sentiments reported by members of the station's audience are consistent with the content found on the station. According to the head of the station, "Radio Citizen is the common man's radio. That is why we make sure that we give them more airtime to air their views than any other station. We have given the ordinary person a forum to participate" (W. Mburu, personal communication, August 14, 2008). One such program on the station is *Bunge la Wananchi* ("The People's Parliament") where listeners call in to contribute to different issues that are affecting the country. In *Bunge la Wananchi* listeners will deliberate on a wide range of issues that are affecting the country. Issues of interest reported include general elections, the constitutional review, a decision by members of the Kenyan parliament to unilaterally raise their perks, corruption in the government, among others. Mr. John Wamae, a primary school teacher, is a fan of this forum.

> *Interviewer: Tell us more about politics.*
> *Wamae: I love politics and that is why I listen to [Radio] Citizen a lot. They have different programs where we participate, talking about different things on politics.*
> *Interviewer: Do you have a particular program in mind.*
> *Wamae: Yeah. My favorite is Bunge la Wananchi. I have called to contribute a number of times. There are always vibrant debates going on and we have different views from people in different parts of the country. During the election period, the debate was so hot but we all get a chance to air different positions.*
> *(J. Wamae, personal communication, August 8, 2008).*

True democratic governance includes a diversity of voices, freedom of speech, and accountability as well. This accountability goes beyond the government and trickles down to the lowest level. For many ordinary people, this is what they demand from teachers, from public servants and administrators such as Chief (a lower administrator in the Provincial Administration system), the local agricultural extension officers or religious leaders. In a country that has consistently scored high on the corruption perception index 147/180 in 2008, 150/179 in 2007, and 142/160 in 2006 (Transparency International, 2009), graft is one form of vice that is common in the system. As a response to such issues, radio stations provide a space where this can be addressed. Through different programs radio gives people the opportunity to comment on the functioning of the government, complain, criticize it, demand accountability from the leaders, and scrutinizes leaders' performance.

For several years, Radio Citizen has had a number of critical programs that are directed to the leaders in various walks of life. One such program was *Wembe wa Citizen* ("Citizen's Blade" in English). Although the program has since been discontinued, it still remains in listeners' minds and has spawned similar programs at other radio stations. The symbolism is of a razor blade and is borrowed from the Swahili expression *kunyolewa bila maji* (to be shaven without water), and refers to an agonizing process. In *Wembe wa Citizen,* ordinary people sent letters to the radio stations with various issues. The station followed up on the issues to establish their authenticity by interviewing the relevant party, or other related parties, after which the problem was aired. Most issues that were brought to light related to complaints such as mismanagement of public resources and public institutions and the mistreatment of people. Two presenters, in a sarcastic mood, took turns to apply a public dressing down to the concerned party. According to Waweru Mburu, Head of Radio Citizen, the program gave the people a forum through which they could deal with various problems they encountered in their everyday lives. The program exposed the failings of junior servants such as Assistant Chief and the Chief who fall within the lowest hierarchy of administration in Kenya as well as senior individuals such as the directors of public institutions, Members of Parliament, Permanent Secretaries, and Ministers. According to W. Mburu, "It was one of the most dreaded programs. If you appeared on the program, you were done and done completely" (W. Mburu, personal communication, August 14, 2008). This type of radio program has enabled the ordinary people to say what they would like to say to the ruling class, a group that they ordinarily cannot reach. The program did not augur well mainly with politicians and well-connected individuals who were featured. Waweru attributes the station's numerous KANU orchestrated closures in the late 1990s to this type of programming. Radio was moving into an area where it had never ventured before by challenging the status quo in an unprecedented manner.

While *Wembe wa Citizen* may not still be on the air, it laid the groundwork for similar types of programming that directly address public issues. Many listeners from Kieni West, for example, tune in their radio every morning to listen to Bahasha FM. On this relatively new station, a program known as *The Boss* is popular because, according to the listeners, it addresses issues of public interest. By appearing on this vernacular radio station, Kikuyu language speakers, many of whom are not proficient in the national languages of Swahili and English, follow issues of local and national interest through this program. Like *Wembe wa Citizen* before it, *The Boss* is based on issues that are raised by the listeners. The radio station will then conduct its own research and investigations before bringing the facts on air. When presenting an issue, many of which are controversial, the stations give the accused a chance to respond to the allegation. For Boniface Maina, a 50-year-old farmer from Kieni West, this is one role of radio he likes.

> *I like Bahasha FM because they tell the news as it is. There is also a program by Muthoni wa Mucomba that is called The Boss. The program highlights people who have erred depending on the complaints they receive. When she (Muthoni) receives complaints, she takes the issue and directs it to the mentioned person, be it a policeman, the chief or even the president. She is able to put forward to the relevant authority issues that the affected people cannot.*
> *(B. Maina, personal communication, July 23, 2008)*

The significance of programs such as *Wembe wa Citizen* and *The Boss* is that they give a voice to people who, ordinarily have no say in the running of affairs that directly concern them. They have no say in much of the decision making and are rarely adequately represented. Their voices as individuals are not likely to carry any weight, neither are they provided with platforms to present their position. In such situations, they are not able to demand accountability. Radio performs this function in another way by amplifying the issue to a local or national level. Broadcasters have a power of their own. They can place a call to a prominent person in a way that an ordinary citizen cannot. Failure of the affected party to respond to an issue would result to them being called out publicly on radio which will lead to negative publicity. Hence, broadcasters are able to obtain responses on behalf of their listeners. By facilitating this type of responsibility, radio in Kenya is increasingly using its power as an activist. It has assumed a role that has traditionally been performed by the civil society. In addition to being mediators, radio presenters take the problems directly from the affected citizenry and personally raise them with the concerned parties. Radio stations thus perform the role of public interlocutors. Unlike most activists, they are able to demand and obtain prompt answers.

Additional Radio Formats Emerge

With the increase in the number of radio stations, the quality of debates on the radio has improved. During the state-controlled broadcasting monopoly, political debates on radio were absent. With the rise of commercial radio, a number of debate-oriented programs have gained roots. Kiss FM, one of the leading urban FM stations has aired a politically charged program *Crossfire*. Highly professionally moderated, the program brings together three prominent personalities with contrasting positions, mostly based on political party affiliation, to debate wide-ranging issues. The program has been particularly successful during the electioneering period. *Crossfire* has hosted some of the smartest minds and addressed some of the greatest debates in Kenyan politics. Although ordinary people rarely participate except through asking questions, the program exposes the listeners to a wide range of issues in the country. *Crossfire* attracts mostly people who understand the English language. Other radio stations have also adopted their own versions of debate programs. Inooro FM, a Kikuyu vernacular station, has a program called *Kiririmbi* ("Flames" in English). Like *Crossfire,* this program brings together politicians from different sides of the political divide to discuss significant issues of the day. The simple act of including political minds who can address issues in the local languages is an important step toward political participation, education and democratization in general. Before the rise of commercial media, a huge section who could not communicate in English or Swahili was left behind. The political discourse was only carried out in these two hegemonic languages making it hard for many ordinary people to follow. Currently, it is possible to communicate on the various issues of public interest in a wide range of vernacular languages.

Radio has also created a platform that has contributed to an increased availability of political and public figures to the Kenyan public. The many radio platforms have put up more demand for leaders and public figures to "speak to the people", making them more answerable to the citizens. This has led to an overall change in the method of governance and how public officials deal with the public. Today government ministers and the heads of governmental bodies are constantly interviewed on different radio stations. They use this opportunity to explain government policies and actions to the citizens. This helps to clarify different issues that the majority of the people would previously not have even heard about. For example, Kenyan government policies are mainly contained in huge complicated documents and the Kenya Gazette both of which are beyond most people's reach. With the increased broadcasting in local languages, leaders use the vernacular languages to explain the policies. This is important because all government documents are usually written in English and rarely translated into Swahili. They are never translated to the local languages which the masses understand.

Radio and the Failed Attempt at Constitutional Reform

Radio stations have also taken it upon themselves to provide pertinent information that would assist the public in making some important political decisions. For example, since 2002, Kenya has been reviewing the country's constitution. The process has witnessed long and protracted debates leading to sharp differences over some key issues that have been hard to bridge. After a five year process of drafting the new constitution, there was a need to hold a national referendum in 2005. The national referendum was to decide whether the new document will be adopted or not. One challenge of holding such a referendum was that only a negligible number of Kenyans had actually read the draft constitution. The dialogue over the constitution had instead been dominated by politicians and special interests.

In the political arena, two camps emerged within the ruling National Rainbow Coalition Party (NARC).Those who advocated for the new constitution, the Banana Team were led by President Mwai Kibaki. Those who opposed the new constitution were led by Raila Odinga (Orange Team). The two teams campaigned vigorously. However, the campaigns were deficient in providing civic education on the contentious issues involved in the proposed reforms. Radio Citizen responded to this need by allocating airtime and inviting experts to review major sections of the Draft Constitution. This role was important because it introduced many people to the particulars of the constitution. On the other hand, the manner in which Radio Citizen dealt with the Draft Constitution was in the end flawed. The station, having listened to both sides of the argument came to a conclusion that the revised constitution was good enough for Kenyans and actively supported its adoption and therefore a "Yes" vote in the referendum. At the same time, different radio stations adopted varying positions providing different viewpoints.

When the national referendum was held in December 2005, the new constitution was emphatically rejected. This happened despite the employment of government machinery to gather support. These results bear witness to the strong influence of radio and the changes in the liberalized market. The multiple stations available have enabled a diversity of voices which are now able to compete with the state-controlled media. Thus, despite the national broadcasters, KBC English and KBC Swahili, being used by the government, as well as a national station Radio Citizen supporting the government, alternative voices could be heard on other radio stations, in addition to other media such as print. This represents a departure from the past when public radio was the only source of information and was used by the state to influence political discourse.

Conclusion

It is evident that many of the developments that have been going on since the mid-1990s are encouraging. Radio has moved away from the control of government officials and well-connected individuals to incorporate more diverse voices. Moving forward however, there are numerous challenges that have to be addressed for radio to fulfill its role as an effective public platform. Freedom in broadcasting, like in other walks of life, comes with added responsibility. Broadcasters have to ensure that the radio political discourse is carried out in a responsible way. In a country where political divisions along ethnic lines thrive, recent experiences have shown that the same can easily seep into the broadcasting system with detrimental effects. The run-up to the 2007 general elections, and their aftermath, exemplify the negative role that radio can play. Following the post-election violence that rocked the country in January 2008, vernacular stations have been implicated for directly fuelling ethnic animosity by inciting their audiences mostly through negligence in facilitating the political discourse. Radio stations, through their presenters and discussion moderators, are noted to have failed to handle responsibly explosive debates on the radio thereby allowing for inflammatory comments (Ismail & Deane, 2008; Commission of Inquiry on Post Election Violence in Kenya, 2008). Listeners interviewed in Kieni West had different views on the role of radio in the post-election violence. Some pointed to outright biases during the election campaign period where stations identified with specific political parties. Others felt that such biases only reflected the political leanings of the listeners, who form the electorate. It is inevitable that stations which target a particular section of the population will reflect their audience's political viewpoint, they argued.

The outcomes of radio's role in the constitutional review process provide an example of the contradictions that abound in the liberalized media market and more importantly some lessons for broadcasters to learn in dealing with critical political issues. The solid position taken by a leading station like Radio Citizen in matters of national interest will always attract close scrutiny and will inevitably be subject to different interpretations. For example, many people saw Radio Citizen as biased in its coverage of the constitutional referendum debates. However, given the prior political positions its owners had supported, and their close association with the Kikuyu ethnic community, most observers were not surprised by the position Radio Citizen adopted. It is important to note that Royal Media, Radio Citizens parent company, has in recent years been accused of preferential treatment of the Party for National Unity (PNU) and the Central Kenya Region. However, the company owns multiple vernacular radio stations broadcasting in different regions of the country. In the 2007 elections campaign, for example, Citizen Television was contracted to air live broadcasts of the unveiling of the manifesto of Orange Democratic Movement (ODM), PNU's main challenger. Thus, while some of the claims may have some grounds; Royal Media Company has played with different sides of political divides in Kenya.

Vernacular radio stations are likely to fall into an ethical dilemma when addressing issues of national interest that have no consensus nationally. Due to diverse political views that are ethnically defined, by the virtue of attracting listeners of one ethnic group vernacular stations are likely to be saturated with that particular group's political opinions and hence display a lack of objectivity. This, as discussed above, is inevitable if vernacular stations are to provide a public platform where citizens can deliberate different issues. On the other hand, ethnocentric political discourses that may emerge are not healthy and do not promote the much needed national unity. Being aware of their delicate positions in political matters, radio stations can enhance their role as moderators in political discourses by pointing to the fact that different political viewpoints exist out there. It is also important those stations to keep the public aware of the historical antecedents that have contributed to these differing viewpoints.

There is a notable level of conflictuality in the Kenyan public sphere, similar to what Wittman (2008) has noted in Senegal. The conflict in Senagalese media is between political, religious, economic, media and regulatory actors. In the Kenyan public sphere, the conflict is mainly between political parties and ethnic groupings, with only a limited role played by the media. The growing multiplicity of media is likely to mitigate these conflicts. The Kenyan media regulator, the Communications Commission of Kenya (CCK), has been accused of passivity, lacking clear-cut guidelines that would counter the potentially negative role of the media in the political discourse (Ismail & Deane, 2008).

The new role of radio in promoting political discourse in Kenya suggests that one communication medium is not adequate to facilitate the exchange of ideas. Radio presents the platform, whereas mobile phones have provided the means through which the public can come together for the realization of a communicative space that permits the circulation of information and ideas. While the distribution of, and access to, information technologies, and the development of a functioning public sphere, presents an important opportunity in developing nations in regions such as Africa, Asia and Latin America some have argued that to create an environment where democratization can take place it is also essential to have a more equitable distribution of economic resources. (Rozumilowicz, 2002; Vanhanen, 2003). In an analysis of democracy around the world Vanhanen (2003) shows that nations with more equitably distributed social and economic goods among different social groups and classes have greater prospects of democracy. Unfortunately, the penetration of communication technologies through improved access in rural Africa in recent years has been achieved without significant changes in the social economic conditions of those rural citizens. Despite this, we can note that information technologies provide rural African populations with an avenue to challenge their establishments through new forms of participation and that this may enhance the overall prospects of democracy in their countries.

REFERENCES

Bourgault, L. M. (1995). *Mass Media in sub-Saharan Africa*. Bloomington: Indiana University Press.

The British Broadcasting Corporation (2007). Country Profile: Kenya retrieved February 17 from 2009 from http://news.bbc.co.uk/2/hi/africa/country_profiles/1024563.stm.

Carey, J.W. (1989). *Communication as culture: Essays on Media and Society*. Boston, MA: Unwin Hyman.

Commission of Inquiry on Post Election Violence in Kenya (CIPEV) (2008). *Report on 2007 post-election violence*. CIPEV: Nairobi.

Dahlgren, P. (2005). The public sphere: Linking the media and civic cultures. In E.W.

Rothenbuhler and M. Coman (Eds.), *Media Anthropology* (pp. 318-327). Thousand Oaks, CA : Sage.

Gadsen, F. (1980). The African Press in Kenya, 105-1962. *Journal of African History, 21*(4), 525-535.

Garnham, N. (2007). Habermas and the public sphere. *Global Media and Communication, 3(2),* 201-214.

Gathigi, G.W. (2009). *Radio listening habits among rural audience: An ethnographic study of Kieni West Division in Central Kenya*. Unpublished doctoral dissertation, Ohio University, Athens.

Gathigi, G. W. (in Press). Setbacks of broadcasting liberalization and partial policy formulation in an emerging democracy: The case of Kenya. In Njogu, K., (Ed), *Media and the 2007 General Election in Kenya*.

Goode, l. (2005). *Jürgen Habermas: Democracy and the public sphere*. London: Pluto.

Habermas, J. (1989). *The structural transformation of the public sphere: An inquiry into a category of bourgeois society* (T. Burger & F. Lawrence, Trans.). Cambridge, MA: MIT Press. (Original Work published 1962).

Ismail, A. J., & Deane, J. (2008). The 2007 general elections in Kenya and its aftermath: The role of local language media. *International Journal of Press/Politics, 13*(3), 319-327.

Karanja, M. (2000). Growth of print media in Kenya. In M. Odero and E. Kamweru (Eds.), *Media Culture and Performance in Kenya* (pp. 57-81). Nairobi: Kenya Chapter of the Eastern Africa Media Institute, and Friedrich Ebert.

Kenya Broadcasting Corporation (2009). *About KBC.* Retrieved on March 21, 2009 from http://www.kbc.co.ke/info.asp?ID=1.

Lippman, W. (1922). *Public opinion.* New York: Macmillan.

Ndlela, N. (2007). Reflections on the global public sphere: Challenges to internationalizing media studies. *Global Media and Communication. 3(3),* 324-329.

Odhiambo, L. O. (2002). The media environment in Kenya since 1990. *African Studies.61*(2), *295-2002.*

Roberts, J.S. (1974). East Africa. In S. W. Head, Broadcasting *in Africa: A continental survey of radio and Television.* (pp. 53-61) Philadelphia: Temple University Press

Rosberg, C.G., & Nottingham, J. (1966). *The myth of 'Mau Mau' nationalism in Kenya.* New York: Praeger.

Rozumilowicz, B. (2002). Democratic change: a theoretical perspective. In M. Price, B. Rozumilowicz and S.G. Verhulst (Eds.).   Media reform: democratizing the media, democratizing the state, (pp. 10-26). London, New York: Routledge.

Scotton, J. F. (1975). Kenya's maligned African press: Time for reassessment. *Journalism Quarterly, 52,* 30-36.

Steeves, J. (1997). Re-democratization in Kenya: "Unbounded politics" and the political trajectory toward national elections. In P. Ahluwalia and P. Nursey-Bray (Eds), *Post-colonial condition: Contemporary condition in Africa* pp 32-54. New York: Nova Science Publishers.

Strategic Research Ltd. (2008). Media Landscape in Kenya. November 2008. Unpublished raw data. Transparency International (2009). Corruption perception Index. Retrieved on April, 12, 2009 from http://www.transparency.org/policy research/surveys_indices/cpi/2006

Vanhanen, T. (2003). *Democratization: A comparative analysis of 170 countries.* London; New York: Routledge.

Wittman, F. (2008). Politics, religion and the media: The transformation of the public sphere in Senegal. *Media, Culture & Society, 30*(4), 479-494.

Chapter 7

The Phasing of Analog to Digital Technology in Nigerian Movie and Broadcasting Industries: A Review of Nollywood and Nigerian Television Authority (NTA)

Cosmas U. Nwokeafor
Bowie State University

Abstract

   The transformation of media technology from analog to digital broadcasting system has significantly impacted the Nigerian movie and broadcast industries. This movement from analog to digital system has provided critical changes to global media broadcasting systems making it possible for Nollywood, Nigerian movie industry and Nigerian Television Authority (NTA) to broadcast and entertain differently. The phasing from analog to digital technology, a revolutionary informational infrastructure, involves digital broadcast recording, multi-channel cable television and satellite networks. It also involves broadcast programming formats which provide a global production opportunity that enables Nollywood and NTA to showcase the cultural heritage and significant events of commendations in Nigeria to international community. This rapid transition from analog to digital systems has decentralized both the television and movie operating systems which have

*introduced a creative and new dimension of information and entertainment
dissemination from Nigeria to the outside world.*

*This chapter intends to examine the impact the transition from analog to
digital has had on Nigerian movie and broadcasting industries by reviewing
literature on the establishment of television and Nollywood. Historical review
of the media/television industries elaborating on the digital broadcast revolution
with emphasis on the digital media and how the transition from analog to digital
technology has significantly changed the Nigerian movie and television
industries will be discussed extensively.*

INTRODUCTION

The establishment of what later became the first radio broadcasting system
in South Africa in the early 1920s paved the way for electronic media system in
the continent of Africa. By 1928 and later part of the 1930s, Kenya, Sierra
Leone, Ghana, and Nigeria heralded the introduction of radio broadcasting
system, a new electronic media system which posed great challenge to the print
media system which was brought along by the colonial leaders. Yushkiavitshus
(1994) argued that although few African nations were proud to welcome the
establishment of radio in the early 1920s and later part of the 1930s as another
dimension to news and entertainment, the 1960s was the period political
transition and transformation in Africa brought with it radio broadcasting
systems. During this period, most African countries emerged from colonialism
to political independence which made it very necessary for them to have an
established radio broadcasting system (Merrill, 1995).

Considering the history and role electronic media systems play in the
development of any society, the presence of radio in the new emerging
democracy in Africa played a dual role; (1) as a tool for national integration and
(2) as a resource that accelerates national development in various African
nations.

The establishment of radio broadcasting system in Africa served more than
the role of national integration and national development; it also provided
information on government policies and activities. Merrill (1995) illustrates the
significant role played by the African radio to include the provision of
entertainment to the colonial leaders and a handful of educated Africans. Radio
broadcasting system was used by the European administrators as a propaganda
tool to secure the loyalty and support of the colonies during World War II.
During the war, radio was used as a necessary conduit through which
information and reports about the performance of participating African soldiers
were provided.

As the establishment of radio broadcasting systems introduced a new
dimension to how news and entertainment was provided in Africa, so was

television in 1959. The first African nation to witness the establishment of television was Nigeria in 1959, followed by Sierra Leone, Gabon, Ivory Coast, and Burkina Faso in 1963 respectively. Television brought different dynamics in the way journalism is practiced in Africa coupled with interactive and creative means of dissemination of news and entertainment. The technology that accelerated the change that assisted in the establishment of television continues to evolve. The change has led to the transference of one phase of broadcasting tool to another, each time with a more improved wavelength. Broadcast technology has gone through various transformations, but one main question that history attempts to address is which factors lead to which change.

Many mass media scholars and technology experts have concluded in their scholarship that in the development of society, technological changes are so rapid and constant that several revolutions have resulted in effect. These revolutions or changes are what Marshall McLuhan referred to as technological determinism, which is the idea that technological changes tend to determine all other economic and social changes in society (Nwokeafor, 2002). Technological advancement in western civilized nations has positively impacted African nations and their electronic media system.

Today in most African nations such as Nigeria, Ghana, Cameroon, Ivory Coast, South Africa, Kenya, Zimbabwe, Zambia, Egypt, Ethiopia, Tanzania, Sudan, Morocco, Uganda, Mozambique, Madagascar, Malawi, Niger, Senegal, Angola, Mali, Tunisia, Guinea, Chad, Somali, Burundi, Benin, Libya, Togo, Eritrea, Mauritania, Liberia, Namibia and many others, the establishment of electronic media systems such as radio and television has come a long way. However, the change that resulted to the digitalization of various broadcasting systems in developed countries such as the United Kingdom, United States, China, Russia, Germany, Italy, and others, have led to a revolution in the mass media industry in the African most populous nation, Nigeria. As Nigerian mass media, most essentially the movie industry, embraces the digital innovation, the level of its product seems to have taken a positive and dynamic overturn.

It is in this light, therefore, that this chapter focuses on reviewing the following (a) the impact of digital technology in Nigerian Broadcasting and movie Industries; (b) how technological innovations have become the driving force in the nation's political, social, and economic growth; and (c) how the technological changes have impacted Nigerian radio, movies (filmmaking) and television industries respectively.

A REVIEW OF THE HISTORY OF TELEVISION
PROGRAMMING AND FILMMAKING IN AFRICA

According to historical account and in keeping with Merrill (1995), the first television station in the continent of Africa was established in 1959 in Nigeria, which opened the opportunity for other African nation's television systems. In 1982, about 29 African countries had television stations which increased to 35 in 1995. However, today at least each African nation has a working television station which is controlled by the government.

Electronic media systems, most importantly television stations in the continent of Africa, are owned by the government who are directly responsible for the operating costs of the stations, thereby exerting control over their services (Nwokeafor & Thomas, 2005). However, technological innovations have made it possible for private-owned television and cable stations to operate in most African nations such as Nigeria, Cameroon, Ghana, South Africa, Kenya, and most other countries in the continent. In Nigeria, for instance, the Nigerian Television Authority (NTA) operates a federal network which is responsible for television programs and production. The federal network circulates its programs and production to all the state affiliates who broadcast the network programs through their stations to the viewing audience.

In Cameroon, the government, after nine months of experimental television transmission, began a controlled transmission of television services in 1985, although things have changed and there are about four privately owned television stations with little government control. In Chad and Niger, transmission of television broadcasting system began in 1987 and 1980 respectively (Merrill, 1995). Gabon's ownership of television is different because the country has a commercial television station that emerged in 1988. This station is different from the national broadcasting organization. In 1993, Botswana launched its television broadcasting system, while in 1961 and 1994 Zambia and Mozambique launched their television stations respectively. The Zimbabwe television station, a two-channel station, became operational in 1980 and on April 27, 1971 by accepting the Meyer Commission recommendation to established television system, South Africa announced the introduction of a television station which did not officially begin transmission until May 5, 1975, and a regular service of South African Broadcasting Corporation (SABC) was officially inaugurated on January 5, 1976.

The television broadcasting service (Merrill, 1995) indicated started off by carrying 37 hours of programming on a single television channel in English and Afrikaans. South African television advertisements only began two years after the official inauguration of the South African Broadcasting Corporation. It is important to note that significant revolutions in television and cable services have changed the phase of the African broadcasting system because, with the launching of PAFSAT and Cable (both coaxial and FIOS) in Africa, a significant number of commercial television and radio stations are providing services to their audiences with little or no government control. Some of these broadcasting services provide services on the web from Africa.

African cinema refers to the film production in countries in sub-Saharan Africa following formal independence, which for many countries happened in the 1960s. Some of the countries which belong geographically to Africa had developed a national film industry much earlier. African cinema has always been discussed to include their directors living in diaspora.

African Film During the Colonial Era

During the colonial era, the continent of Africa was represented in cinema by Western filmmakers. During this period cinema about Africa shot during the colonial period included jungle epics such as *Tarzan and the African Queen*, and various adaptations of H. Rider Haggard's 1885 novel titled *King Solomon's Mines* (Pfaff, F, 1988).

In the French colonies, filmmaking was forbidden to Africans. The first francophone African film, *L'Afrique sur Seine* produced by Paulin Soumanou Vieyra, was shot in Paris in 1955. Prior to independence, only a few anti-colonial films were produced. Examples of this include *Les Statues Meurent Aussi* by Chris Marker and Alain Resnais. This film was about European robbery of African art, which was later banned by the French for 10 years. Another colonial era film, *Afrique 50*, produced by Rene Vauthier was about the anti-colonial riots in Cote D'Ivoire and in Upper Volta (now referred to as present-day Burkina Faso). Many of the ethnographic films produced in the colonial era by Jean Rouch and others were rejected by African filmmakers because they distorted African realities (Armes, 1987).

African Film from the 1960s, Through the 1980s and Beyond

The first African film to win international recognition was Ousmane Sembene's *La Noire de*, which is also referred to as *Black Girl*. This movie showed the despair of an African woman who has to work as a maid in France. This movie, produced by Sembene, a native of Senegal and considered to be the father of African cinema, occupies a most essential place in the birth of African film making. African film created its own forum in 1969 when they organized the first African film festival, FESPACO, in Burkina Faso. Today, the African film festival takes place every two years in alternation with the film festival Carthago in Tunisia. FESPACO was formed in order to focus attention on the production, promotion, distribution, and exhibition of African films industries. From its inception, the Federation of African Filmmakers was a critical partner organization to the OAU, now AU. It looks at the role of film in the political-economy and cultural development of African states and the continent as a whole (Pfaff, 1988).

Med Hondo's *O Soleil O*, shot in 1969, was overly recognized; however, it was politically less engaged than Sembene, who chooses a more controversial film language to show what it means to be a stranger in France with the wrong skin color. Djibril Diop Mambety's sophisticated comedy *Touki-Bouki,* released in 1973, about a young couple in Dakar who want to make a trip to Paris at all costs, is still considered as one of the best African films ever made.

Souleymane Cisse's *Yeelen's* movie released in 1987 and Cheick Oumar Sissoko's *Guimba* in 1995, both in Mali respectively, were well received in the West. Both filmmakers have been criticized for adapting to the exotic tastes of western audiences. Many films of the 1990s — for instance, *Quartier Mozart* produced by Jean-Pierre Bekolo in 1992 from Cameroon — are situated in the globalized African metropolis. The first African summit took place in South Africa in 2006 and was followed by the Federation of African Filmmakers' (FEPACI) 9th Congress.

African filmmakers often have difficulty accessing African audiences. The commercial cinemas in Africa often have to book blindly and show primarily foreign films from European countries and the United States of America. There are still limited venues where African audiences have access to African films, such as at the Pan African film festival in Ouagadougou, Burkina Faso. Most African filmmakers still rely heavily on European institutions for financing and producing their films. Today, a commercially viable video production has been set up in Nigeria, known as Nollywood.

The political approach of African filmmakers is clearly evident in the charted u eineaste africain (Charta of the African cineaste) which the union of African filmmakers FEPACI adopted in Algiers in 1975. From the annals of its inception to the present time when technological innovations have taken control of the world frontier, African cinema has always been seen as a part of third cinema, which resulted in African filmmakers of contemporary times stressing solidarity with progressive filmmakers in other parts of the world. Their agenda, therefore, was to, in the words of Souleymane Cisse, "show that people in Africa are human beings and to help them discover the African values that can be of service to others" (Boughedir, 1987).

The role of the African filmmaker is often compared to traditional Griots whose primary aim is to express and reflect communal experiences. It is obvious that patterns of African oral literature often recur in African films as is shown in foremost African novelist, Chinua Achebe's novel *Things Fall Apart,* which is globally recognized. The literature and story created structured by Achebe is currently reflected in a movie (Balogun, 1987). African film has also been influenced by traditions from other continents such as Italian neo-realism, Brazilian Cinema Novo, and the theatre of Bertolt Brecht.

TABLE 1
AFRICAN MOVIE DIRECTORS BY COUNTRY

Movie Directors	Country
Sarah Maldoro & Zeze Gamboa	Angola
Jean Odoutan & Idrissou Mora Kpai	Benin
Idrissa Ouedraogo, Gaston Kabore, Dani Kouyate, Fanta Regina Nacro, Appoline Traore, Orissa Toure, Pierre Yameogo, Sanou Kollo and Pierre Ruamba	Burkina Faso
Jean-Pierre Bekolo, Bassek Ba Kobhio, Jean-Pierre Dikongue, Jean-Marie Teno and Francois Woukoache	Cameroon
Fernando Vendrell and Francisco Manso	Cape Verde
Didier Ouenangare	Central African Republic
Issa Serge Coelo and Mahamat Saleh Haroun	Chad

Desire Ecare, Fadika Kramo Lancine, Roger Gnoan M'Bala, and Jacques Trabi	**Cote d"Ivoire**
Mweze Ngangura, Balufu Bakupa-Kanyinda, Joseph Kumbela and Zeka Laplaine	**Democratic Republic of Congo**
Salah Abu Seif, Youssef Chahine, Yousry Nasrallah, Ezzel Dine Zulficar, Sherif Arafa, Tarek Al Erian, Atef El Tayeb, Khaled Youssef, Ali Badrakhan, Dawood Abdel Said, Magdy Ahmed Ali, Marwan Hamed, Amr Arafa, Barakat, Ehab Mamdouh, Sandra Nashat, Enas El Deghedy, Adel Adeeb, Mohamed Khan, Ehab Lamey, Shady Abdel Salam, Hala Khaleel, Khairy Beshara, Ali Ragab, Hady El Bagoury, Radwan El Kashef, Ashraf Fahmy, Samir Seif, Ali Abdel Khaleq and Nader Galal	**Egypt**

Haile Gerima	**Ethiopia**
Imunga Ivanga	**Gabon**
Kwaw Ansah, King Ampaw, John Akronfrah and Fara Awindor	**Ghana**
David Achkar, Gahite Fofana and Mohamed Camara	**Guinea**
Flora Gomes	**Guinea-Bissau**
Souleymane Cisse, Cheick Oumar Sissoko, Abdoulaye Ascofare and Adama Drabo	**Mali**
Med Hondo, Abderrahmane Sissako, and Sidney Sokhana	**Mauritania**
Oumarou Ganda	**Niger**
Ola Balogun, Eddie Ugboma, Amaka Igwe, Zeb Ejiro, Lola Fani-Kayode, Bayo Awala, Izu Ojukwu, Greg Fiberesima and Tunde Kelani Jide Bello	**Nigeria**
Judy Kibinge, Jane Muneme and	**Kenya**

Anne Mungai	
Ousmane Sembene, Paulin Soumarou Vieyra, Djibril Diop Mambety, Moussa Sene Absa, Safi faye, Ababacar Samb-Makhbaram, Ben Diogaye Beye, Clarence Delgado, Ahmadou Diallo, Bouna Medoune Seye, Moussa Toure, Mansour Sora Wade and Samba Felix Ndiaye	**Senegal**
Abdisalam Aato	**Somalia**
Gadalla Gubara	**Sudan**
Anne Laure Folly	**Togo**
Lionel Ngakane, Seipati Bulani-Hopa, Mickey Dube, Gavin Hood, Zola Maseko, Sechaba Morejele, Morabene Modise and Teddy Matthera	**South Africa**
M.K. Asante, Jr.	**Zimbabwe**

Murphy, D. (2000). "Africans Filming Africa: Questioning Theories of an Authentic African Cinema" Journal of African Cultural Studies 13 (2): 239-249.

The history of African Television programming, which started in Nigeria in 1959, and filmmaking in 1960s, has been on analog system until the recent digital revolution made possible by the advent of modern technology, which has ushered an enhanced media production that shows an enhanced video, audio, and quality pictures with speed. Digitalized technology has brought with it a tremendous development in the way television and filmmaking are produced in a contemporary African media system most importantly in Africa's most populous nation, Nigeria.

The Digital Broadcast Revolution

The transformation of media technology from analog to digital tape recording is providing critical changes for global media broadcasting systems. This revolutionary, informational infrastructure involves digital broadcast recordings, multi-channel cable television and satellite networks, and broadcast programming formats which provide historical significance to the social, economic, and rich culture of Africa (Nwokeafor & Thomas, 2005).

This digital media movement is one of the most powerful technological marvels in the world. Over the last decade, digital technology has escalated into a multi-billion dollar industry in most of the Asian and European regions. This technological globalization has provided corporate America with unlimited opportunities to expand and share its technologies with other countries. For example, countries like Russia, Italy, England, Germany, China, Japan, and the developing nations of Africa are transmitting and receiving programs from around the globe.

The innovation of expensive high-tech cable and satellite systems provides African countries the unique opportunity to broadcast their programs on television, radio, and the Internet. Digital media information and communication technologies are big businesses for entrepreneurs seeking new global opportunities. As a result, the technological industry is selling and designing broadcast digital television and radio systems in African countries by replacing the old analog systems with satellite relays, digital TV, radio transmissions and Internet networking systems.

This evolution of broadcasting global trends in the electronic media technological process provides what Nwokeafor & Thomas (2005) referred to as intriguing ways in which programs are stored, distributed, and recorded around the world. This relaying of programs and information from one point to another is called "terrestrial relays," which has unique ways of relaying media signals by using interconnection wires and coaxial fiber-optic cables. For example, cable television, telephones, and other data engineering systems require coaxial cables. The fiber-optic cable, however, digitally processes information by using very thin glass strands to convey modulated light beams capable of carrying thousands of telephone calls and television signals. Discussing the future of television, Doyle (1992) opined that:

> Digital TV will transmit the audio and video coming into people's houses in computer language — zeros and ones — instead of the current analog information that is transmitted over the airways. Most experts predict that the way this digital information will get into consumers' houses will be over fiber-optic cable installed by the phone company. Digital fiber-optic cable is capable of handling one hundred times the information carried on today's coaxial cable. It will allow consumers to dial-up a virtually unlimited number of TV programs, to transmit live and taped video pictures from their personal TV to other TVs anywhere in the world, and to access enormous libraries of data and information. The living room TV becomes an interactive home computer, but that's just the beginning of the revolution (p. 158).

Thus, with the growing number of broadband services, and the demand by consumers for faster networking informational systems, cable television systems throughout the world are replacing coaxial cables with optical fiber systems which have positively impacted the broadcasting system in the continent of Africa.

Therefore, broadcaster's heading into the 21st century are taking full advantage of the fiber optic cable revolution (Head, Spann, & McGregor, 2001, pp. 126-128). The growing number of households in African countries provides broadcasters the opportunity to deliver numerous sports, news, entertainment, and special interest cultural programs to massive consumers and viewers in a matter of seconds with the use of fiber-optic cables linked to satellites, wireless cable, and the Internet system around the world.

The world of communications moves forward with great speed into the 21st century. The utilization of compelling high-tech electronic devices has revolutionized television, radio, cable broadcasting system, the Internet, mobile phones, and mobile devices in civilized nations, which is gradually filtering into various African countries. Shrivastava (2005) indicated that the power of digital media has changed the meaning of information on demand. Numerous cultural societies have the ability of communicating with each other 24-hours a day, seven days a week, regardless of where they live.

The advent of digital media system in today's technology-driven society has made it much easier to retrieve, analyze, share, move, and store information faster than ever before. Digital signal processing allows communication satellite networks to transmit hundreds of signals to customers around the globe. Shrivastava (2005) points out that fiber-optic convergence is rapidly shifting from analog technology to the digital environment. According to Shrivastava:

> *The new media sphere has greatly increased our communication choices. Narrowcasting, interactive, educational and other networks now respond to hundreds of different needs, interests and tastes. Multimedia systems are broadening the horizons of artistic and intellectual creativity through video art, holography and virtual reality. Electronic images are replacing traditional forms of sharing and recording memory* (p. 3).

Transition from Analog to Digital Programming

Informational and electronic consumers are buying high-tech products and software that are capable of retrieving, moving, and creating quality programs that fit their needs. As a result, engineers around the world are making significant progress toward the digital revolution by replacing analog media production equipment with sophisticated digital, technical, editing, and broadcasting machines. Feldman (1997) reports that "a good way of getting a sense of what analog information and digital information are is to imagine 'analogue' as an expression of our experience of the real world while 'digital' expresses a world belonging exclusively to computers" (p. 1). Television engineers have been renovating and restructuring editing and analog studios to digital facilities across the western civilized nations. Ide, MacCarn, Shepard, and Weisse (2005) reported that:

> *Over the past decade, television production and broadcasting have been moving from analog to digital. The analog method, which transmits sounds and pictures through continuous wavelike signals or pulses of varying intensity, is being replaced by digital capture of transmission in which sounds and images are converted into groups of binary code* (p. 3).

The approach to digital signal processing has changed the broadcast production industry approach to producing and formatting programs. For example, during the 1990s, linear editing systems required that technicians shuttle through hours and hours of tape to play and log desired selections of tape. Today, digital technology provides several digital video tape formats, featuring better video quality and sharper imaging capabilities. This breakthrough in digital tape format recording provides electronic consumers and professional production companies with a variety of options, including mini-

DV, DV-CPRO, Digital-8, and DVD (digital video disc). It is obvious that this cutting-edge technology has impacted both peoples' lives and the television and radio industries in the continent of Africa.

Moreover, digital distinctive special components allow for mathematically applying formulas to recreate audio and video signals (Davie & Upshaw, 2003). Feldman (1997) illustrates five key factors involving digital unique characteristics: *(1) digital information is manipulatable, (2) digital information is networkable, (3) digital information is dense, (4) digital information is compressible, and (5) digital information is impartial.* Feldman further explains that if we translate analog information into a digital form, we'll be able to manipulate real world images into representations of our own imaginations. Within seconds, users of the media can shape their own experience into digital products.

Digital Television and Radio Systems

Digital television has revolutionized the way millions of household viewers receive and interact with their televisions. Digital TV's cutting-edge technology enables consumers in both the developed and developing countries to enjoy greater clarity during their personal and private television program experiences. H.M. Hobbs (personal communication, December 21, 2001) asserts that transmitting television to homes with digital technology is occurring in several countries around the world. She further explains that digital television is being transmitted by satellite, cable, and terrestrial means; it provides viewers with better reception quality, increased program choices, multi-view camera angles, and interactivity. Beacham (2005) notes that redefining the business of television and digital technology puts consumers in total control of their electronic environment. He further points out that "viewers are subscribing to new pay HDTV and video-on-demand (VOD) services at a brisk rate in countries like the United States, and once they experience the new technology, few turn back" (p. 26).

Digital television technology converts sound and pictures into digitized signals encoded and compressed for transmission by satellite and optical fiber. For example, Head, Spann, and McGregor (2001) declare that:

> *Compressed signals are decompressed by an intermediary cable system head-end decoder before passing the signal on to a household subscriber, which is digitally received by home television cable systems; thus, allowing viewers to be able to select from hundreds of signals, providing virtually unlimited program choices* (pp. 141-145).

Digital television's vast and expanding networks are dramatically changing and cultivating the way information is presented to viewers around the world. The Cable News Network (CNN) for instance can be accessed around various African countries today. In Nigeria, for instance, CNN is among the top television programs that brings news and entertainment to the homes of the subscribers of cable. Also, joining this digital revolution is the future of digital radio and Internet accessibility. For example, World Space Corporation announced its digital audio broadcast system, PANOS, a new Internet radio provider. This new digital radio system has the capability and means to transmit to the remote places in digital form. The impact of this digital Internet and radio technology offers features which "cover a wide range of social and economic and political issues detrimental to the image of African countries. These issues range from under-age drinking in Zimbabwe, gun violence and gangs in South Africa, advance pay-off (otherwise referred to as "419") and healthcare in Nigeria (The Internet Meets Radio, 2005, p. 1).

Digital audio broadcasting is on the cutting edge of technology; however, researchers suggest that it's not moving as swiftly as digital television. For example, Bachman (2005) reports that consumers who regularly listen to terrestrial radio constitute a nine percent lower rating than those consumers who listen to traditional radio. In addition, Bachman further states that those consumers who listen to "on-demand radio (iPods, satellite radio, Internet radio) spend two hours and 33 minutes each day listening to traditional radio, which equates to an average of two hours and 48 minutes per day among persons aged 12 and older" (p. 1). This innovation in radio might be very new in Africa, but it is believed that it will gradually transit to the various capital cities in most African countries.

Meanwhile, advanced radio technologies are strongly focusing on satellite and Internet radio with companies like XM Satellite Radio and Sirius Radio in the United States. According to Urban and Brandt (2005), these two innovative giants are challenging traditional radio listeners by providing commercial-free music, multi channels, and digital technology for better sound quality, uninterrupted reception, pre-installed auto receivers, and music formats to meet the demand of consumers' musical tastes.

Satellite companies in the United States, for instance, have launched a major change in the radio industry during the mid 1990s by broadcasting multi-channel digital signals from satellite to ground-based receivers which will impact the broadcasting industry in various African countries. The high-tech satellite systems allow the transmission of 150 channels from XM Satellite's listeners and 120 channels from Sirius satellite listeners. XM and Sirius satellite channels provide a variety of formats, which include weather, sports, talk shows, football, and baseball. Moreover, the companies have projected that in the year 2010 they will have over 50 million customers all tuned to on-demand audio radio (Urban & Brandt, 2005).

Digital Audio Technology

The demand for improved audio efficiency has forced media companies to be more competitive in the development of audio sound and digital technology. Connelly (2005) points out several major factors relating to this subject. He reports that digital audio eliminates a number of major problems associated with recording and storing analog audio, and that digital audio has the capability of being stored, manipulated, and played back through a series of devices. Digital audio also can be stored magnetically on a computer hard drive, a flash memory card, or digital audio. As a result, tape digital production technology has changed the way audio is transmitted and received to the Internet systems whereas radio programs and commercials are digitally transferred from one point to another in a matter of seconds.

National broadcast companies that invest billions of dollars in radio station ownership are replacing their analog equipment with expensive digital machines and computers with the power of doing the work in half the time and with fewer staff members. Conceptually, digital audio technology accommodates a wide array of production applications. As a result, broadcasting stations around the world are restructuring their production facilities with digital broadcast production equipment, including digital audio computer systems, digital production studios, consoles, editing and production systems, special effects, audio compressors, and recorders.

Reese and Gross (2002) explain that digital technology will have a tremendous impact on the future of radio and audio production environment. They record how:

> Digital technology has revolutionized how the radio production person can record, edit, and otherwise manipulate an audio sound signal. The days of pushing buttons to start a tape recorder are quickly being replaced with manipulating a mouse or keyboard and viewing a computer monitor screen to accomplish the tasks of audio production. From the advent in the early 1980s of the compact disc player, to the total digital production studio of the early 2000s, radio has eagerly embraced digital technology (p. 19).

As the infrastructure develops, digital and audio technological revolution are shaping the quality and production of the way listeners receive their information, news, sports, weather, music, and other format choices. The broadcasting industries are shifting their technological innovations to a more high-tech digital technological production society. Digital application will improve on attracting local, national, and global audiences. The development of these applications has improved significantly and impacts the global broadcasting system most importantly broadcasting system in various countries in the continent of Africa.

Companies like Dolby, Sony, Panasonic, Tascam, and others are designing high-speed mechanisms and digital program management systems for both radio and television. Innovative upgrade systems set performance standards for creating and managing customizable quality for products and programs for both digital radio and television.

Brief History of the Nigerian Television Authority (NTA)

The history of the Nigerian Television Authority (NTA) can be traced back to the modest beginning on October 31, 1959 when the Western Nigerian Television (WNTV) beamed out the first television signals in Nigeria. Barely a year after, in 1960, the Eastern Nigerian Television (ENTV) was born, which was followed after two years in 1962 by the Radio Television Kaduna (RTK). In 1962, the Federal Government, under the leadership of President Nnamdi Azikiwe and Prime Minister Tafewa Belewa, established the Nigerian Television Services (NTS) in Lagos. This development gave a much needed boost to television broadcasting. In 1973, three years after the end of the civil war, Midwest Television (MTS) came on board while Benue/Plateau Television (BPTV) Jos made history by commencing transmission in color from inception in 1974.

In May 1977, with the promulgation of Decree 24 by the Federal Military Government, the vision that became a reality in Ibadan in 1959 metamorphosed into a giant Network of NTA Stations. The Nigerian Television landscape has been significantly transformed with about 28 NTA Stations across the country utilizing a huge transmitter Network.

The inauguration of Nigerian Television Authority (NTA) in May 1977 empowered the organization that is today the only body to undertake television broadcasting in Nigeria. With the authority invested in NTA, all other existing state television stations were taken over and incorporated with it. The Authority was organized on the six-zone structure such that each zone consists of three stations, except for one, which is made of four stations. The production centers exist in each state to contribute programs to the zonal output. Today, Nigerian Television Authority/NTA is the largest Television Network in Africa and the oldest and most accomplished indigenous broadcast outfits in Nigeria (www.africine.org).

Nigerian Television Authority (NTA), generally renowned as Africa's window to the world, is operated on Megahertz networks 4 (MHz-4) which functions on a full feature network that brings around-the-clock coverage of serialized dramas, educational programming, sports, and a host of talk shows. Due to the delay of the United States Federal Communications Commission

(FCC) mandated digital transition, NTA was not available via broadcast (over the air) until June 12, 2009. As the largest television network operating in the continent of Africa, NTA is available through cable and teleco. As the world television operating systems are undergoing sporadic changes, so is the case with NTA, which could be watched in the United States under channel 454. With the recent technological development coupled with the process of digitalization, NTA fanatics, who are citizens of Nigeria who reside in various countries of the world, strongly supported the recent changes that are taking place within the Nigeria Television Authority.

According to a Saturday, December 9, 2006 article on Nigeria world titled "Upgrading Nigeria Image through Nigerian Television Authority (NTA), Tourism, and Nigerians Abroad," the Executive Director of NTA Programs, Peter Igho, stated that "The NTA online network has 26 fully fledged stations with three in Lagos. It covers approximately 80 percent of the total land area of Nigeria with a viewership of over 50 million." Igho (2006) showed that presently, NTA has six zones, South-South (Benin); North-Central (Kaduna); North-West (Sokoto); South-East (Enugu); North-East (Maiduguri); South-West (Ibadan), while Lagos and Abuja operate independently as the seat of business and the seat of Government respectively. NTA programs are very entertaining and educative, while the news is very in-depth, covering the whole of Nigeria.

Nigerian Television Authority (NTA) Programs

As the strongest television voice and the most popular in the continent of Africa, some of NTA programs, in addition to the News, include Sports, Current Affairs, Entertainment — Drama which features Soap Operas, Children's Adventure, Cartoons, Specials, Comedy, Musicals, Series and Serial; Variety and light Entertainment — such as Talk Shows, Quiz and Debates; Family Support Services; Educational Support Services; Traditional and Cultural Ceremonies. Other programs include: Traffic (Land), Traffic (Air); Fitness Drills; Business News; "Izozo" (Exposing the evils of Prostitution and child trafficking); "Another Opportunity" (Ex-convicts' new life); "Flying High" (educating Nigerians on the different aspects of our national life, history and culture as well as promoting and awareness of pride as a Nigerian); "Aiguo Basinmwin" (drama set in Benin city to highlight the conflicts between traditional beliefs and Christianity in the colonial era); "Grassroots TV" (Interaction between the government and rural areas); "I Need to Know" (HIV/AIDS crusade); "NDDC News" (Niger Delta development programs), among others (Igho, 2006).

As a government-owned body in charge of television programming in Nigeria, some of NTA programming can be viewed online through Africast while some of its news bulletins are carried on Africa Independent Television. Considerable amounts of NTA programming are relayed in turn to the United Kingdom by BEN Television in the United Kingdom and the United States respectively. Sky Digital also makes it possible to provide news and entertainment to Nigerians resident in the United Kingdom. The presence of digital technology has made NAT a unique powerhouse in the media and entertainment industries in Nigeria, most importantly in the continent of Africa. The quest to improve the bastardized Nigeria image by some past and present Nigerian leaders at home and abroad is taking another dynamic leap. The Federal Government of Nigeria launched Nigeria Television Authority International, which according to Peter Igho (2009), the executive director of NTA programs a right step at the right directions. As a television station in a class of its own, NTA will continue to be in the forefront of innovation as it strives to become among the best on the global landscape with creative programmers, services, news and entertainment (Igho, 2009).

NIGERIAN TELEVISION AUTHORITY (NTA) BRANCHES AND NETWORK CENTERS

Television services rendered by the Nigerian Television Authority could be abstracted through its numerous network centers and affiliate stations in various western nations of the world. These stations are as follows:

TABLE 2

Nigerian Television Association Network Centers	Network State
NTA-Aba	Abia State
NTA - Abeokuta	Ogun State
NTA – Abuja	Federal Capital Territory
NTA – Plus Abuja	Federal Capitol Territory
NTA – Ado-Ekiti	Ekiti State
NTA - Akure	Ondo State
NTA – Asaba	Anambra State

NTA – Awka	Anambra State
NTA – Bauchi	Bauchi State
NTA – Benin	Edo State
NTA – Calabar	Cross River State
NTA – Damaturu	Yobe State
NTA Dutse	Jigawa State
NTA – Enugu	Enugu State
NTA- Gombe	Gombe State
NTA - Gusau	Zamfara State
NTA - Ibadan	Oyo State
NTA - Ife	Osun State
NTA – Ijebu Ode	Ogun State
NTA – Ilorin	Kwara State
NTA International	United States, Europe and Neighboring African nations
NTA – Jalingo	Taraba State
NTA – Jos	Plateau State
NTA – Kaduna	Kaduna State
NTA – Kano	Kano State
NTA - Katsina	Katsina State
NTA – 2 Channel 5 Lagos	Lagos State

NTA – Channel 10 Lagos	Lagos State
NTA – Lafia	Nasarawa State
NTA – Lokoja	Kogi State
NTA - Maiduguri	Borno State
NTA – Makurdi	Benue State
NTA – Minna	Niger State
NTA - Ondo	Ondo State
NTA – Oshogbo	Osun State
NTA - Owerri	Imo State
NTA – Port Harcourt	Rivers State
NTA – Sokoto	Sokoto State
NTA – Uyo	Akwa Ibom State
NTA – Yenagoa	Bayelsa State
NTA – Yola	Adamawa State
NTA - Sapele	Delta State

NOLLYWOOD – Nigeria's Movie Industry

The cinema of Nigeria is a nascent film industry in Nigeria, which has grown and developed to great heights in the last 20 years to become the second largest film industry in the world behind the United States' film industries. According to Hala Gorani and Jeff Koinange, former staff of CNN, Nigeria has a 250 million dollar movie industry producing about 200 videos for the home video market every month.

Nigerian cinema, Freeman (2007) reports, is Africa's largest movie industry with the value and number of movies produced annually. Although Nigerian films have been in existence since 1960s, the rise in affordable digital filming and editing technologies has stimulated the country's video film industry. The Nigerian film industry, known as Nollywood, may not have similar ranks with the United States' Hollywood, but rather surpassed Bollywood, the Indian movie industry, in popularity and turnover of movie products. Nollywood has come of age since the early 1990s when the late Alade Armoire and Kenneth Nnebue introduced the home video in Nigeria. The movie industry today in Nigeria can boast of over 20 films released into the demanding market every week (Freeman, 2007).

The release of the box-office movie *Living in Bondage* in 1992 by NEK Video links in the Eastern Nigerian city of Onitsha set the stage for other films and home videos which exploded Nollywood into a booming industry. One of the first Nigerian movies to reach international renown was the 2003 release *Osuofia in London*, starring Nkem Owoh, the famous Nigerian comedic actor. The huge success of Nollywood has pushed foreign media off the shelves and its products are marketed all over the continent of Africa and the rest of the entertainment world. The first Nollywood films were produced with traditional analog videos, such as Betacam SP, but today, movie production in Nollywood has gone through tremendous changes where digital technology has replaced analog systems. The primary distribution centers of these movies are Idumota on Lagos Island, and 51 Iweka Road in Onitsha, Anambra State (Guardian Newspaper, 2006).

The Guardian article (March 2006) cites Nigeria's film industry as the third largest in the world in regards to earnings, bringing in about 200 million dollars annually. However, recent data has shown that Nollywood is currently the second largest movie industry in the world. It outsells Hollywood films in Nigeria and many other African countries. Nollywood's biggest competitor in Africa is the Ghanaian film industry. Nigerian filmmakers often times collaborate with Ghanaian actors and filmmakers. Van Vicker a popular Ghanaian actor has starred in many Nigerian movies and famous Nollywood actress Genevieve Nnaji has also starred in many Ghanaian films.

According to Frank Ikegwuonu, author of Who's Who in Nollywood, about "1200 films are produced in Nigeria annually." More and more filmmakers are heading to Nigeria because of competitive distribution system and a cheap workforce. Further, Nigerian films seem to be better received by the market when compared to foreign films because they are more family oriented than the American films (www.nigeriaentertainment.com).

Renowned Nigerian Actors/Actresses

As filmmaking and movie Industry has come a long way in Nigeria so are its actors. Notable among them are: Hassanat Akinwande, Regina Askia, Kanayo O. Kanayo, Liz Benson, Ini Edo, Pete Edochie, Rita Dominic, Omotola Jalade Ekeinde, Desmond Elliot, Chioma Chukwuka, Stella Damascus-Aboderin, Richard Mofe Damijo, Kate Henshaw-Nuttal, Osita Iheme, Chinedu Ikedieze, Baba Suwe, Oby Kechere, Jide Kosoko, Genevieve Nnaji, Ramsey Nouah, Oge Okoye, Sam Loco-Ife, Nkem Owoh, and Dolly Unachukwu.

DIGITAL TECHNOLOGY'S IMPACT ON NIGERIA'S TELEVISION AND MOVIE INDUSTRIES

The 21st century movie and advertising production is raising the bar when it comes to the world of digital cinema and marketing production. Writers, producers, directors, editors, and engineers are setting new standards in the post production industry. With DVDs (digital video discs) reaching sales in the billions, digital technology has become the most remarkable new technology which enables movie and advertising producers to design the most intriguing cinematography and advertising products imaginable.

In most developed countries in Europe and the United States, the digitalizing process has become the order of time. As this developed nations move toward a complete transition to digital technology, production outcome seem to have changed considerably. In the United States, for instance, film director, George Lucas, who is responsible for the hit film *Star Wars*, created one of the most innovative and inventive films in the world (Nwokeafor & Thomas, 2005). For example, Lucas used the process of digital technology and special effects when making the film *Attack of the Clones*. The production quality, as well as the level of control of all the special effects which tend to be real in appearance, makes the production standout. The digital movie (film) revolution allows filmmakers to be more in control of transitions, utilizing cutting-edge digital technology to capture challenging production images. This development, brought about by the advent of new technology, has created a dynamic way by which the movie industry's productivity is being evaluated in today's changing society.

According to Roberts (2005), "digitization" in the movie industry is unique when it comes to integrated multiple formats, editing, directing, shooting films, advertising, and television productions. Roberts further opined that, "Possibly the most interesting topic brought about by the increasing use of digital technology is the introduction of digital characters. Films such as *The Phantom*

Menace and *Toy Story* have introduced audiences to characters made entirely from digital sources. Although George Lucas' Jar Jar Binks was extremely annoying to many, the character alone showed just what could be done with emerging digital technology. In the anxiously awaited *Lord of the Rings* trilogy, directed by Peter Jackson, so much effort has been put in to ensure the world of Middle Earth is as detailed as the original novels. Peter Jackson explains, "My same philosophy applied to digital effects as to the overall design. I wanted the monsters to feel real right down to the dirt under the fingernails of a Cave Troll." Digitization is giving directors the chance to be more believable in creating their digital characters." (Nwokeafor & Thomas, 2005).

Thus, digital technological achievements in the development of television and films have revolutionized the visual concepts, and the numerous aspects of film and television viewing. Digital technology includes high definition TV, multi-channel audio, video processing, streaming, web serving, production editing, broadcast news, mobile and satellite functionalities. As a result, we come to understand that new digital technological production is a socially complex process, because each one of its elements is internally differentiated, and appeals to traditional viewers seeking visual and audio effectiveness during their private viewing times (Castells, 1997). Therefore, the movement toward diversity in digital communication (McLuhan and Powers, 1989) forms a bond with consumers seeking its high-tech products, specialized software systems, digital video disk (DVD's), radio, television cable, advertising, and satellite programs. This new advancement in the digital technological revolution is a multifaceted system designed to service the customers' communication desires, interests, and needs.

The digital transformation and commercialization have vigorously provided profound challenges and changes within the digital age. Digital media has dramatically altered the way people watch television in the developed countries which is significantly impacting same media audience in developing countries such as Nigeria, Ghana, Cameroon, Kenya, South Africa, Egypt, Ethiopia, and a lot more other African countries. The broadcast business and technological society have provided viewers with ways to share, record, buy, exchange, and distribute digital contents (Nwokeafor & Thomas, 2005). It has transformed the mass media industry in the world which has significantly impacted the production world of developing countries movie makers as well their audience.

Herman and Chesney (1997) as quoted by Nwokeafor & Thomas (2005) argued that throughout the world, commercialization of national television systems has been regarded as an integral part of economic liberalization programs, and that the digital media business creates opportunities for a number of countries, including the continent of Africa and Nigeria is taking lead in such transformation that is currently impacting its television, movie and advertising industries respectively.

The mid 1990s through 2009 have witnessed the booming of the "video-film" industry in Nigeria, Ghana and now most recently in Ethiopia. Nigerian "video films" are not films produced in traditional ways of cinema, but rather stories recorded on home videos. A typical director of video-film does not have a traditional filmmaking experience or background. Some of these indigenous film directors range from wealthy merchants with access to the required capital necessary to produce a movie project to theater actors who have the dramatic theater background (Gabriel, 1982).

The digital age has opened up opportunities for Nigerian filmmakers to use digital video, which captures high quality images and sound, and makes post-production equally accessible. Digitalization brought about by the advent of the new technological advancement addresses both the financial and distribution challenges previously faced by Nigerian filmmakers. It has also greatly expanded accessibility and significantly changed the landscape of the aesthetics, form and content of Nigerian movie industry. Nigerian filmmakers have taken advantage of the digital age as well as the market niche created by the video-film industry to produce their films on a small budget and direct video distribution of their films within the 36 states and their neighboring African countries (Gabriel, T. 1982).

Despite the short period of time the Nigerian movies have been in existence, the industry and its producers are at a crucial crossroads and have made significant impact in the movie industry across the country and other neighboring African countries. This supports the claim by Mbye Cham's (1996) contention that:

> In spite of its youth and the variety of overwhelming odds against which it is struggling, cinema by Africans has grown steadily over this short period of time to become a significant part of a worldwide film movement aimed at constructing and promoting an alternative popular cinema, one that is more in harmony with the realities, the experiences, the priorities and desires of the society which it addresses (6).

It is, of course, obvious that digital technology has increased the access needed by Nigerian movie producers to produce higher-quality films, which has to a larger extent flooded the Nigerian market and other parts of African countries including the U.S. and European markets respectively.

Summary and Conclusion

It could be argued that the cost for new digital technology is reaching beyond the financial capabilities of some African communities. Nevertheless, Africa is merging into the informational and technological age with transmission into digital television and advertising broadcast programming, as well as moviemaking, as a huge economic market which has a very large and prosperous audience, both internally and in the global market community. Nwokeafor & Thomas (2005) quoting Johnson-Odim (2002) report that digital imaging and other technologies have made it cheaper for African movie producers to produce and distribute their products throughout Africa and other countries around the world. This trend opens the doors to African movie and television producers to join with other media professionals in the development of national television broadcast and advertising programs, as well as the contemporary movie industry that has hit the ground of movie entertainment running.

The main goal of this study was to explore the impact of digital media communication technologies in the continent of Africa's movie, broadcast, informational, and technological communities. The presence of radio and television broadcasting systems in the continent of Africa has served more than the role of national integration and national development. It has provided information on government policies, political agenda, and economic activities. It has also provided entertainment to the people. The broadcasting industry in African countries has served as propaganda tool for the government to secure the loyalty and support of their people. Digital media cable organizations around the world are replacing analog systems with powerful digital production distribution and transmission capabilities. Digital devices, including cell phones, television, radio, and DVDs, are being sold and marketed to consumers throughout the globe. This communication phenomenon provides a historical and political shift for developing countries seeking the need to improve their technological and informational infrastructure with reliable and faster digital signals, instructional TV, interactive television, and digital broadband Internet access.

The digital multi-media revolution is becoming an integral part of our growing global society and constitutes a significant need in the way information is exchanged, accessed and stored. The implications of this new emerging digital media technology have become a central part of developmental initiatives throughout the continent of Africa. Access to information is considered liberating to those individuals who are hungry with anticipation of having accessibility to technological resources.

Dutton (1996) claims that access to information is regarded as liberating; communication systems promote new forms of community, education and training needs; structuralism offers new resources and interests; and evolution will change to new cultural forms. Thus, the foundation of this argument is that audiences in Africa are growing, and the need for access to more information has escalated to phenomenal dimensions. We find that information and communication digital technologies open doors of vision and representation of the beauty, splendor, and brilliance of the present, past, and future of the rich cultural and political heritage of Africa.

REFERENCES

Armes, R (1987). Third World Filmmaking and the West. Berkeley University of California Press. pp. 381.

Balogun, F. (1987). The Cinema in Nigeria. Enugu: Delta Publications. Pp. 144.

Bachman, K. (2005, March 23). *Research: On-demand nibbling at traditional radio.*

Retrieved March 28, 2005, from http://billboardradiomonitor.com/radiomonitor/ news/business/ratings_research/article_display.jsp?vnu_content_id=100085 4312.

Boughedir, F. (1987). Le Cinema Africain de A-Z. Brussels: Editions OCIC. pp.206.

Castells, M. (1997). *The rise of the network society* (Vol. 1). Malden, MA: Blackwell Publishers.

Cham, M. (1996). African Experiences of Cinema – Edited by Imruh Bakari and Mbye B. Cham. London: BFI Publication (p.1).

Connelly, D. (2005*). Digital radio production.* New York, NY: McGraw-Hill.

Davie, W. R., & Upshaw, J. R. (2003). *Principles of electronic media.* Boston, MA: Allyn and Bacon

Doyle, M. (1992). *The future of television: A global overview of programming, advertising, technology and growth.* Lincolnwood, Illinois: NTC Business Books.

Dutton, W. H. (Ed.). (1996). *Information and communication technologies: Visions and realities.* New York: Oxford University Press.

Feldman, T. (1997). *An introduction to digital media.* London: Routledge.

Freeman, C. (2007). "In Nollywood, lights, camera, action is best case scenario." The Daily Telegraph. http://www.telegraph.co.uk/news/ worldnews.

Gabriel, T. H. (1982). Third Cinema in the Third World: The Aesthetics of Liberation by Teshome H. Gabriel, Ann Arbor, Michigan: UMI Research Press, p. 23

Head, S. W., Spann, T., & McGregor, M. A. (2001). *Broadcasting in America: A survey of electronic media* (9th ed.). Boston, MA: Houghton Mifflin Company.

Herman, E. S., & Chesney, R. W. (1997). *The global media: The new missionaries of corporate capitalism.* New York: Cassell Wellington House.

Ide, M., MacCarn, D., Shepard, T., & Weisse, L. (2005). *Understanding the preservation challenge of digital television.* Retrieved April 2, 2005, from http://www.digitalpreservation.gov/index.php?nav=3&subnav=9

Igho, P. (2009). Upgrading Nigeria Image Through Nigerian Television Authority, (NTA), Tourism, and Nigerians Abroad. Nigeriaworld.

Ikeagwuonu, F. (2006). Who's Who in Nollywood Nigeria Movie Industry (www.nigeriaentertainment.com)

Johnson-Odim, C. (2002, December 5-8). *Africa in the information and technology age.* Retrieved April 6, 2005, from http://www.africanstudies. org/asa_papercalltheme.html

McLuhan, M., & Powers, B. R. (1989). *The global village: Transformations in world life and media in the 21st century.* New York: Oxford University Press.

Merrill, J. (1995). Global Journalism: Survey of International Communication. (3rd ed.) New York: Longman Publishers. New Nigerian Cinema: An Interview with Akin Adesokan (2006). Retrieved from www.Indiana.edu on May 27, 2008. Nigeria's film industry, The Economist

Nwokeafor, C. U. (1992). Development Communication in the Nigerian Mass Media: A Study of Selected Publications. Unpublished doctoral dissertation, Howard University, Washington, D.C.

Nwokeafor, C. U. (2002). Strategic Technological Changes in Contemporary Advanced Information Society: A link between African-Americans and Africa in the Diaspora. A paper presented at the Southern Interdisciplinary Roundtable on African Studies Conference Proceedings. Kentucky State University, Frankfort, Kentucky.

Nwokeafor, C. U. & Thomas, O. (2005). The Impact of Digital Technology in African Changing Mass Media Market: A Review of Nigerian Radio and Television Industries. A paper presented at the Southern Interdisciplinary Roundtable on African Studies (SIRAS) Conference Proceedings. Kentucky State University, Frankfort, Kentucky.

Ogan, C. (1982). Development Journalism: "The Status of the Concept." Gazette. pp. 3-12.

Pfaff, F. (1988). Twenty-Five Black African Filmmakers. Westport, CT: Greenwood Press. pp. xiii.

Reese, D. E., & Gross, L. S. (2002). *Radio Production Work text: Studio and equipment (4th ed.).* Woburn, MA: Focal Press.

Roberts, P. (2005). *Digital cinema.* Retrieved April 4, 2005, from http://www.dvdanswers.com

Shrivastava, K. M. (2005). *Broadcast journalism: In the 21st century.* Elgin, IL: New Dawn Press.

Step Aside, L.A. and Bombay, for Nollywood, New York Times.

The Internet Meets Radio: New content forms for rural audiences. Retrieved April 6, 2005, from http://www.balancing act-africa.com/news/back/balancing-act58.html.

The Guardian Newspaper (March 2006). Nigeria's Film Industry the third largest in the world in terms of earning.

Urban, R., & Brandt, N. (2005). *XM, Sirius gaining traction.* Retrieved April 4, 2005, from http://www.mercurynews. com /mld/mercurynews 11300756.htm

Yushkiavitshus, H. (1994). Unpublished, untitled paper read at the International
    Press Institute, 43rd Annual General Assembly, Cape Town, South Africa,
    February 16.

Chapter 8

Media and Peace-building in Sudan

Hala A. Guta

INTRODUCTION

On January 9, 2005, the Government of Sudan (GOS) and the Sudan People's Liberation Movement/Army (SPLM/SPLA) signed a peace agreement that ended one of history's longest civil wars. The war had left two million people dead and more than four million displaced (Jok, 2004). A new interim constitution approved by the National Assembly in July 2005 heralded a new era of peace. This interim constitution states that Sudan is a democratic, multi-cultural, multi-racial, multi-ethnic, multi-religious, and multi-lingual State; "it is an all-embracing homeland wherein races and cultures coalesce and religions co-exist in harmony" (Sudan Constitution, 2005). These constitutional stipulations are ideals; but for these ideals to be realized, all Sudanese people, authorities, as well as institutions must be committed to the promotion of social cohesion and deepening trust and accords among different groups.

Indeed the signing of the Comprehensive Peace Agreement (CPA) marked a moment of historic importance for a country that has been at war for half a century. Although another conflict continues in Darfur, in the western part of the country, the signing of the Comprehensive Peace Agreement filled people with hope that the agreement would end suffering in a country that had been embroiled in a civil war. This hope, however, did not last long because violence broke out again in July of 2005 after the accidental death of then Vice President, Founder, and Chief of SPLA/M, John Garang. These violent outbreaks, which were mainly between Southerners and Northerners, left 45 dead and more than 360 injured. Since that day, commonly known as "Black Monday," hopes for lasting peace and ethnic solidarity have slumped and skepticism regarding the hitherto fragile peace process has grown. Half a century of civil war has left Sudanese society with deep ethnic divisions. For sustainable peace in Sudan to be a reality, the structural factors that underlying conflict need to be analyzed and addressed. Using framing analysis this study aims to understand how radio contributes to peace and social cohesion by investigating the frames that the radio uses to frame issues of peace and conflict in Sudan.

Historical Background of Sudan's Conflict[1]

Sudan is the largest country in Africa with an area of 1 million square miles. Its population is approximately 37 million (Sudan Central Bureau of Statistics, 2007). Sudan is characterized by its diversity; it is a multiethnic and multi-religious country. The largest ethnic categories, Arabs, constitute nearly 40 percent of the total population, and are mostly Muslims. Major Muslim (but non-Arab) groups are Nubians in the far North, nomadic Beja in the Northeast, and the Fur of the West. Southern non-Muslim groups include Dinka (more than 10 percent of the total population and 40 percent in the south), Nuer, and numerous smaller Nilotic and other ethnic groups. Seventy percent of the country's population is Sunni Muslim, mostly in the North, 25 percent hold indigenous folk beliefs, and Christianity accounts for five percent of the population, mostly in the South and Khartoum (Library of Congress, 2004).

Sudan's past is closely tied to its present challenges. The historical process of dichotomizing the country into the Arab North and African South dates from the 7th century. At the time, the Arab-Muslim Empire invaded the Sudan and concluded peace accords with Northern people that established remote Arab control over the country and opened communication channels with the Arabs. Through conquest, intermarriage, trade, and settlement, Northern Sudan underwent Arab-Muslim assimilation. Arab migration and settlement toward the

---

[1] For the purpose of this paper, the term "Northern Sudan" is defined according to Mukhtar (2004) which defines the North not as a geographical North, but rather the ideological and political North, whose geographical confinements are limited to the Muslim, Arabic speaking, central riverain Northern Sudan. For more information on this please consult Mukhtar, Al-Baqir (2004), The Crisis of Identity in Northern Sudan: A Dilemma of a Black people with a White Culture. In Lobban, Carolyn and Rhode, Kharyssa (Eds) *Race and Identity in the Nile Valley: Ancient and Contemporary Perspectives*. Trenton, NJ : Red Sea Press

south was hindered by the tough geographical terrain and harsh tropical climate. The relationship between the Arabs and Southerners was thus limited to those who were engaged in the slave trade (Deng, 1995; Khalid, 2003).

In 1820, joint Turkish-Egyptian forces invaded the Northern regions of the Sudan. Promises of gold and slaves to build his empire were the main motives of Mohamed Ali Basha, the governor of Egypt. During this era, slave traders used the North as a base for their operations, carrying out incursions into the Southern regions. Resistance to the Turks and Egyptians came from both the North and South, resulting in a successful revolt in 1884 led by Mohamed A. Al Mahdi. In spite of the Islamic nature of the Mahadist revolution, "the south, though it did not convert, saw the religion of the Mahadist as a tool for liberation" (Deng, 1995, 11). The Mahadist regime, however, greatly disappointed its supporters from the South by continuing, like its predecessors, the slave raids (Daly & Sikainga, 1993; Deng, 1995). Indeed, as stated by Deng (1995) "Islam was turned against the South, thus becoming a divisive element" (p.11). Suliman (1995) notes:

> The memory of the brutal slave trade conducted mainly by mercenaries of the Northern Jellaba has lived on in the culture of the South. The experience of such aggression by Arab Muslims against Black Africans gave rise to Southern resistance to Islam and the embrace of Christianity, which Southerners perceived as being on their side against oppression (p.1). The dichotomy of the slave-master relationship between the North and South in the Mahadist regime deeply shaped the later development of the political and social sphere later.

This division is further enforced during the 58 years of colonization under an Anglo-Egyptian administration (1898-1956). During colonization, both Northern and Southern Sudan were administered as separate colonies under a Governor General. This separation of administration reinforced Arabism and Islam in the North. Southern Sudan, however, was ruled as an African colonial territory, where African culture and Christianity were encouraged. In addition, the British introduced the concept of "Closed Districts" whereby the British closed the South to Northerners, including Northern government officials (Sarkesian, 1973). Closed Districts included Southern Sudan, the Nuba Mountains of Southern Kordofan and the Funj areas of the Southern Blue Nile. Britain's declared justification for the "Closed District" policy defended it as means of protecting Southerners from slave traders from the Northern part of the country. Along with this, British colonizers formalized a "language policy" that allowed vernacular indigenous languages to be taught in primary schools in Southern Sudan where English was designated as the official language.

Consequently, Arabic was not used in schools and government offices in Southern Sudan (Biong, 2003).

In 1947, the British abruptly reversed their policy and determined that Southern and Northern Sudan would become one independent country. During colonialism, the British government concentrated economic development in the North, whereas the South was neglected. For the British rulers "the North promised return on foreign capital [through its agricultural products, especially cotton]; it thus had a claim on the government's disbursement of funds for education, health services, and general development which the South had not" (Dally & Sikainga, 1993, 6). As the South was highly underdeveloped and its educational opportunities were limited, the independence movement was led by Northerners (Deng, 1995). During the independence negotiations with the colonizers, the South was initially excluded from the handover of power and from the negotiations with Egypt (Dally & Sikainga, 1993; Deng, 1995; Khalid, 1990; Khalid, 2003). As Khalid stated, "The exclusion of the Southerners from the Cairo negotiations was perhaps the most disastrous decision taken by Egypt and the Northern parties" (Khalid, 2003, 55). One group of Sudanese was treated as more Sudanese than the other. During independence, the national assembly appointed a committee to draft a national constitution; only three of its 46 members were Southern Sudanese (Deng, 1995, 137). A wedge was further driven between a people with long standing historical suspicions. The Southerners were discontented. Subsequently, the Southerners' demand for federalism was not only rejected but also outlawed. Dissatisfied and denied the option of federalism, the Southern Sudanese revolted in 1955. This dissatisfaction became one of the main factors that contributed to the first civil war in the Sudan (1955-1972).

Sudan entered into the era independence with a long history of mistrust, marginalization, and exclusion. Successive post-independence governments continued the pattern of exclusion. The British separation policy, in addition to the heritage of the master-slave history, had "led to a sense of alienation that made Northerners and Southerners see each other as foreigners" (Deng, 1995, 111). Northerners had undergone centuries of assimilation into Arabic and Islamic cultures. Since independence, in an attempt to reverse the British separation policies, Northern dominated governments often made, and continue to make, attempts to extend this process of assimilation to the other regions of the country, including the South and the West. Successive post-independence central governments have adopted different policies aimed to constructing a united Sudan, with Arabic and Islamic cultures as the key determinants for national unity (Khalid, 1990, Sarkesian, 1973). As stated by Biong, "The ruling Northern elite saw the religious and cultural diversity of Sudan as a threat to unity and strove to eliminate it ... as such diversity was perceived as tantamount to racio-cultural hegemony" (Biong, 2003, 4). Since independence, Arabic has been considered the national language and the official medium of instruction in government, commerce, education and in the media (Deng, 1995; Lesch, 1998).

Hence, the Arabic language has special significance in the context of the Sudanese conflict. Being the language of the Quran, "Arabic culture ... is automatically linked to faith in minds of most Sudanese" (Lesch, 1998, 21). These attempts of the Northern-dominate governments effectively marginalized non-Arab cultural identities and created a sense of alienation.

The war resulting from the Southern revolt of 1955 was resolved in 1972 via the Addis Ababa Peace Agreement, which gave the South regional autonomy (Dally & Sikainga, 2001). Although the war was successfully resolved, President Numeiri breached the terms of the agreement. In September 1983, he instituted the Islamic Sharia as the supreme law of the land. Consequently, anti-Sharia groups, mainly in the South, formed the Sudan People's Liberation Movement and the Sudan People's Liberation Army (SPLM/SPLA), in order to fight against the government, for political power and social equality.

The conflict in Sudan took a new dimension when, a radical Islamic faction in the army, with the collaboration of the National Islamic Front (NIF) took over power on June 30, 1989. This new government introduced a new perspective to the Sudanese problem by dividing the country into Muslims and non-Muslims (Kufar) citizens, and it transformed the political conflict into a religious one by introducing the concept of Jihad (holy war) against real or perceived Kufar. The country shifted from a neutral position of a secular state to a religious, specifically Islamic, state. Soon the war in the South moved northward into non-Arab areas in Darfur in the Western region of the country, thereby adding a racial dimension to the conflict.

All these factors — the heritage of master-enslavement history, British policy, and preservation of the pattern of exclusion by successive post-independence governments — prevented the Sudanese of the North and the South from interacting with each other and identifying with each other. This resulted in deep polarization among ethnic, religious, and regional lines (Khalid, 2003). It is essential, thus, that post conflict social institutions in Sudan, such as media, education and religious institutions, engage in addressing these cultural aspects of Sudanese life that legitimize prejudices and eventually lead to violence.

Sudanese Electronic Media Landscape

Radio and television in Sudan are governed by the state-owned media corporation Sudan's Radio and Television Corporation, SRTC, which is the only broadcaster with transmission facilities inside Sudan. Private broadcasting can use its facilities after getting a license. SRTC broadcasts throughout Sudan, including the South, through four repeater transmitters and regional stations. Sudan National Radio, also known as Radio Omdurman, broadcasts 24-hours a day and can be received throughout almost all of Sudan although there are some areas where reception is poor (SRTC, 2007).

Radio is by far the most accessible medium in most of Sudan. An assessment conducted by Sudan Radio Service (SRS) of radio listening habits in South Sudan, concluded that almost 81 percent of households in South Sudan have access to radio (SRS, 2005). Other research done in West Darfur, the Nuba Mountains, and some other areas of the Upper Nile confirmed that there are radios in most villages (IMS, 2003). In some smaller communities, some arrangements are made in the community for satellite receivers, TVs and generators, or other power systems in order to enable the community to meet in a common place at certain times to watch various programs. In the Nuba Mountains, these are called "peace clubs" (IMS, 2003, p. 27). Although there is a lot of doubt about the credibility of the "state-owned" radio and TV, Sudan National Radio remains the most listened to radio station in the country (SRS, 2005).

Literature Review
Peace Studies

This study draws on Johan Galtung's concept of cultural violence (Galtung, 1964; Galtung, 1990; Galtung, 1996). Galtung makes clear distinctions between three dimensions of violence: direct violence, structural violence and cultural violence. Direct violence can be thought of as the physical act of violence, while structural violence is the type of violence that results from social injustices. Cultural violence can be attributed to "those aspects of culture, the symbolic sphere of our existence ... that can be used to justify or legitimize direct or structural violence" (Galtung, 1996, p. 1). Galtung's concept of the violence triangle is considered a transformation in the field of peace studies.

Galtung (1964, 1990, 1996) introduces three concepts of violence: direct violence, structural violence, and cultural violence. To change the vicious triangle of violence, we need to work with a virtuous triangle of peace. "This virtuous triangle," argues Galtung (1990) "would be obtained by working on all three corners all at the same time, not assuming that basic change in one will automatically lead to change in the other two " (p. 302).

Although direct violence can be stopped by a peace agreement or a cease-fire, cultural violence can survive long after an effective cease-fire (Bratic, 2005; Galtung, 1990). Since cultural norms are normally embedded in social institutions, it is essential that post-conflict social institutions be critically examined. Any aspects of culture that legitimize violence should be identified to prevent recurrences of direct violence[2]. While political negotiation deals with direct violence and policies deal with structural injustices, addressing cultural violence "requires attitude change" (Bratic, 2005, p. 68). Cultural violence is normally embedded in social institutions and can, therefore, survive long after

---

[2] Bigombe *at al.* (2000) reports that 31 percent of the civil wars in the world resume within the first 10 years of the end of the conflict (p.323).

the effective ceasefire and thus become a real obstacle to peace (Bratic, 2005, p. 239). For Sudan to achieve a sustainable peace, it is essential that structural imbalances, socio-economic disparities, and cultural aspects that legitimize violence, inherited in societal institutions (media, education, family, etc.) be identified and addressed.

Broom (2006) discusses how conflicts, even after resolution through political peace agreements and ending of direct violence, leave societies suffering from distrust, trauma and grievances that last long after conflict resolution and can be transmitted through generations. Conflicts, especially those along ethnic and religious lines, can deeply divide societies and become embedded in cultural norms; thereby creating vicious cycles of cultural-direct violence. Cultural violence creates negative interdependence, whereby each party sees the elimination of the other as a prerequisite for its own survival. When considering the effects of conflict, it is essential to address that polarization and distrust among conflicting parties. In conflict situations, media institutions can be manipulated to perpetuate cultural violence; on the other hand, they can also be used to promote cultural peace.

The relationship between communication — and mass media as an instrument of mass communication — and peace is well articulated in the UNESCO constitution, which reads: "Since wars begin in the minds of men, it is in the minds of men that the defenses of peace must be constructed." Media represents one of the most important sources of information that help people to understand the world around them.

Media's role in inciting and escalating violence has been the subject of numerous studies in the field of mass communications (Allan & Seaton, 1999; Seib, 2005). The case of the hate radio station Radio-Television Libre de Mille Collines, that fuelled the genocide in Rwanda in 1994, is one illustration of the role of media as provocateur in conflict situations (Kellow & Steeves, 1998). Since many scholars have concluded that media can incite conflict, it is then logical to assume that media can influence peace building as well. Media can be a double-edged sword in the context of peace and conflict, argues Hattotuw (2002):

> *The media can emphasize the benefits that peace can bring, they can raise the legitimacy of groups or leaders working for peace, and they can help transform images of the enemy. However, the media can also serve as destructive agents in a peace process, and can choose to negatively report on the risks and dangers associated with compromise, raise the legitimacy of those opposed to concessions, and reinforce negative stereotypes of the enemy* (p. 1).

Bratic (2005) in his research about 40 peace media projects around the world concludes that integration of media within peace-building projects can have a significant impact in creating peaceful societies. However, despite the role of modernized Sudanese mass media institutions can play, as Awad (2002) notes, little research have been done on the influence of the Sudanese mass media and their contribution to the consolidation of the fragile peace in Sudan. However, the nature and the extent of mass media effects on audiences are still a matter of debate among scholars. Because of this debate, varieties of approaches and theoretical frameworks have been adopted in communication research to explore mass media influence on society and audiences.

Framing Theory

Framing theory is one approach that seeks to understand the way the media influence audience. According to framing theory scholars, "mass media actively set the frame reference that readers or viewers use to interpret and discuss public events" (Scheufele, 1999, p. 105). Media framing research considers communication a process that results from the interaction between media and recipients. However, rather than studying media effects on individuals, framing scholars seek to understand the dynamics of interaction between the story organization and presentation and the audiences' experiences, perceptions and orientations (Entman, 1993; Entman, 2007; Goffman, 1974; Garber, 1994; Scheufele, 1999).

The term "frame" has been used in many disciplines, from social psychology to political science. However, according to Goffman (1974), the term "frame" was first coined by the social psychologist Bateson (1972) in his article "A Theory of Play and Fantasy." Bateson considers human communication a map of interaction and meaning that guides our interaction by constructing the cognitive structures that we use to make sense of the world around us. Goffman (1974) later used the term "frame" to describe the organization of social experiences in order to make sense of them. Goffman (1974) defines frames as interpretive devices or schemas that individuals use to "locate, perceive, identify and label" things together in order to make sense of them (p. 21). Goffman (1974) acknowledges that frame construction is influenced by individuals' personal and past experiences, contexts and cultures.

The literature on framing proposes that framing is influenced by personal, social, and institutional factors. Individuals' perspectives and experiences are key factors in the interpretation of any event.

Goffman (1974) states that the schemata of interpretations, which individuals use to organize a particular event, can be called a primary framework. A primary framework, according to Goffman (1974) is "one that is seen as not depending on or harking back to some prior or original interpretation...[it] is one that is seen as rendering what would otherwise be a meaningless aspect of the scene into something that is meaningful" (p. 21).

Thus, a primary framework is the frame that individuals use to, interpret, characterize and create meaning of the events and experiences around them.

However, Goffman (1974) differentiated between two classes of primary frameworks, natural frameworks and social frameworks. Natural frameworks, according to Goffman (1974) are unguided frameworks; they are purely physical with no interference from an outside agency. Social frameworks "can be described as 'guided doings.' These doings subject the doer to 'standards'" (Goffman, 1974, p. 22). These standards vary according to one's culture, social status, setting, and personality. Individuals apply primary frameworks to make sense of a given event. However, since these social frameworks are "guided doings," they are not isolated from the event itself and cannot be built in isolation from one's culture, experiences, and perceptions.

Media Framing

The term "frame" has been referred to as schema in many scholarly works (Goffman, 1974; Garber, 1984; Plaster, 2002). Frames, as cognitive constructs, are becoming increasingly influential in media studies. Thinking of media as a channel of information diffusion, the framing approach is useful for understanding how information is perceived; thus, it informs audiences' interpretations of messages presented to them. Framing scholars argue that the way information is organized and presented affects the cognitive processing of information; therefore, it affects which frames or schema individuals apply to understand and interpret an issue (Reese, 2001). According to framing theory, information will remain neutral and meaningless until some frame has been applied to it.

Entman (1993) states that "to frame is to select some aspects of a perceived reality and make them more salient in a communicating text, in such a way as to promote a particular problem definition, casual interpretation, moral evaluation, and/or treatment recommendation for the item described" (p. 52). He notes that framing essentially involves selection and salience, and he defines salience as "making a piece of information more noticeable, meaningful, or memorable to audiences" (p. 53). Framing theory suggests the way an issue is selected and made salient impacts the way audiences create meaning from it. It is worth noting, however, that it is not only selection and salience that matter, but also exclusion.

Unlike agenda setting and priming, which are based on a theoretical foundation that sees salience as making issues more prominent in people's minds, framing "is based on the assumption that how an issue is characterized in news reports can have an influence on how it is understood by audiences" (Scheufele & Tewksbury, 2007, p. 11). Framing does not only focus on adressing if an issue is reported or not, but how it is reported is also a matter of interest to framing reaserchers. Framing deals not only with object salience but also with object attributes. For example, Mhtani (2001), reviewing studies about the relationship between Canadian media and minorities, illustrates how the coverage of minorities in Canadian media sets frames that only serve to humiliate minorities. Canadian media, according to Mhtani (2001), although covering minorities' issues, continue to broadcast negative and stereotypical images of them. The issue is not whether minorities' issues are salient in the media or not, but what attributes are linked to the salience. The negative attributes that are linked to minorities set certain frames through which the representation of minority can be understood.

Selection and salience may lead to adoption of totally different frames for the same news story, as in the case of the 1999 NATO Air Strikes on Kosovo. An analysis of how the strikes were framed in Chinese media in comparison to U.S. media reveals that while the Chinese newspapers framed the air strikes as a violation of Yugoslavia's sovereignty and territory, the U.S. newspapers framed the air strikes as humanistic aid to Albanians to stop the ethnic cleansing initiated by Serbians (Yang, 2003).

The literature on framing suggests that different factors influence the construction of media frames. Among these factors are power relationships and cultural associations, as well as organizational culture and journalistic work routines. Ideological and hegemonic factors influence which frames are more prominent in the media. The literature on media framing suggests that centers of power as well as the ruling elite's interests can influence promotion of certain frames in mainstream media. There is a growing body of scholarly research focusing on the news coverage of minorities and social movements. These studies have focused on how certain aspects of realities are highlighted in order to produce frames that are in agreement with authorities or dominant groups' constructs of social reality (Avraham, Wolfsfeld & Aburaiya, 2000). However, Benford and Snow (2000) find that social movements are also producing counter-frames and reframes such as the injustice frame.

Cultural association is another factor that might influence construction of certain frames. The coverage of the controversy of the Mohamed cartoons in a Danish newspaper is one illustration of how culture influences the production of frames. While most of the Western media used the "press freedom" frame, Arab media used the "respect" frame to address the controversy. The framing difference reveals a cultural difference in the angle from which each side is approaching the issue; thus, it results in different characterization frames that are an important element when addressing issues of peace and conflict.

Journalists do not always deliberately select the frames that they are applying to a certain issue. Reporters report on what they see. However, since one of the frame functions is to organize information in order to make sense of it, reporters seek to fill in missing pieces in what they see in order to make the story understandable to their audiences. Journalists' past experiences and current location combined with the work routines and the political and economical interests of news organizations set what attributes of news are selected and emphasized. For instance, Kuypers and Cooper (2005), in their research about the mass media coverage of the Iraqi war, illustrate how journalists' location (embedded or behind front lines) plays a role in which attributes they select and make salient, and, accordingly, which frames are applied. The study compares embedded and behind the front lines reporting and finds that embedded reporting focuses on the weakness of the Iraqi army resistance, thereby assigning the victory frame to the representation of the war. Behind the frontline reporting, on the other hand, focuses on war causalities and the potential of Iraqi forces to counterattack. This study demonstrated how different attributes are selected and structured in frames.

Organizational culture can dictate journalist practices and work routines and, consequently, the framing of the news. Organization of information can frame the same issue differently. Thus, the way news is selected and how certain attributes of an issue receive salience influences the reception and meaning derived from such events. In his book about the British media framing of the War in Bosnia, Kent (2006) explains how the "objectivity" and "balance" routine that was practiced by British journalists resulted in production of "moral equalization" frame, a frame that shied away from naming a responsible agent for the atrocities in Bosnia.

Frames or schemas perform four basic functions: 1) selection or salience; 2) evaluations and organization, so that the information presented fits into the established system; 3) filling in the missing information from previously established frames and perceptions; 4) seeking solutions, and these solutions are normally based on past scenarios and experiences (Entman, 1993; Garber, 1984; Plaster, 2002):

- Defining a problem: the first function of frame is to define the problem in order to make sense of what is going on. That is for media as well as audiences. For media, defining a problem is to set the context of the problem. By defining the problem, media set for audiences the parameters of how to think about the issue being covered.

- Organizing information to fill in missing pieces from previous experience: the second function is to use what is at hand and organize it in a frame, which is influenced by past experience and perception, in order to fill in the missed information. Reading in news we can identify this function by looking at how journalists associate one piece of news with previous issues that are somehow related to the issue being covered.

- Evaluation: the third function of framing is to make evaluations and causal interpretations. By framing, media and audiences try to assess the issues to create an interpretation and /or suggest solutions or actions.

- Suggesting solutions

Framing in the Context of Peace and Conflict

In terms of conflict and peace, Beer (2001) discusses how framing theory can offer insights in terms of understanding the patterns of cognitive behavior and the meaning of conflict and peace. Beer (2001) states, "the cognitive meaning of war and peace is the schema [frame]-the idea, the thought- that represents and constructs it" (p.8). Frames can be understood as a schema or "a cognitive structure consisting of organized knowledge about situations and individuals that has been abstracted from prior experiences" (Graber, 1984, p. 23). In conflict situations, frames are the interpretive lenses through which disputants see, conceptualize, and interpret the conflict. It is important to understand that frames are not objective devices, but rather a subjective perception or "view that one person [or group] has of what is going on" (Goffman, 1974, p. 8). Framing does not only influence how an individual sees conflict from his or her point of view, but also the way he or she understands "the motivations of the partners involved, and how the conflict should be settled" (Gray, 2003, p. 12).

The literature on framing suggests that the way issues of peace and war are framed can influence the way they are understood and eventually addressed (Avraham, Wolfsfeld & Aburaiya, 2000; Benford & Snow, 2000; Reese, 2001; Watkins, 2001). Many scholars state that the way issues are framed can contribute to either conflict escalation or conflict transformation (Pinkley, 1990; Shmueli et al. 2006). Scholars identify different types of frames that contribute to intractability. For instance, Shumueli et al. (2006) identify the following frames as salient in conflict situations: the identity frame, the characterization frame, the power frame, social control and conflict management frame, the risk and information frame, whole story frame, and the loss and gain frame.

Although different frames can escalate conflict, Coleman and Rider (2006) note that most of the conflicts are identity-based conflicts, in the broader sense of identity. Therefore, the infusion of the cultural peace perspective through social institutions is effective in conflict management. In this aspect, media play a significant role in either reducing or escalating conflict by the way they frame issues of identity. As argued by Bratic (2005) "inherently media are responsible for good or bad interpretations of the things outside our immediate perceptions; in wars, media frame our enemy for us" (p. 69). In this context, mass media, among other social institutions, plays an essential role in defining Us and Them. The representation of We and Others through mass media is influential in shaping collective public opinion. Keen (1991) states: "We first kill people with our minds, before we kill them with weapons" (p. 18). If we think of media as part of the cultural institutions that create "the symbolic sphere of our existence," then media play influential role in creating or transforming cultural violence.

Johan Galtung, in developing a framework of peace journalism, emphasizes these concepts and argues that the way conflict is framed differentiates peace journalism from war journalism. By highlighting peace initiatives, focusing on peace makers, toning down ethnic and religious differences, and focusing on people's suffering, the peace journalist works toward preventing further conflict. On the other hand, war journalism focuses on "our" suffering and frames the conflict as and Us/Them dichotomy (cited in Lynch & McGoldrick, 2005).

Methods and Data Collection

This study applies framing analysis to investigate radio frames regarding issues of conflict and peace to understand the possible influence of media frames peace-building in Sudan. For data collection, a composite of a six-day sample from each month for the period from November 2008 to February 2009 was selected, with a total of 30 days sampled. One news podcast for each day of the sample was randomly selected. Only news story that deal with any issue regarding peace or conflict in Sudan were transcribed. Fifty-seven stories were transcribed. The breakdown of the number of stories was as follows:

October	17
November	11
December	7
January	9
February	13

Framing Analysis and Frames

Tankard (2001) identifies three empirical approaches to conduct framing analysis. The "Media package approach" is one in which the researcher develops a paragraph that includes the keywords and common language that would help identify the certain frame (Gamson & Modigliani, 1989). The second is "framing as multidimensional approach," and in this approach, various elements or dimensions of the story are recognized and included in the framing analysis. The third approach is the "list of frames approach" in which the researcher identifies a list of frames and defines each frame by specific words, catchphrases, and images. After compiling the list of frames, coders will be asked to conduct framing analysis and place each story in the list of frames. For the purpose of this study, the multidimensional approach was applied to conduct framing analysis for media messages.

Gamosn & Modigliani (1989) argue that media discourse is presented in a "set of interpretive packages" or frames that serve as the central organizing idea of any news story (p. 3). On the other hand, "every political issue has a relevant public discourse ... that [is] used in the process of constructing meaning" (Gamosn, 1988, p. 165). In terms of media frames, these organizing ideas or frames can be thought of as themes that "[connect] different semantic elements of a story (e.g., descriptions of an action or an actor, quotes of sources, and background information) into a coherent whole" (Pan & Kosicki, 1993, p. 59). A theme is a "pattern" that recurs in a specific text, and can be used to describe or interpret an aspect of the phenomena under study (Boyatzis, 1998; Roberts, 1997). Using the multidimensional approach, I was looking for three dimensions in each news story: Master narrative or storyline, language, and frame sponsorship or selection of sources quoted and quotations.

Thinking of frames as interpretive devices, framing analysis poses a methodological challenge. Any news story has a manifest and a latent message. Any text can have multiple meanings; therefore, different frames can be extracted from the same text (Graber, 1989; Gamson, 1989). Gamson (1989) suggests using the preferred reading in framing analysis in order to solve the methodological dilemma. The preferred reading is the meaning that is intended by the sender and it is usually represented in the story line. In journalists' practices, a story is organized according to an "inverted pyramid" structure. According to this inverted pyramid, the information in the news story is arranged in descending order of importance. The most important point is placed at the beginning of the story in the lead sentence or paragraph. Thus, master narrative, or story line, can be identified from the lead paragraphs. In this case, the most important point of the message can be found on the news summary that precedes the detailed news cast. Regarding the language use and frame sponsorship, notice was taken of the words choices, number and affiliations of sources quoted, quotes selected, and thematic or episodic tendencies of coverage.

In qualitative frame analysis "categories are not predefined, which allows categories to emerge as the researcher becomes immersed in the data" (Perkins, 2005, p. 67). I used an inductive or data driven approach to identify frames. News stories were recorded, and then stories dealing with peace and conflict issues were transcribed. I read the transcripts several times to identify frames using the framing definition and criteria described earlier. I conducted a preliminary analysis during which the master narratives, main themes, language use and sources, and quote selection were noted. From this preliminary analysis notes and findings were categorized. Transcripts were read again, notes and findings from the preliminary analysis were analyzed to identify the frames.

Findings

Since I am using a multidimensional approach, notice was taken of three dimensions in any news story: the master narrative, the language, and the frame sponsorship. In terms of frames sponsorship, it was apparent that SNR, as many state-owned radio stations, is used as mouthpiece for the government. Frames are mainly government sponsored. Officials are the main sources who are quoted and, in rare cases when others are quoted, these quotes support the officials view point. Though such findings are expected from a state-owned radio station, an interesting observation is that it is one side of the government that is sponsoring the frames. Since the signing of the CPA, the government comprised of Sudan People Liberation Movement and the National Congress

Party as the main partners, in addition to smaller political groups, including Darfurian movements who recently joined the National Unity Government. A further analysis reveals that in terms of frames sponsorship, the national Congress Party is the dominating sponsor. Very few SPLM officials were quoted in the sample analyzed.

From a language dimension, it is visible that language choice was consistent with the frames and master narrative applied and it supports the preferred reading. That is to say language choice was carefully considered to send certain messages to the audience. Certain phrases were associated with certain frames, as explained below.

Three major themes were found regarding the master narrative: the Comprehensive Peace Agreement (CPA) and its implementation, Darfur Conflict, and the International Criminal Court (ICC). Though the ICC theme could be classified as part of Darfur conflict theme, I chose to have as a separate theme because a different frame was applied every time reference was made to the ICC. Darfur conflict dominated the news. Out of the 57 stories there were 29 stories about Darfur, followed by 12 stories about the CPA, and7 stories about the ICC. The remainder of the stories were general stories with either no specific focus or a different focus such as Eastern-Sudan Peace Agreement. Major frames found were:

➤ Structural justice frame: This frame can be described as "peace means development" frame. This frame links issues of peace to development and characterizes development and structural justice as a guarantee to achieve sustainable peace in Sudan. This frame is used frequently when reporting about the CPA implementation. Progress on the implementation of the CPA is always characterized and linked to development projects and proportion of national budget allocated to development projects in War-affected regions. While structural justice is an integral part to peace-building in Sudan, there is absence of any mentions of cultural violence/peace. The radio is shying away from talking about cultural issues and eventually characterized the peace process in terms of ceasefire and power sharing and wealth sharing.

➤ Unity frame: Within this frame the political sphere of Sudan is represented as united. Disagreements and conflicts are denied. When this frame is applied, leaders from different political groups are quoted, for example in a newscast on 10/29 El Sadiq E Mahadi (leader of Umma Party which is an opposition political party) was quoted praising and commending the Sudanese people Initiatives meetings.[3] Two days later, on 10/31, M. Osman El Margheni (leader of the Democratic Unionist Party, another opposition political party) was quoted calling the Sudanese political parties to participate in the same initiative.

---

[3] A government-sponsored initiative on Darfur which meant to lay a foundation for Doha peace talks in Qatar at the end of 2008

This unity frame is used even when lack of unity is apparent to assert the frame. For instance, reporting that some Darfurian armed groups did not participate in the initiative meetings would challenge the unity frame, so the radio would add a note to the story stating that though the Darfurian armed groups did not participate in the meetings, their viewpoints were fully considered. News stories featuring meeting by coalitions such as National Unity Political Parties coalition are frequent to support such frames that assert that political sphere in Sudan is united.

➢ The unity frame plays in accordance with another frame that is conflict frame. Under the conflict frame there are sub-frames: Conflict between Sudan and ICC, Conflict between Sudan and the Western world, Conflict between the West/ Arab and African countries. Language choice for this frame includes phrases such as "Sudan is targeted," "Conspiracies against Sudan," and "Western domination." These phrases are normally used in contrast with positions of Arabic and African countries to stress the dichotomy and the conflict between the two sides. For instance, in Arab Justice ministers' meeting in October 2008, Sudanese Justice minister A. Basit Sabadrat was quoted expressing Sudan's confidence in his Arab "brothers" in supporting Sudan against the ICC indictment of President Omar El Bashir. When reporting about Arabs and African countries, the media's language choice always reflected support and a sense of brotherhood. Phrases such as "brothers" and "support in the face of West/ICC/ Western domination, etc." were used.

➢ Sovereignty frame: This was a very blatant frame specially in discussing ICC issue or international intervention in Sudan. This frame is used to counter the justice frame that is normally used by political opposition or supporters of ICC intervention. Although, according to personal interview with one of the news editors, there is an explicit policy that the ICC issue should not be given much attention in the news, the sovereignty frame is so blatant. The sovereignty frame is one of the frames that Hertog and Mcleod (2003) describe it as an "ego-involving" frame. One major phrase was used with this frame, that is "the president, the symbol of national sovereignty," resonates well with Sudanese culture of pride and self-sufficiency. It is a provoking metaphor that deeply embedded in Sudanese culture and was well-utilized in this context.

Conclusion

Sudan National Radio as a state-owned radio works as a mouth-piece for the government. To be more specific it works for the National Congress Party, a key player in the Sudanese National Unity Government. Thus frames that are adopted and sponsored by the government are the ones that broadcasted by the radio station. The radio explicit policy is to support peace-building efforts in Sudan. Yet, the practice reveals that the radio is war-oriented rather than peace-oriented. Coverage of conflict is more dominant than coverage of peace efforts. Darfur, as a conflict region, is more dominant in the news than the implementation of the Comprehensive Peace Agreement (CPA). Conflict frame is a dominant frame. Though the radio uses unity frame, but this frame is used in a dichotomized way of perceived "united" supporters against a perceived enemy or opposition.

Framing analysis does not only focus on what is included, but equally what is excluded. The coverage of peace and conflict issues on Sudan Nation Radio ignores the root causes of the Sudanese conflict(s) and shies away from any mentions of cultural injustices. Coverage of the CPA treats it as "a done deal" and focuses only on what could be termed as structural peace incentives such as development projects. While these are important aspects of the peace building efforts in Sudan, media role, as a societal institution, can be greater. Sudan conflict(s) are deeply rooted and the Sudanese society is deeply divided after half a century of war. Media (radio in this case) can do a better job by covering the peace initiatives at the grassroots level which target more the cultural aspect of the conflict.

REFERENCES

Allan, T., & Seaton, J. (1999). The media of conflict: war reporting and representations of Ethnic violence. London: Zed Books

Avraham, E., Wolfsfeld, G., & Aburaiya, I. (2000). Dynamics in the news coverage of minorities: the case of the Arab citizens of Israel. *Journal of Communication Inquiry, 24(2)*, 117-133

Awad, M. O. (2004). *Transition from war to peace in Sudan*. Switzerland: University of Peace Beer, F (2001). *Meanings of war & peace*. College Station: Texas A&M University Press

Benford, R., & Snow, D. (2000). Framing processes and social movements: an overview and assessment. *Annual Review of Sociology, 26*, 611–639.

Boing, L. D. (2003). Education in southern Sudan: war, status and challenges of achieving Education For All goals. Paper Prepared For UNESCO EFA Monitoring Report.

Boyatzis, R. (1998). Transforming qualitative information: thematic analysis and code development. Thousand Oaks, CA: Sage Publications

Bratic, V. (2005). In search of peace media: examining the role of media in peace developments of the post-cold war. Unpublished Doctoral Dissertation, Ohio University

Broom, B J., & Hatay, A. (2006). Building peace in divided societies: the role of intergroup dialogue. In Oetzel, J. & Ting-Toomey, S. (Eds.). *The Sage handbook of conflict communication: integrating theory, research and practice.* Thousand Oaks, CA: Sage Publications

Coleman, S.W.; Rider, E. (2006). International/intercultural conflict resolution training.

In Oetzel, J.; Ting-Toomey, S. (Eds.). *The Sage handbook of conflict communication: integrating theory, research and practice.* Thousand Oaks, CA: Sage Publications

Daly, M.W. & Sikainga, A. (1993). *Civil war in the Sudan.* London: British Academic Press.

Deng, F. (1995). *War of visions: conflict of identities in the Sudan.* Washington, DC: The Brooking Institution.

Entman, M .R. (1993). Framing: towards a clarification of a fractured paradigm. *Journal of Communication, 43(4)*, 51-58

Entman, M. R. (2007). Framing bias: media in the distribution of power. *Journal of Communication, 57(1)*, 163-173

Galtung, J. (1964). An editorial. *Journal of Peace Research, 1*, 1-4.

Galtung, J. (1990). Cultural violence. *Journal of Peace Research, 27(3)*, 291-305

Galtung, J. (1996). Cultural peace: some characteristics. In From *a culture of violence to a culture of peace* (Ed.). Paris, France: UNESCO

Gamson, W. A.,& Modigliani, A. (1989). Media discourse and public opinion: a constructionist approach. *American Journal of Sociology, 95,* 1-37.

Gamson, W. A. (1988). The 1987 Distinguished lecture: a constructionist approach to mass media and public opinion. *Symbolic Interaction 11,* 161–74.

Gamson, W. A. (1989). News as framing. *American Behavioral Scientist, 33,* 157–61.

Gitlin, T. (1980). *The whole world is watching: mass media in the making & unmaking of the new left.* Berkeley, CA: University of California Press

Goffman, E. (1974). Frame analysis: an essay on the organization of experience. New York: Harper & Row

Graber, D. (1984). Processing the news: how people tame the information tide. New York, London: Longman.

Graber, D. (1989). Content and meaning. *American Behavioral Scientist, 33,* 144–52.

Graber, D. (1994). Processing the news: how people tame the information tide. In Davis, R. (Ed.). *Politics and the media.* New Jersey: Prentice Hall.

Gray, B. (2003). Framing of environmental disputes. In Lewicki, R.; Gray, B.; Elliott, M. (Eds.). *Making sense of intractable environmental conflicts: concepts and cases.* Washington, DC: Island Press

Groff, L.,& Smoker, P. (1996). Creating global/local cultures of peace. In *From a culture of violence to a culture of peace* (Ed.). Paris, France: UNESCO

Hattotuwa, S. 2002). The role of the media in peace processes. *Paper presented 14th World Congress of Environmental Journalists.* Accessed 11/15/2007 from Http://www.Cpalanka.Org/Research_Papers/Role_Of_Media_In_Peace_Processes.Pdf

Hertog, J., & McLeod, D. (2003). A multidimensional approach to framing analysis: a field guide. In Reese, S., Gandy, H. O., & Grant, E. A. (Eds.). *Framing public life: perspectives on media and our understanding of the social world*. Mahwah, N.J.: Lawrence Erlbaum Associates

Jok , M. (2001). *War and slavery in Sudan*. Philadelphia, PA: University Of Pennsylvania Press Keen, S. (1991). *Why peace is not covered*. Media and Values, 56, 18.

Kellow, L.,& Steeves, L. (1998). The role of radio in the Rwandan genocide. *Journal of Communication, 48(3)*, 107-128

Kent, G. (2006). Framing war and genocide: British policy and news media reaction to the war in Bosnia. Cresskill, NJ: Hampton Press

Khalid, M. 1990). The government they deserve: the role of the elite in Sudan's political evolution. New York, N.Y.: Routledge

Khalid, M. (2003), War and peace in Sudan: A Tale of Two Countries. London: Kegan Paul

Kuypers, J.,& Cooper, S. (2005). A comparative framing analysis of embedded and behind-the-lines reporting on the 2003 Iraq war. *Qualitative Research Reports in Communication, 6(1)*, 1-10

Lesch, A. (1998). *The Sudan: contested national identities*. Bloomington, IN: Indiana University Press

Library of congress (2004). Country Studies: Sudan. Retrieved 04/08/2005 from: Lynch, J.,& McGoldrick, A.(2005). *Peace journalism*. Stroud: Hawthorn

Mahtani, M. 2001). *Representing minorities: Canadian media and minority identities*.

Halifax, Nova Scotia: Department Of Canadian Heritage for the Ethnocultural, Racial, Religious, and Linguistic Diversity and Identity Seminar

Mukhtar, A. (2006). *Identity and conflict in Sudan*. Presentation at Ohio University, Athens, Ohio

Pan, Z.,& Kosicki, G. (1993). Framing analysis: an approach to news discourse. *Political Communication, 10*, 55-75

Perkins, S. C. (2005). Un-Presidented: A qualitative framing analysis of the NAACP's public relations response to the 2000 presidential election. *Public Relations Review, 31(1)*, 63-71

Pinkley, R. (1990). Dimensions of conflict frame: disputant interpretations of conflict. *Journal of Applied Psychology, 75 (2)*, 1990, 117-126

Plaster, S. (2001). *When women run: the press and framing of female senatorial candidates*. Unpublished Doctoral Dissertation, Ohio University, Ohio.

Reese, S., Gandy, O., & Grant, A. (2003) (Eds.). *Framing public life: perspectives on media and our understanding of the social world*. Mahwah, N.J.: Lawrence Erlbaum Associates

Roberts, C. (1997). Text analysis for the social sciences: methods for drawing statistical interferences from texts and transcripts. New Jersey: Lawrence Erlbaum Associates

Sarkesian, S. C. (1973). The Southern Sudan: A reassessment. *African Studies Review, 16(1)*, 1-22

Scheufele, D. A. (1999). Framing as a theory of media effects. *Journal of Communication, 49(1)*, 103 -122

Scheufele, D., & Tewksbury, D. (2007). Framing, agenda setting, and priming: the evolution of three media effects models. *Journal of Communication, 57(1)*, 9-20

Seib, P. (2005). *Media and conflict in the twenty-first century*. New York: Palgrave Macmillan

Shmueli, D., Elliott, M., & Kaufman, S. (2006). Frame changes and the management of intractable conflicts. *Conflict Resolution Quarterly, 24*, 207-218.

Sudan Constitution (2005). Retrieved February 5, 2006 from: Http://Www.Sudanembassy.Org/Default.Asp?Page=Thisissudan_People

Sudan Radio Service (2005). *Audience survey report*. Nairobi, Kenya: Minds

Sudan Television and Radio Corporation (STRC) (2007). Retrieved 11/6/2007 From www.Srtc.Gov.Sd/
Sudan Central Bureau of Statistics (2007). Sudan in Figures 2002-2006. Khartoum: SCBS.

Suliman, Mohamed. *Civil War in Sudan: The Impact of Ecological Degradation.* http://www.sas.upenn.edu/African_Studies/ Articles_Gen/ cvlw_env_sdn.html

Tankard, J. (2001). The empirical approach to the study of media framing. In Reese, Stephen Gandy, H. Oscar, Grant, E. August (Eds.). *Framing public life: perspectives on media and our understanding of the social world.* Mahwah, N.J.: Lawrence Erlbaum Associates

Watkins, S.C. (2001). Framing protest: news media frames of the million man march. *Critical Studies in Media Communication, 18*, 83-101.

Yang, J. (2003). Framing the NATO air strikes on Kosovo across countries: comparison of Chinese and us newspaper coverage. *Gazette: The International Journal for Communication Studies, 65(3),* 231-249

Chapter 9

Media and Conflict: A System Analysis of Mass Media Technology's Impact on Africa's Democratic and Economic Systems

Cosmas U. Nwokeafor
Bowie State University

Abstract

The rate at which violence and conflict raise their ugly heads in various African countries is so alarming that one ponders how the media have been able to handle their coverage. As democracy evolves in various African countries, and continue to grow, the media system in African nations have the liberty to report local, state and national news most importantly those news with violent contents. There have been numerous conflict emanating from ethnic, religious, and various organized unions who are generally identified for their use of different strategies or tactical means (ranging from threats of violence, intimidation, to outright rebellion) to threaten the existing democratic governance in their nations. Some of the ethnic, political and religious violence are sometimes organized by angry groups whose intent is to dismantle the government in power. This group of few self-serving citizens has been accused of being agents of divisiveness and manipulation who have directly or indirectly engaged their cronies in acts of violence, which has generated both ethnic and religious tensions in their nations. This chapter attempts to review conflicts and therefore address some questions as to (a) what the role of the media is in reporting these conflicts, and (b) the extent at which the media system has been successful in covering these conflicts.

INTRODUCTION

The African media system plays a unique and significant, if not often invisible and taken-for-granted role in the coverage of conflicts and violent acts perpetrated by various African nations' organized groups, whose motive has been to scuttle the nascent and to some countries old democratic governance. The rate of these conflicts in Africa, most importantly in the African most-populous nation, Nigeria, is so alarming that one ponders how the media system has been able to handle the coverage of such conflicts while paying attention to the pressing needs of the citizenry. The democratic government in power in Nigeria, Ghana, Cameron, Sierra Leone, South Africa, Ethiopia, Liberia, Kenya, Zimbabwe, Angola, Uganda, Tanzania, Gambia, Zambia, Rwanda, Sudan, Senegal, Togo, Somalia, Cote D'Ivoire and many other countries of the region, has strived hard to provide the benefits of democracy to its citizens (economic, political, and social needs of the people). Since the assumption of power to their respective authoritative positions, African leaders have promised security and transparent leadership to its citizens, but the result of this promise has been very difficult to empirically measure.

In the case of Nigeria, for instance, the year 1999 ushered in a dynamic democratic dispensation whose goal of transparency was far-reaching and never achieved. However, various ethnic, religious, and organized group conflicts taking place in various states of the federation in the case of Nigeria, as reported by the mass media, poses a great challenge to achieving transparency. It makes governance and life difficult for both the leaders and the citizens who are very eager to embrace the dividend of democratic governance.

The question of conflict in Africa has become a way of getting strong rejection of government viewpoints and opposition across to the leaders. For the purpose of this chapter, an address as to what extent the media system has been able to handle the coverage of conflict should be revisited and re-evaluated based on the basic relevance of the functions of media in a democratic system. The argument as to whether the African media system has given enough coverage to conflicts in the region of Africa will be discussed with a review of existing literature to explore the extent to which constant conflict has almost led to the destabilization of the various African democratic governance, thereby creating political and economic hazard in the second largest continent in a changing global system.

Purpose of Study

The purpose of this chapter, therefore, is to examine existing literature to ascertain how media coverage of conflict in Africa as documented by scholars has impacted its political and economic system. Attempts will be made to discuss in detail the advent of mass media technology in Africa, and to redefine its impact to include political movements, and social and economic dimensions as important indices which must be given priority consideration in the large context of African development.

Research Questions

There have been several studies conducted, books and articles written in an effort to evaluate the coverage of conflict by mass media technology in Africa. Studies (Acayo & Mnjama, 2004; Kariithi, 1995; Merrill, 1995; Nwokeafor, 1992; Obotette, 1984; Pye, 1963) and preponderant web publications and scholarly articles have shown that African mass media have truly covered conflicts in various African nations; however, some of these coverages have not addressed significantly how some of the conflict issues have impacted political and economic spheres of the continent. Even when these conflicts are covered, they are not given equal attention based on whom and at what level the conflict issues are being covered.

The reason behind this has been attributed to intimidation of journalists by the political system. In most cases, because of evidence which claims that government leaders, even in the recent democratic dispensations in most African nations, have intimidated and undermined journalists who are sometimes petrified to practice. Afraid of being censored and sometimes completely banished from their practice, their coverage of conflict or violent issues fails to reflect the exact account of the news, which denies the reading and listening public access to truth and clear picture of an existing conflict. This chapter, expecting to contribute to the growing body of knowledge, and extrapolating from the discussions of the problem and attendant issues, is guided by the following questions.

(1) To what extent does the mass media in Africa cover conflicts without bias?

(2) Does the mass media in Africa cover conflict at national and state levels equitably as it does at the local levels?

(3) Who controls and sets the media agenda in the continent of Africa?

Significance of Media Paradigm

The statement by Schramm according to Nwokeafor (1992) that "unless a nation uses its mass media to develop spiritual and human potentialities, it cannot develop much else..." (p 41-42) forms a strong foundation upon which this chapter is based. Looking at the extensive nature of media development in various nations of Africa today as technology directs the economic and social structures. This chapter, therefore, supports the issue that mass media system should define political, social, and economic potentials that exist in the continent of Africa if its economic viability will be attained. It is obvious, therefore, to argue that there is a relationship between mass media use and political, social, and economic development in the continent of Africa. This relationship may probably be mutual and reciprocal. The assumption of a mutual relationship tends to ignore not only the impact of the structural constraints, but also the need to evaluate how the continent benefits from true media independence and democracy. Nwokeafor (1992), therefore, argues that:

> *"If mass media especially the newspaper and electronic media systems are indispensable tools in structuring the political process which, in turn, assists in enhancing the course of social and economic development, the importance of establishing a kind of media structure that would address conflict issues without bias (RQ #1) thereby contributing in the acceleration of development programs cannot be overemphasized"* (p.96).

The assumption of this chapter is that African media systems do cover conflict issues; however, the democratic system may have some encroaching impact on both the level of coverage and the extent of the report of the coverage. The impact of this type of mass media coverage becomes very worrisome, and obviously supports the significance of this chapter. The big question, therefore, is to what extent does the mass media in Africa cover conflict news issues without bias? A review of available literature relating to media conflict and its possible impact on Africa's political, economic, and social systems will follow.

Review of Literature

Extrapolating from a vast literature on mass media and conflict and looking at the impact of such coverage on the political and economic systems in Africa, the primary objective of this review, therefore, is to functionally address the problem militating against a democratic practice of journalism in Africa. Leaders in various African nations should have a high level of political and economic understanding of their nation to rise to the need to readdress, reassess and rediscover the direct impact of mass media system in governance in African region. The literature review will include African mass media in a Democratic governance, media stability and security in Africa, and the role of mass media in Africa's political and economic transformation.

African Mass Media in Democratic Governance

One of the greatest lessons learnt in the new millennium by African media practitioners and mass media scholars is the revisiting of the critical role the mass media plays both in the sustenance and strengthening of the African democratic process and the progress made on the political and economic sphere. Okoro (1995) opined that post-independence initiatives in African nations have demonstrated the effectiveness of various forms of media in the process of attaining political and economic transformation, creating cultural awareness, and establishing social cohesion. The role of mass media has been empirically determined as a facilitator of growth and development. One of the fundamental defects of early development plans in Africa has been attributed to the inadequate role assigned to the mass media and to some extent the intimidation and suppression suffered by mass media practitioners.

Nwokeafor (1992), therefore, argued that the role of mass media in any country is to mobilize human resources by substituting new norms, attitudes, and behaviors for old ones in order to stimulate increased social, economic, and political productivity. Nwokeafor (1992) quoting Rogers and Shoemaker (1973) opined that mass media technology is used to increase the acceptance of an innovation. Rogers and Shoemaker's ideological principles may have been 36 years old, but still seem to resonate among current scholars. Contemporary scholars and mass media theorists maintained that the appropriate mass media strategy to be applied by African media practitioners should be the one that makes use of the general media system to affect a two-way communication process between the government and the public. They also believed that the use of appropriate mass media technology, emphasis on national development, fulfillment of basic needs, productive use of local resources, and political and economic development defined by the people and their environment would help to facilitate the expected outcome of media systems role in Africa.

Mass Media Stability and Security in Africa

One of the most recognized functions of mass media is its ability to transport news from one destination to another. Nwokeafor (1992) described the mass media as the vehicles for transferring new ideas and models from one part of the African country to another. Advancing the speculation that, mass media serves the function of a talking drum that circulates information from the urban to rural areas, in process helps in the dissemination of development ideas and assists in the transference of modern technology. Through the transference of new ideas and technological innovations permeating all parts of African nations since the beginning of Independence, Africa has changed and its various nations succumb to various conflicts, which makes it nearly difficult for any kind of confidence to nation building to exist.

In order to stabilize African nations and bring confidence and sense of belonging to the people, the various African governments must establish a mutual relationship with the mass media and allow them to operate independent of the leaders and political system. The eventual move toward press and mass media freedom in African nations would give autonomy to mass media practitioners to cover news and development issues without censorship or intimidation. The freedom of media practitioners to cover news and events at both national, state, and local levels would support Merrill's (1995) definition of freedom of the press and mass media as the right for media practitioners to speak, broadcast, or publish without prior restraint by or permission of the government. African leaders and various government agencies should allow mass media practitioners to perform their journalistic responsibilities without direct intimidation or micromanagement. They should not be controlled nor given parameters that would measure the extent of their coverage of any issue including conflicts no matter who may have been involved in the news.

African mass media should be devoid of encroachment and control. There must be stabilized and secured media practice, which in turn may result to political and economic development in various African nations. Stability in the context of this chapter is understood to mean the relative constancy of an environment within which a slow, dynamic system evolves through the normal and harmonious interplay of social, economic, political, and even cultural factors without major disturbance.

Stability, according to Mogekwu (1995), provides an air and feeling of durability and firmness of purpose. It brings to a certain degree a state of constancy than it could provide a foundation for the building of trust because one can perceive in a stable environment, firmness in purpose and character. Stability, therefore, is a precursor to security and is discussed as a state of being without anxiety that guarantees safety and freedom from danger which helps in the building of confidence. As the African leaders allow the mass media in Africa to function with freedom in the center, it will stabilize the mass media system and afford them the required security to operate adequately.

THE ROLE OF MASS MEDIA IN AFRICA'S DEMOCRATIC AND ECONOMIC TRANSFORMATION

In the past four decades, the continent of Africa has suffered low annual economic and political growth which, according to Kariithi (1995), is due to (among other factors) a virtual collapse of productive sectors, massive reduction in local and foreign investment, a crippling external debt, the militarization of the polity, poor and lack of patriotic-minded leaders, and depressed global commodity prices. African countries have also experienced deterioration in international trade, and high inflation, while most of the leaders and a few well-to-do citizens were living on gold and splendor. The majority of the population is completely trailing on the edge of disengagement from the global economy.

Poverty, coupled with poor health and security issues has made life very unbearable and uncertain for African citizens. The essence of absolute awareness and knowledge among the citizens is to reduce suffering and uncertainties, which have become a typical lifestyle in a continent endowed with numerous mineral resources. The mass media in various African nations play numerous vital responsibilities, which include the transferring of new ideas and models from one African nation to another and also from one local entity in a specific African nation to the other.

According to Wilbur Schramm in his book *Mass Media and National Development* (1964), villages in African nations are drowsing in their traditional patterns of life and the urge, therefore, to develop politically, economically, and socially usually comes from seeing how the well-developed nations of the world or the more fortunate people live. The mass media in African nations, therefore, functions as a bridge to a wider world and is entrusted with the task of preparing individuals for rapid political, economic, and social change by establishing a climate of modernization.

The African leaders use the mass media in a one-way and top-down communication to disseminate modern innovation, and report the outcome of their duties to the people. Despite the one-way and top-down system of communication used by African leaders, mass media practitioners in Africa use the media as a conduit to report conflicts and its effects on the public. As a result of these responsibilities (magic multipliers of development benefits, harbingers of modernizing influences, among others), the role played by the mass media in African nations includes, but is not limited to, the acceleration and easing of the long, slow social and political transformation required for economic development. The role of mass media in various African nations is significantly monumental to the regions political, social, and economic transformation. In the context of the literature abstracted for this chapter, it becomes imperative to state in categorical terms that the role of the media in Africa is to identify and cover problems such as conflicts that are sometimes detrimental to basic human needs and issues related to the security of the various nations.

In the process of identifying and covering these problems, which include conflicts such as the mayhem of the 1990s in Rwanda; various political, social, religious, and inter-ethnic conflicts in various African nations such as Nigeria, Liberia, Somalia, Sierra Leone, Ethiopia, Zimbabwe, Angola, Uganda, Sudan, South Africa, and Ghana among the least, the mass media has been challenged through the process of media coverage in making attempts to provide specialized information designed for the solutions of these conflicts. The position of this chapter, therefore, is to determine to what extent the African mass media coverage of conflict reflects a significant concern of the issues without bias, which addresses the first research question; and seek answers on the second research question as to how they give significant attention to these conflicts at national, state, and local levels.

Reports from African journals on conflict resolution have significantly shown that the media system has fallen short in covering these conflicts as it should because of the numerous sanctions and censorship by the various African governments. In various instances, like in the most recent conflict and political upheavals emanating from Zimbabwe, the government has used its authority to intimidate journalistic coverage and the publication of what is currently happening on the ground (Acayo and Mnjama, 2004). In Madagascar, the political rift that recently brought a new, undemocratic government into power uses the government security and authority (power) to intimidate media coverage. In Rwanda, the upheavals and cruelty perpetrated by the government and most heartless security personnel can never be covered as it should. In most of these conflicts and crises, foreign media practitioners were only in good states to cover the malaise to the international community. As a result of the peace agreement and the most recent resolutions reached between the government and international peacekeepers, things are changing rapidly.

Definition of Conflict and Types

According to the American Heritage College Dictionary, conflict is defined as a state of disharmony between incompatible or antithetical persons, ideas, or interests. It is a psychic struggle resulting from the opposition or simultaneous functioning of mutually exclusive impulses, desires, or tendencies. Conflict is the balancing of vectors of powers and of capabilities to produce effects. It is a distinct category of social behavior where two parties are struggling to get something they both cannot have. Conflict has also been defined as the pushing and pulling, the giving and taking, the process of finding the balance between powers (confrontation of powers). Conflict can be treated broadly as a philosophical category denoting the clash of power against power in the striving of all things to become manifest. Conflict can be identified both as a potentiality or a situation, as well as a structure or a manifestation and as an event or a process

Conflict Types

There are various types of conflicts such as neighborhood conflict; housing conflict; family conflict; parent/youth conflict; community conflict; racial and cross-cultural conflict; and organizational conflict. Neighborhood conflict includes noise, pets, shared common areas, and other disturbances in the neighborhood, excluding domestic violence. Housing conflict develops between landlords and the tenants, roommates, and in apartments, condos, houses, and mobile home parks. Family conflict may include divorce or child custody, and financial and estate distribution between members of a family. Parent/youth conflict is classified as misunderstanding between youth, peer relations, school, neighbors, and employers. Community conflict is associated with new development and land use issues. Racial and Cross-Cultural conflict includes interracial conflict, cross- racial confrontations, and religious conflict, while organizational conflict consists of private nonprofit agencies, community groups, city groups, and ethnic rivalries. These various categories of conflict could result to various violent behaviors in society.

In Africa nations, for instance, the extent of media coverage of neighborhood, housing, family, and parent conflicts are not as prevalent as the community, racial, cross-cultural and organizational issues, which have dominated most violent acts perpetrated by some dubious citizens not only to challenge the authorities, but sometimes to seek means of balancing powers. Some of the perpetrators of these conflict acts do so for selfish reasons. Acayo and Mnjama (2004) in their study titled "Print Media and Conflict Resolution in Northern Uganda" found that Acholi and Langi communities were deprived of their ability to get rich from looting other Ugandans. Museveni (1997) contends that the reason why the rebels in the north, organized on a tribal basis, was to fight for control of national government over the nations' resources.

Community, racial, cross-cultural, and organizational conflicts in Africa have resulted sometimes in various unrest and violence which the media has not given significant attention or coverage to. The position of this paper, therefore, seems to opine that if coverage is not significantly done, was it because of bias, or just that the media failed to give coverage of the conflict? In most instances, when conflicts arise from organized groups or communities — such as in the case of Nigeria, the Movement of the Ogoni People from the Rivers State (1990 –1998) that led to the eventual public execution of the leader Mr. Ken Saro Wiwa — the media coverage of the conflict that resulted to the death of Wiwa looked more upon his death than the causes. This type of media coverage tends to give a one-sided report of an issue of great magnitude that resulted in the eventual termination of a community leader's life. As the story of the death of Wiwa evolved, it cast blame on the government in power as being responsible and using its power to sanction any media outlet that tells the story as it is.

It also failed to report adequately as to who was involved in the final decision that resulted to the public execution, which goes back to reflect on the questions addressed by this chapter. Was the extent of coverage of the Wiwa's dilemma a result of media intimidation by the powers that be, or the level of relationship between the government and the media? The rationale of the leader of the Movement for the Actualization of the Sovereign State of Biafra (MASSOB), an organized group from Eastern Nigeria who was asking for an independent Igbo nation or the organized leader from Bayelsa, Alhaji Asari

Dukubo, who was also advancing Saro Wiwa's beliefs, were not adequately covered by the Nigerian media in avoidance of government intimidations.

African media systems have been silenced during military dictatorship in the coverage of conflicts. The reporting of significant news items which include conflicts are dictated by the military leaders whose relationship with the media seem not to be cozy. Coverage of news and conflicts during an undemocratic military dictatorship has always been determined to a larger extent by the type of conflict and who has a stake in such conflict or violence. However, Nwokeafor (2001) argued that the end of military dictatorship in some African nations that has resulted to democratic dispensation in the recent times has set an agenda for a rethinking of the social, economic, political, and journalistic relations. He agreed that democratic dispensation will lead to transparent relationship between the government and the media practitioners. The reality of this claim, no doubt, has been far-fetched because even with a democratically elected government in power, the media intimidating situation may have slowed down but still in practice. This relationship will determine the coverage of conflict and news items more by their newsworthiness than the people in the news, a practice, which will eventually impact positively the political, social, and economic development of the region.

Mass Media and Coverage of Conflict in Africa

Conflict has become an on-going and common phenomenon in the history of African democracy. According to historical records, the first African nation to embrace democracy in 1958 was Ghana (Gold Coast) seconded by Nigeria in 1960. Other African nations gained their independence from their respective colonial leaders during the early to later 1960s. Many of these countries gained their independence by encountering their colonial leaders, which sometimes resulted to some kind of conflict. In the case of Nigeria, for instance, the 1940s witnessed an upsurge in political movements from the formation of the Nigerian Youth Movement (NYM) to the inauguration of the National Council of Nigeria and Cameroon (NCNC), the Action Group (AG), and the Northern People's Congress (NPC), (Nwokeafor, 1992).

The organized political movements in Nigeria led to various conflicts and threats to peoples' lives and property that posed a challenge to peace and stability. These organized movements led to the emergence of great political minds like Dr. Nnamdi Azikiwe, Chief Obafemi Awolowo, Alhaji Abubakar Tafewa Belewa, and many others who represented their respective (NCNC, AG, and NPC) parties. The position of these founding fathers led to the first election in Nigeria in 1959, and their respective political agenda instigated various oppositions and conflicts in a nation after nearly 49 years since independence, which is still divided across political, religious, and ethnic boundaries.

The experience of Nigeria is very similar in other African nations such as Ghana, Cameroon, Kenya, South Africa, Madagascar, Kenya, Sierra Leone,

Ethiopia, Eritrea, Zimbabwe, Ivory Coast, Liberia, Rwanda, Somalia, Angola, Uganda, Sudan, Egypt, Congo -Kinshasa, Morocco, Algeria, Mozambique, Gambia, Namibia, Tanzania, Tunisia, Chad, Benin, Togo, Central African Republic, Mauritania, Lesotho, Mali, Zambia, Cote d'Ivoire, Burkina Faso, Malawi, Niger, Mali, Libya, Botswana, Guinea-Bissau, Gabon, Swaziland, Comoro, and a host of other countries that make up the 54 nations of the region of Africa.

On October 1, 1960, Nigeria, like most other African nations, became independent and the struggle to control the benefits of power was highly intensified with rioting and organized disturbances at political meetings. There were also major conflicts between the Northerners and Southerners, which has created hatred and inter-ethnic rivalry. During this period of increased political movement in Nigeria, and most of the recent political, social, religious, and inter-ethnic conflicts, the mass media has been instrumental in its coverage of these conflicts, but how much becomes a crucial question. In Ghana, for instance, Dr. Kwame Nkrumah, the first democratic President of the Republic of Ghana, went through a tussle, a struggle that sent the expatriates packing from the former Gold Coast. He fought convincingly to bring about freedom and independence to Ghana. The struggle went through with the presence of various conflicts, sometimes within the various ethnic units in the country.

In Somalia, Rwanda, Sierra Leone, South Africa, Zimbabwe, and various other African nations between the early 1980s to the later part of the 1990s, and for over 30 years in the case of South Africa, following the Apartheid controversy, conflict has raised its ugly face in one instance or the other. This conflict, most of the time politically motivated, has not been covered by the media as it should, due to the level of control and manipulation by the government in power. In most of these nations today, peace had long returned and a democratic system is rigorously practiced. A case in point is South Africa, which is today led by a democratic-elected black president.

Since independence, African nations have gone through series of conflicts and violence that have challenged and sometimes stifled the continents political, social, and economic development. In the 1990s, the nation of Rwanda saw the bloodiest conflict in the phase of Africa that claimed thousands of lives. In Sierra Leone, the more than 10-year-old civil war that destroyed the entire country left children maimed, and a great number of them without their parents. In Liberia, the long-lasting war completely rendered the nation impoverished. In Kenya, South Africa, and many other African nations, the AIDS epidemic has contributed to a massive conflict that has left the continent in confusion. In South Africa, for instance, the more than 25 years of apartheid destroyed hundreds of thousands of black South Africans. The conflict, which was politically motivated, was not given adequate coverage in South Africa, as was the case in various other European countries. The reason behind this lack of coverage during the unrest and undemocratic era in South Africa and the other nations was not that African journalists could not perform their journalistic duties; rather, they were intimidated by the government in power during the periods in discussion, who sometimes denied them the opportunity to publish relevant news issues from their respective countries.

In Nigeria, for instance, in spite of the 1960s that ushered in the Tiv rebellion (1960-1964) — the January 1966 military coup, the 1966 ethnic violence against the Igbos in the North, a second coup in July 1966; the 1967-1970 civil war that claimed more than one million lives — there are most recent coups in the 1970s, '80s, and '90s that led to changes in military leadership and resulted in conflicts and political instability in the nation. The unending Niger Delta conflict, popularly known as the Movement for the Emancipation of the Niger Delta (MEND); The Movement of the Ogini People, an organized group in Rivers State; the Odua People Congress from the Southwest; the Movement for the Actualization of the Sovereign State of Biafra (MASSOB); the Chris Uba greed for the Anambra State treasury and its devastating effect on the citizens of the state; Dr. Chris Nwabueze Ngige, the former governor of Anambra State (2003-2006) and his continuing tussle with the Uba family and the leadership at the federal level not to bring down Anambra State to a disaster area resulted to considerable conflict.

Nigerian Labor Union, Nigerian Students' Union, and many other organized group conflicts in the North, West, Southeast and South-South of Nigeria, which may have claimed many lives, are crucial conflicts that may have been given attention and coverage by the media; however, the contention of this chapter lies on the question of the extent of coverage of these conflicts without bias and how the media may have given the coverage significant attention at the national, state, and local levels. In an attempt to address the key questions posed by this chapter, it is relevant to review the performance of African mass media in the context of covering conflicts. (1) To what extent does the mass media in Africa cover conflicts without bias? It is obvious to note that most conflicts covered by the media in most African nations are sometimes subdued, intimidated, and stories and facts are sometimes blatantly not reported as they should be. Most African journalists, sometimes for fear of intimidation and threats on their lives, present conflict stories with some bias. The demise of popular newsmagazine editor Dele Giwa on Oct. 19, 1986 supports the premise of this question by showing that, as a result of fear or threat, most of these journalists attempted to refrain from coverage of such issues or conflicts. (2) Does the mass media in Africa cover conflicts at national and state levels equitably as it does at the local levels? The coverage of conflicts at the national and state levels seems to have taken more considerable time and visibility than some of the local conflicts. However, in some local crises, such as the Movement for the Emancipation of the Niger Delta (MEND), coverage has risen over 95 percent because of the severity of the issue, according to a *Daily Sun News Online* (May 5, 2009) report. MEND News attracts both local, state, national, and international interest because of what is at stake — oil.

The focus of the Federal Government has always been to protect the oil, as a result of which this special, local conflict, which has translated to a national conflict, receives quite a tremendous coverage. (3) Who controls and sets the mass media agenda in the continent of Africa? The media in the continent of Africa has performed the function of both watch-dog as well as a conduit for dissemination of political aggrandizement and propaganda by politicians. In some cases, the media were considered the vehicles for transferring of new ideas and models from one developed nation to various countries in the continent of Africa. The media has been used for information dissemination from urban areas to the rural countryside. Melkote (1991) posited that the media were used in one-way and top-down communication by African leaders to disseminate modern innovation to the masses. As a result of their leadership role and authority, they control and sometimes set the media agenda.

The recent political saga in Kenya and Zimbabwe, which resulted in conflicts that claimed lives of the citizens, may have been covered by international media more than in these countries because of the fear of repercussion journalists may suffer from the government; although in these two mentioned nations, the dissenting group leader was settled by being allowed to ascend the mantle of leadership, which was a form to close the political-gap which may not have been covered as adequately as it should. In Sierra Leone and Liberia, the various crises that resulted to a high-level conflict were not given thorough coverage because of the fear of intimidation, sanction, and even death. For example, the killing of innocent citizens and the maiming of young children and various inhumane atrocities done to women by soldiers were only covered by some foreign observers and journalists. These threats, in most instances, resulted in inadequate as well as insufficient coverage of news.

AN ANALYSIS OF THE PERFORMANCE OF AFRICAN MASS MEDIA TECHNOLOGY IN A DEMOCRATIC AND ECONOMIC SYSTEM

The history of mass media services and its performance in the continent of Africa dates back to the late eighteenth century, when Napoleon occupied Egypt (Merrill, 1995); however, the Royal Gazette in Sierra Leone, established in 1801 in Sierra Leone, was among the oldest and earliest African mass media. Reviewing the history of mass media system in Africa empirically suggests the level of its performance in a continent whose government has leaned more toward military dictatorship than democracy.

The record of the origin of mass media system in Africa beginning with the Royal Gazette in Sierra Leone, Royal Gold Coast Gazette and Commercial Intelligencer in Ghana (1822); the Liberian Herald in 1826; the Iwe Irohim, in

Nigeria, in 1859; La Bastille and Blaise Diagne in Senegal; L'Eveil des Camerounais and La Pressed u Cameroon in 1955; Abidjan Matins in Ivory Coast; La Presse de Guinea in Conakry Guinea; Journal Official de La Republic du Togo, in Togo; Ebano and Poto Poto in Equatorial Guinea; Le Journal du Katanga in the present day Republic of Congo; Provincia de Angola in Angola; the South African Journal and Het Nederduitsch Zuid-Afrikaansch Tydschrift (1824) in South Africa; Ebifa Mu Uganda and Muno first published in 1907 and 1911 respectively; and most of other African dailies set the stage for a multitude of other various African nations weekly and daily newspaper that were founded later by indigenous African leaders, most of whom were journalists themselves (Merrill, 1995, Nwokeafor, 2001).

The presence of these indigenous and early newspapers was a pride to the various African nations. However, these newspapers were established for the same reasons the expatriate medium were established. They serve as the megaphone of the indigenous leaders who used these newspapers to publish their self-acclaimed political agenda. These news media were used to advance their political dreams and also intimidate their opponents. Literature has shown that in considerable times, these newspapers have served the purpose of the government in power which supports Ogan's (1982) position that African journalism is a "government say-so-journalism" because of the pattern of their publications that tend to support and not criticize the government in power. (pp. 3-12).

In most instances, conflicts that report the government in power in a negative state cannot be published. Journalists have in the past been censored, banished, and sometimes killed for being objective in their practice regarding whose sword is guard. In 1986 in Nigeria, for instance, a promising and renowned journalist Dele Giwa was killed by a time-bomb because of his style of journalism, which was timely and objective and most times critical of the government in power. In many other African countries, journalism and journalists have gone through tough times because of their objective approach to an issue or news item that may be critical to the government or leaders of various communities.

The dawn of the present millennium has ushered new democratic dispensations in most Africa Nations. This applies to Nigeria, Ghana, South Africa, Cameroon, Sierra Leone, Liberia, Zambia, Mali, Tanzania, Namibia, Malawi, Botswana and a lot more others whose democracies were either new or have been in existence for quite some time. These democracies have allowed journalistic freedom to a certain extent. One of the dividends of democracy is press freedom; however, the evaluation of media performance in some African nations seem encouraging with a lot more loopholes. Mass media systems, it is believed, perform better in a democratic governance than in a military dictatorship. Looking at the research questions addressed in this chapter, which looked at the extent of coverage of conflict by media without bias and the level of significant attention given to conflict on a national, state, and local levels respectively by the media, the argument, therefore, is whether the mass media in African nations has performed independently without instruction from the government not to cover events that are damaging to the nation.

Nwokeafor (2001) reported an on-line Guardian Newspaper Opinion Poll (GOP) in Nigeria which showed that one year after the1999 democratic election, about 80 percent of the population polled scored the media high in performance, while 72 percent expressed approval of the reportage of issues. A breakdown of the population showed that 98 percent of the respondents from the South-South region of the nation rated news media performance high, while 80 percent commended the level of news coverage across the nation. In the Southeast, media performance and the level of coverage scored 45 percent and 69 percent respectively. In the Southwest, the figure seems close with 44 percent and 58 percent. In the Northeast, the figure recorded was 38.9 percent and 61.1 percent, where as in the North-Central, the role of mass media and their performance level scored 35.3 percent and 66.5 percent respectfully.

The cumulative score of response to the rating of the performance of mass media according to the poll in Nigeria shows that 26 percent rated the mass media excellent, 43 percent good, 21.2 percent average and 5.4 percent poor. Seventy-two percent of the population polled approved the performance of the mass media, while 14.5 percent disapproved. The results of the poll not only suggest that mass media functions much better during a democratic system, but also shows that coverage of conflicts and other related news are done with less intimidation.

The result of the Nigerian opinion poll on the performance of mass media could be attributed to other African nations who practice democracy. The poll results demonstrated a common belief that one of the benefits of democracy is the level of media freedom to operate. Although the founding fathers who established the first newspapers used them for their selfish political reasons, just like their expatriate counterparts who they accused of the same exercise, and used the news medium as their megaphone to promote their political agenda. Democratic governance in most African nations has contributed immeasurably in the way mass media practitioners perform their professional responsibilities; however, there is still more work to be done in the area of media freedom because some of the current African democratic leaders are former military leaders.

Technological innovation has also contributed tremendously in the high record of performance by the African media system, which has resulted in more improved ways of sending and receiving data, as well as the online capabilities. The high-powered means of generating data for news publication, and most importantly, the transition from analog to digital structures, has not only defined contemporary media systems in Africa, but also has significantly improved the practice of journalism in African nations. Today, the process of retrieving data from online data bases to support publications, interviewing sources regardless of distance, or validating an actuality for a specific news bite could be accomplished in a dialing of a phone number or accessing a website. Full coverage of a news bite or validation of a news item could be accomplished on a timely basis. The alarming speed at which the African media system professionals operate in today's world, which is attributed to the enhancement of technology, has to a larger extent impacted the democratic, social, as well as economic systems in the world's second largest continent.

In various parts of Africa in contemporary times, political parties have used the television, radio, newspapers, and even the electronic mailing systems to advance their political agendas. Politicians can effectively reach their audience in a timely basis through the media. Political campaigns are organized easily with the use of various media paraphernalia. In Nigeria for instance, these politicians use television, radio, and newspapers to disseminate their campaign messages. Their campaign messages are tailored to specific audiences or voters and they are able to reach them in a timely manner regardless of distance. Information retrieval is more enhanced in contemporary times. Media programs are more entertaining and adequately available. Various African politicians target their voters through the means of television programs and use the Internet based on affordability to tell their political stories. The improved media programs, such as the popular African movies, have been used to target voters. A good example is Nollywood in Nigeria, which has significantly improved the use of the media products to reach a diverse audience.

NOLLYWOOD

Nollywood is the movie industry in Nigeria that produces all the movies that are currently flooding the African continent, as well as the international community markets, with culturally-oriented movies. The industry, as the name suggests, is fashioned from the United States of America's Hollywood — the industry that controls the movie products of the world. The Nollywood industry in Nigeria has made the movie market, an aspect of the mass media, to transport ideas and issues of pertinence to the grassroots level, thereby keeping the critical mass in Nigeria and the continent of Africa informed of the cultural endowment, as well as to link Africans in Diaspora with their respective homes by the nature, theme, and background of the movies. In Ghana, Cameroon, Kenya, South Africa, and most other African countries, the Nollywood success has spurred a lot of positive movie-making, management, and dissemination of cultural information to the grassroots level. It is, of course, true to say that the management of the movie industry in the African region has to a significant level positively impacted the economic well-being of those countries.

Most Nigerian movies, for instance, and some others produced in other African countries, have stormed African markets tremendously. Nigerian movie producers have collaborated with their counterparts in Ghanaian, South Africa, Ivory Coast, Liberia, and Cameroon in the production of relevant movies that depict real democratic processes in Africa. They have used actors and actresses from these mentioned African nations to produce movies that have either mimicked the political process, or how rudely intoxicated leaders have used the political process to impoverish their people. In Nigeria, for instance, *The Last Vote* was a movie that shows how a state government under the leadership of its health commissioner has usurped his authority and flooded the market with expired drugs that kill a good number of pregnant mothers who are undergoing prenatal care from the hospitals.

Movies, a form of news and information, have been used as a mass media outlet to inform the citizens of some of the ills of the political system in various African nations. These movies have stormed the African, and most recently the international markets, with relaxing, cultural, emotionally-driven and comic contents. These movies, as a source of information, have to a larger extent impacted the democratic and economic mainstay of the continent regardless of the piracy quagmires. The negative impact of piracy in the production and marketing of these movies has tremendously affected the proceeds the producers ought to have derived from making those movies. One of the drawbacks of the advancement in technology has to deal with accessibility and capability of reproducing these movies without authority from the label owners and royalty to the owners of the products by some busybodies who are reproducing these movies and making huge profit off of them without permission from the owners. Although the development in technology has to some extent helped in the improvement of both democratic and economic systems in African states, the drawbacks have also significantly impressed upon both media users and producers, who have continued to fight a lost battle with piracy.

The contemporary technologically-enhanced African media systems have changed the way African media cover conflicts associated with the various nations of the continent of Africa. It is, of course, obvious that most media practitioners in today's Africa could use the Internet as a convenient means of disseminating their products to their targeted audience. The case of blocking the airwaves or their means of reaching their audience may have met its low by the existence of technological outfits that have created a totally different means by which information could be transmitted to and from audiences. In order to read or retrieve conflict issues in any of the African nations, a simple push of the computer button (Google.com) could bring the information even closer to the comfort of the audience's home or office.

Contrasting the historical overview of early mass media in Africa and looking at the extent of usage of media products today, there is considerable evidence to show that improved technological structures have significantly impacted African democratic and economic processes. The Nollywood movie industry in Nigeria has ushered a new and dynamic media culture which has changed the way African citizens use the mass media products. In Nigeria as other parts of Africa, the products from Nollywood have transformed African media audience and tremendously increased their usage. These changes have also created jobs for a diverse population, thereby enhancing the economic well-being of the continent of Africa. The movie industry as a form of mass medium uses the airwaves in the form of reenacting real political issues and most of the corruptions perpetrated by politicians in the various nations of Africa. In so doing, mass media serves as a conduit through which corruption and abuse of power are directly disseminated even to the grassroots level. The African movie producers, by producing movies that indirectly portray the corrupt motives of the government and their allies, to an extent play the watch-dog role as well as a whistle-blower function to most of the ills that have adversely affected the entire continent of Africa.

Summary and Conclusion

Conflict and various violent acts have been synonymous with various activities and events in African nations where organized groups have been responsible for unsteady government and fraudulent activities that have derailed the political, social, and economic development of a continent with versed resources. The 1966 through 1970 civil war in Nigeria, the devastating war in Sierra Leone that lasted for more than 10 years, the conflict activities in Rwanda, Liberia, Somalia, and Northern Uganda over who will be the primary beneficiary of Uganda's wealth, and many other violent related activities in various African nations have tremendously impacted the political, social, and economic system, thereby making it very difficult for sustainable development.

In Kenya, where the recent state of the democratic election kept the country in near standby, as well as in Zimbabwe, where a similar election outcome resulted, turmoil and incessant conflict remain to plague the nations regardless of the recent resolve. It has placed a politics of dissention between political parties and affiliations where citizens have been fragmented and sometimes resort to violence and conflict in resolving common issues. In South Africa, the tenure of the immediate past President came to a quick end in 2007 and the result of the conflict has resulted in factions who are loyal to different leaders. In Madagascar, just recently, the conflict that arose as a result of the undemocratic appointment of a leader who replaced a democratic-elected leader may have not been adequately covered by the media because the culture of media coverage has always been to protect the powers that be. In most instances when coverage of conflict is allowed in most of the nations of Africa, they are doctored such that the real issues may not be allowed to be freely published. The leaders and government in power use the mass media to shield themselves and protect their political agenda.

The position of this chapter, therefore, has established the fact that media coverage of conflict in African nations practicing democracy has improved; however, there is much work to do in those nations still under military dictatorship. African nations are considered a vibrant continent concerned with the political, social, and economic growth of its people. To attain such growth, the media has a deserving role to play, which includes the role of providing access and channels of communication between the federal, state, and local governments and the people without any interruption or bias. The mass media in African nations should cover conflicts and violent issues (at any level) without intimidation by any organized group or government in power, by performing its watch-dog role and being free to sound a genuine alarm without frustration by any government in power, or the most affluent in the community.

The Madagascar issue must be freely covered by its media without bias, The Nigerian media system should operate as it presently does without any sensational censure by any organized group or elected government no matter who or what made the news. The violence caused by the war and mayhem in Sierra Leone that resulted in several years of conflict, corruption, and intimidation must be covered by the country's media system independent of the government in power. The religious and organized group conflict in the Northern states of Nigeria must be adequately reported by the mass media regardless of who is the President of the nation.

The Bakassi protracted conflict between Nigeria and Cameroon should be covered to its depth and resolve brought to the open, regardless of who is at fault. The economic tailspin that is currently challenging the global community and has drastic measures in most African countries should be covered freely by the mass media regardless of how the government may be involved in it. It is when the mass media in Africa is allowed to practice independently (press freedom), as it is obtained in western civilized countries, that the benefits of democracy will be felt by the citizens of Africa in their respective nations, as well as in Diaspora. The peaceful existence of mass media systems and the freedom to practice journalism as indicated in the theory of journalism by African journalists would go a long way to transforming both the democratic and economic systems. No sooner than African journalists are free to practice their profession than the expected peaceful co-existence of the people of Africa will be attained.

The African mass media have come a long way and still have a lot of catching up to do. The most recent acceptance of democracy and the advent of improved technology have, to a larger extent, contributed to a more professional journalistic practice. The government in power should separate their democratic authority from control of the mass media. They must allow media practitioners to set the media agenda. When African mass media takes its proper place in the practice of journalism, where peaceful democratic and economic systems achieve their respective places in the global front, then democracy and its benefits will have been sustained. The advancement in technology and various technological innovations which have permeated various African nations, even at the grassroots level, have made it possible for news and information, as well as performance and entertainment, to travel globally and make some significant changes in the way people react to each other and conduct businesses.

REFERENCES

Acayo, C. and Mnjama, N. (2004). The print media and conflict resolution in northern Uganda. *African Journal On Conflict Resolution*, 4 , 1 31-32.

The American Heritage Dictionary of the English Language. (4th ed.) Houghton Mifflin Company.

Kariithi, N. K. (1995). Questioning the policymaker: The role of mass media in shaping Africa's economic future. In Charles Okigbo (ed.) *Media and Sustainable Development*. 363-366.

Merrill, J. (1995). *Global Journalism: Survey of International Communication* (3rd ed.) New York: Longman Publishers.

Melkote, S. (1991). *Communication for Development in the Third-World: Theory and Practice.* Newbury Park, CA: Sage Publications, pp. 38-50.

Mogekwu, M. (1995). Media, stability and security: Imperatives for sustainable development in Africa. In Charles Okigbo (ed.) *Media and Sustainable Development*. 300-302.

Museveni, Y. K. (1997). Sowing the mustard seed. In Gerwel & Malan (eds.) *African Journal on Conflict Resolution*, 4, 1. Durban, South Africa. 31-32.

Nwokeafor, C. U. (2001). The African Print Media in a New Millennium: An Appraisal of the impact of a transparent democracy. Southern interdisciplinary roundtable on African studies conference proceedings publications. Kentucky State University. 5-7.

———— (1992). *Development communication in the Nigerian mass media: A survey of selected publications.* Unpublished dissertation, Howard University, Washington, DC.

Obotette, B. E. (1984). *Mass communication for national development in Nigeria: Analysis of content and structure.* Unpublished Dissertation, Howard University, Washington, DC.

Okoro, E. (1995). The mass media and political development. In Charles Okigbo (ed.) *Media and Sustainable Development.* Nairobi, Kenya.

Pye, L. W. (1963). *Communication and Political Development.* Princeton: Princeton University Press.

Rogers, E. M. and Shoemaker, F. F. (1973). *Communication of Innovations: A Cross Cultural Approach,* New York: Free Press.

Schramm W. (1964). *Mass Media and National Development.* Stanford, California: Stanford University Press.

Yushkiavitshus, H. (1994). Unpublished, untitled paper read at the International press institute, 43rd Annual General Assembly, Cape Town, South Africa, February 16.

Chapter 10

Communication, Civil Society, and Democratization in Africa: Perspectives on Political Development

Ephraim Okoro
Howard University

Abstract

A significant number of scholars and researchers believe that political establishments and governments in the developing nations of the Sub-Saharan Africa region should desist from interfering with ownership and control of the press and its functions in the attempt to achieve sustainable national development. Contending that development strategies in the twenty-first century are pluralistic, complex, and culturally diverse, African society must adopt a strategic communication model that is independent of government interest and control. This paper suggests the concept of media-participation-integrative model that is grounded in agenda-setting role of the press. The paper specifically focuses on the instrumentality of the press in advancing and promoting political practice and democratic reforms in the region. Past and present relationships between the press and governments in the context of nation-building have been counter-productive, largely because of mutual distrust and incompatible objectives, which have stalled development reforms. Based on assessments of the quality of politics and governance in recent years, this paper then argues that to sustain political development in the Sub-Saharan African nations, the concepts of "free enterprise" and the "marketplace of ideas" should be nurtured by the present governments. It then concludes that in a free-market democracy, the citizens must be adequately and objectively informed and participate in the decision-making process.

INTRODUCTION

The surge in despair over African political and economic prospects at the turn of the twenty-first century raises alarming concerns about political reforms. The continent has been the focus of some of the most dramatic political changes over the past three decades. The concerns of many African citizens range from what has changed to what was the nature and quality of the change. In the overall development agenda, there are also concerns regarding what strategic efforts and initiatives are in place to build institutions, reinforce the legal system, support citizens, and provide appropriate economic policies and oversight (Gyimah-Boadi, 2004). Furthermore, the changing nature of politics in Africa, the task of nation-building in the post-independent African nations, the quality of their democratic governance, and the role or ability of the media to set public agenda remains a fundamental challenge in the current African political renewal. Together with democratic failures and deficits in the developing African countries is the inability of their media to promote democratic values and strategies to enhance political process and ethnic integration. Gyimah-Boadi concludes that the "unprecedented surge" in Africa's civil society is a critical element that has emerged as a key force in their political development agenda. It was strongly suggested that relaxing of media censorship in the continent will be instrumental to fostering the much needed political reforms and consolidation. Past and current communication scholars (Megwa, 1988; Nwokeafor & Nwanko, 1993) have argued that standards of democratic performance in the Africa will remain undesirable and below global expectation until the mass media is involved in the process of transformation.

In the wake of democratization and political reforms in many parts of the developing world, communication scholars (Salawu, 2009; Megwa, 2009; Agbaje, 2004)) maintain that the media, specifically the press, can play a critical role in identifying and advancing development and political needs toward sustainable democracies in the African region. Over the years, media practitioners and researchers (Okoli, 2009; Mazula, 2004; Nwokeafor & Nwanko, 1993) have stressed that there is a significant correlation between politics and communication, and that the relationship between the two entities can be improved through effective, ethical, and efficient communication patterns. These studies focused extensively on the effectiveness of the media in promoting Africa's political experiments in the competitive global economy.

Recent literature on political and national development indicates that post-independence initiatives in Africa, specifically in Nigeria, Cameroon, Ghana, and Sierra Leone indicate a serious need for effectiveness of various forms of media in the process of attaining political transformation, creating cultural awareness, and establishing social and ethnic cohesion. Some of these development studies (Nwanko, 2000; Nwokeafor, 2000; Van de Walle, 2004; Onwumechili, 2009) emphasize that communication was instrumental for the rapid and consistent development of advanced societies. In some developing nations of Africa, the concepts of political development and modernization have dominated national priorities for the past two or three decades, largely because of the impact of globalization. The World Bank and other international organizations (The World Bank, 2006; Bread for the World Institute, 1998; The World Bank, 2001; The Central Bank of Nigeria, 2008) have devoted a significant amount of time to development activities and programs in the Sub-Saharan Africa, and have advanced recommendations intended to improve democratic practice and reforms in the entire region. These various institutions and scholars identified the central role of the mass media in key developments in African politics, especially in their bid toward the integration of pluralistic and disparate communities.

It is widely argued in academic research that development programs and efforts in the twenty-first century should include the mass media, especially the new technological innovations that have rapidly and systematically changed the information dissemination processes. Since some of the basic recurrent needs of developing nations are to achieve political stability, ethnic integration, and political reforms, it is crucial to analyze the performance and structure of media content, contexts, and delivery channels. Some historical studies (Omu, 1978; Opubor, 1974; and Ugboajah, 1987) contend that the fundamental preoccupation of the mass media in the developing countries should be to foster and encourage national harmony, reconciliation of deep-rooted ethnic differences, and the propagation of national solidarity. Similarly, nationally-recognized experts such as Lerner (1963), Nwanko (1973), and Casmir (1991), among others from a wide range of subject areas in which communication research has been used to address social, economic, and political problems persist in their conclusion that that the mass media and the new technological innovations must be involved in the process of national development and political reforms in the emerging African democracies.

Empowering the media to play their traditional role of disseminating and sharing information is central to any form of development. The uses or role which the citizens expect the mass media to play in a democratic process vary, depending on the type of societies and the sophistication of the citizens. According to McQuail (1987) and Unger (1991), societies are significantly different in value systems, attitudes, and political interests; therefore, public expectation or use of the mass media for political reform and gratification differ. Nevertheless, studies of the past few years indicate a high degree of uniformity in the roles which societies and people anticipate of the media. McQuail synthesized media use in four broad categories as follows: information dissemination, cultivating personal identity, promoting integration and social interaction, and providing entertainment.

The Concept of Development

Uche (1991) explains that various scholars operationalized economic, national, and political development in a number of different ways. Opubor (1974) sees development as involving the creation of opportunities for the realization of human potentials. Rodney (1974) describes it at the individual level as increased skill and capacity, greater freedom, creativity, self-discipline, responsibility, and material well-being. Beltran (1974, p.11-27) analyzes development at the national level as "a directed and widely participatory process of deep and accelerated changes in the economy, the technology, the ecology, and the overall culture of a country, so that the moral and material advancement of the majority of its population can be obtained within conditions of generalized quality, dignity, justice, and liberty." Awa (1989) explains that development experts define it in operational and measurable terms, adding that development must meet and uplift basic personal human and societal needs and expectations.

Over a period of time, scholars (The World Bank, 2006; Casmir, 1989; Graber, 1990) have taken the position that national development must ultimately lead to political development in order to ensure stability and economic growth. Therefore, political development in the context of this paper is conceived in accordance with Wilmot (1981, p.3) as "the action of men attempting to bring political meaning and order into an institution where power is being exercised." The World Bank report (1989), "Sub-Saharan Africa from Crisis to Sustainable Growth," points out that African nations have long seen greater regional integration and cooperation as prerequisites for sustainable political development, but that the objective of political reform and democratization may not be easily achieved if the mass media are unable to disseminate knowledge and information freely and independently. Further, new and improved technology of the twenty-first century is certainly a gateway to reach the critical mass at a more faster and convenient pace, thereby enhancing African democratization and political progress. The World Bank's report further stressed that too often the level of political consciousness and participation in Africa is stymied, sometimes deliberately so, by lack of information about government policy and activities.

As developing nations (Nigeria, Cameroon, Ghana, etc.) continue their efforts toward political advancement in the current decade, a critical part of the larger problem facing their development efforts and ambition is the type of role that is played by the communication channels, specifically the press and the new media. As channels that disseminate contemporary ideas, political issues, and refine traditional practices and values, the new media assist in reshaping and analyzing conflicting societal norms. For example, in the Unites States and other parts of the globe, the growing need to distribute goods and services, deliver consumers to advertisers with low cost content has dramatically shrunk the space for domestic and international mainstream news about government activities, political developments, and public policies (Bennett, 2003; Patterson, 2003). Furthermore, traditional and new media are recognized as agents capable of instituting a level of consistency and uprightness, and ethical practices needed to transform a society's social and political orientation.

Golding (1974), Fair (1989), Denton & Woodward (1990) stressed that an independent, objective and effective mass media system could sustain the type of political reforms instituted in the developing nations. By creating a high level of public awareness, identifying appropriate standards of public behavior and responsiveness, and accentuating the need for collective action, the media promote and sustain public interest and participation in the political process. For example, during national and local government campaigns and elections in Nigeria and other African nations, the media have the responsibility of performing these important functions objectively and consistently. Similarly, researchers (M'Bayo, 2000; Graber, 1989; Boas, 2000; Okigbo, 2000) recognized the complex and awesome efforts involved in the quest for modernity and democratization, and have determined empirically that the media can create an environment for effective political communication by providing balanced analysis of issues and sensitizing citizens to the values of unity and cooperation in diversity. Research evidence (Nwanko, 2000; M'Bayo & Mogekwu, 2000) indicates that the concept of national integration is an achievable political goal, but the media must be empowered to educate the citizens about its importance in the overall scheme of national reform agenda.

Mass Media, Politics, and Agenda-setting

In recent years, developing nations have been encouraged to employ the services of mass media systems to transform or redeem old values, attitudes, and behaviors that have impeded the process of modernity and modernization. As Denton and Woodward (1990) noted, there can be little doubt that even in a pluralistic, ethnic, or tribal environment the mass media collectively exert a considerable influence in determining agenda of political issues that will be given prominence in a society, both in developing and developed nations of the world. Harry West and Ellen Fair (1993), in their comprehensive examination of the processes needed to democratize, urbanize, and transform traditional African communities to modern status, acknowledged and stressed the importance of the effectiveness of the mass media as the single most critical agent capable of engendering public awareness and participation, and generating political change. Characterizing the mass media as innovators, analyzers, and mobilizers of transformation, West and Fair (1993) encouraged traditional societies to redefine the role of the media because in the modern era, their unique source is instrumental in creating and projecting new values and ethics as well as motivating collective responsibility. Accordingly, the focus of this paper is on the agenda-setting role of the African media in promoting political development, raising public awareness of political issues, or fostering national integration.

A vast array of mass communication literature of the past decades is replete with reemergence of the dominant influence and effects of the mass media in the political process, specifically focusing on the agenda-setting function of the media (Megwa, 2009; Solawu & Isola; 2009; McLeod, 2009; Rice & Atkin 2002; Lippman, 1992; McCombs & Shaw, 1992). As developing nations embark on the process of democratization, African scholars (Nwanko, 2000; Nwokeafor, 2000; M'Bayo, 2009) have reached the consensus that to achieve a reasonable measure of political development in the continent, local and national governments must reposition and empower their media with the responsibility of interpreting and setting the public agenda. Without the acquisition of this critical function, the expectations of the media role in development may be far-fetched and unrealistic.

Theoretical Framework: Media Agenda-Setting Paradigm

While studies conducted in recent years (McCombs & Reynolds, 2002; Lin, 2002; McLeod, 2009; Stewart & Rawlou, 2009) provide analytical approaches relating to issues of the press, political development, and socialization, other political communication researchers were concerned about the absence of precision in the conceptualization and operationalization of the agenda-setting role of the media — the power of the media to influence issues, shape and restructure societal values, define political objectives, construct knowledge, and create symbolic reality. As the emerging corpus of communication research indicates, the press is an influential and a significant segment of the social and political process that creates issue salience. This function is achieved through a selective process in which the media construct a broad framework within which a political structure can operate and develop (Megwa, 2009; Nwokeafor, 2000; Casmir, 1991; Rogers & Dearing, 1988).

McLeod (2009), Lin (2002), Graber (1990), and McCombs & Weaver (1977) demonstrate that agenda-setting is concerned with raising public awareness and managing information, a combination of which results in the chain of effects perpetuated by the mass media. The basic notion of agenda-setting is that the press has the power to structure public issues, and can exert some influence on public consciousness, cognition, and behavior. Three decades ago, Paulette Henry (1989) noted that while government and media officials have the power to determine issues and policies that can influence the social fabric of a nation, the press operates in a unique capacity of watchdog of public interests. In other words, exposure to the mass media increases information and knowledge acquisition among the citizens and enables them to make informed decisions and judgments. Therefore, efforts at political development can translate into reality in a society where the press is capable of setting public agenda. Another theoretical implication of the agenda-setting function of the press was provided by Graber (1980, p.8), who views political socialization as a function that resides in the domain of the press. As this researcher defines it, political socialization "is a process that involves the learning of basic values and orientations that prepare individuals to fit into their cultural milieu." Advocating the agenda-setting role of the press as a necessity for political development, Graber states that families/parents were thought to perform the socialization role; but increasingly and consistently, research evidence (Mukasa, 2000; Okigbo, 2000; Megwa, 2009) shows that recently new orientations, opinions, and perceptions that citizens acquire during their lifespan were shaped by the information supplied by the communication media.

For example, Okigbo explains that Africans have progressed from one phase of human development to another over the years, and stresses that such developmental stages in Africa could not have been achieved and sustained without an effective communication system as well as a functional civil society. Referring specifically to the role of the press in Nigeria, Okigbo cites national mobilization and the transition from military rule to democratic governance as well as the awakening of political consciousness in Nigerian citizens. The author states that Nigeria's first president (a newspaper publisher and an outstanding journalist) Nnamdi Azikiwe, identified a clear parallel between the exemplary achievements of the pioneer Nigerian journalists and the intellectual as well as material developments of the country, especially with regard to the crusade for political development. This remarkable achievement occurred through communication's strategies of raising political and social consciousness by zeroing in on an energized and informed civil society.

Describing the contributions of the media to democratic politics, Epstein (1974, p. 129) identifies surveillance, interpretation, and political socialization as functions that are collectively provided by the mass media in the form of news reports and analysis, which they provide to government and to a larger societal context. Without the performance of this function, Epstein argues "the daily agenda of reports produced and called "news" is not the inevitable product of chance events; it is the result of the decisions made within a news

organization." Analyzing the agenda-setting role of the media, Nwafo Nwanko
(1992) synthesizes the process of "issue emergence" and relates it to the
formation of official or government agenda. By selectively, objectively, and
repeatedly presenting information articulated by the "silent majority," the
national press sets the tone for what eventually becomes the official agenda for
the public. Distinguishing between political communication and information
dissemination, Nwanko describes the press as an inevitable channel associated
with both concepts.

Departing from the traditional agenda-setting paradigm, and using the 1983
session of the Missouri state legislature as a case study, Megwa and Brenner
(1988, p.41)) examined the coverage in the metropolitan and community
newspapers to determine whether there was any influence of news sources on
the agenda-setting role of the press. This study found that "the legislature did
influence the contents of the two newspapers, and that the contents reflected the
priorities of the legislature." While conceding the position of the press in the
agenda-setting process, Megwa and Brenner indicate that there were forces that
influenced the press in the agenda-setting function. As they put it, "the mass
media (specifically press) agenda-setting power is a by-product of a social
interactive process, a persuasive process, involving the source and the media on
the one hand, and the media and audience on the other."

The Media, Political Development, and Democratization in Africa

It was argued in a recent study (Shivute, 1995) that the relationship existing
between governments and the mass media was largely determined by the role
that the media were expected to play in the process of political reform,
development, and nation-building. Shivute emphasized that in developing
nations, an additional role for the media is acting as support for development
and citizenship, and this added function has given rise to the concept of
"developmental theory" of the press. Indeed, a significant use of communication
for political development would entail a certain degree of cooperation between
governments and the media; it also implies a measure of control and authority in
the dissemination of news and information. In keeping with the preceding
philosophy, a communication scholar, John Lent (1977) pointed out that
developing nations were not firmly established; therefore, they needed time to
cultivate their democratic and social institutions.

During this cultivation period, stability and unity should be sought and
carefully negotiated; criticism should be minimized or reduced, and public faith
in the democratic governance and in government institutions as well as in
polices should be encouraged. Similarly, media institutions should cooperate,
according to this guided press concept, by stressing positive development-
specific news, ignoring negative societal characterization, and supporting

governmental agenda and ideologies. Hence, McQuail (2006) sees political development as a multi-dimensional and symbiotic experiment that requires a process of societal change designed to improve the quality of life of a society and citizenship.

Media Role in Post-Independent Africa

As the debate on national and political development in Africa continues to take different dimensions, political communication scholars over the years (Agbaje, 2004; Gyimah-Boadi, 2004; Casmir, 1991; Entman, 1989) emphasize the need for the simultaneous functions of the media in sustaining development efforts, promoting lasting ethnic relationships, and reinforcing a sense of national identity. Concurrent with the preceding perspective, the earlier works of Lerner (1958), Pye (1963), and Schramm (1964) advocated the utilization of the media channels to influence and mold human attitude, behavior, and political orientation. Furthermore, mass communication literature delineates other scholars (Nwosu, 1992, Nwokeafor, 2000; Megwa, 2009; M'Bayo, 2009) who validated the role of the mass media in promoting the need for ethnic and national integration that subsequently leads to political development.

This role is critically important in African nations where democratization and political reforms, according to Gyimah-Boadi (2004) remain incomplete and inadequate. As currently exists, African democracies have been charged with entrenched corruption, intense political conflict, and marginalization. Therefore, based on media role in highly advanced countries, the media in Africa should be involved in the political and social reform processes in order that they can serve as agents to dismantle negative images and stereotypes which characterize the continent.

Some researchers share the concept of media centrality in transforming, improving, and sustaining political status quo, especially in the developing nations of Africa. Kpundeh (2004), Mazula (2004), and Hedebro (1982) contend that the function of the media in mobilizing human resources, molding or replacing old norms and dispositions enhances human productivity and consequently increases labor efficiency in the global competitive economy. As Hedebro points out, except for natural disasters, changes in the modern societies as well as in developing countries may not take place without the strategic intervention of the mass media. This is because effective communication strategies are usually designed to support and promote development initiatives and efforts. The authors stress that in socialization to politics, the press does not only transmit values and information, it also reinforces values that are supportive of democracy and civil debate.

The utility of the mass media in the quest for political development in Africa has continued to receive increasing attention and recognition from researchers across the disciplines (Onabajo, 2009; Nwokeafor, 2000; Nyamnjoh,

2009). There appears to be a dramatic realization or a renewed consciousness concerning the position of the media in Africa's political-national development, as globalization gains significant recognition and support by world leaders. It is no longer questionable whether or not media systems are powerful and can contribute to global awareness, economic growth, and intellectual sophistication.

Empirical studies of the past decades (Kasoma, 2000; Okigbo, 2000; Okoro, 1993) were consistent in demonstrating that in distant societies of Africa where a large proportion of the population resides in localities that are far from their families, churches, and other community affiliations, the mass media serve as agents for transmitting information and news needed to balance the knowledge gap, and to stimulate the level of interest and participation in the development of rural and urban areas. Therefore, it is important that the media structure in developing nations be set free from any form of external and internal control as well as pressures in the slanting, framing, and dissemination of news. Yoroms (2009) recent study lends credence to the charge that the ineffectiveness of the media in politics and nation-building in many African countries is largely due to the overwhelming political influence compounded by irresistible government control mechanisms. For example, Onwumechili and Nwokeafor (2000) and Nwanko (2000) stress that the overt and covert controls faced by the media in Nigeria were systematically designed by ruling governments to curb and control media performances, which have made it exceedingly difficult for some media channels, especially the press, to contribute productively to democratic politics. The inconsistencies, contradictions, double-standards, and lack of accountability in the political processes in many Nigerian states are largely attributable to the weaknesses of the media to provide objective news content as well as in the coverage of corrupt practices.

After years of persistent marginalization and systematic control, the media in most of Sub-Saharan Africa have begun to emerge as the key institution in the pursuit of democracy and political reforms. Significant research evidence (Gyimah-Boadi, 2004; Nimmo and Swanson, 1990; Ungar, 1991; Martin and Chaudhary, 1983) indicates that the majority of citizens in developed nations of the world acquire their political information and knowledge from the communication media. For example, during campaigns and elections the press is usually preoccupied with the analysis and comparisons of actions and views projected by citizens.

Nimo and Swanson (1990, p.8), in an analysis of communications effects on citizens' political knowledge, sentiments, and behaviors state that: "Studying how, through communication, politicians and journalists influence voters' decision-making blinds us to the larger and more important truth that media portrayals of elections constitute dramatized rituals that legitimize the power structure in liberal democracies."

More than anywhere else, the contributions of the media in development appear more glaring and influential during electioneering campaigns because of their analytical skills and interpretation of issues and events. In modern societies nowadays, the educative role of the press has become a significant part of the democratic process. Citizens in all walks of life depend on the news media for current economic, social, and political events. Historically, political communication literature on Africa has shown the inadequate utilization of the media in fostering political development. Past studies (Uzomah, 1989; Ndolo, 1987; Momoh, 1985) point out that a government of a new state, such as Nigeria, faced with the problem of validating its legitimacy, and of creating a feeling of "nationhood" among disparate groups, can utilize the mass media to achieve its national and political objective. But by deliberate control or relegation of media systems to mere "megaphones" or conduits in many developing societies, there has been an increasing low or unfavorable public perception about their credibility to inform and educate the public on significant political and national issues.

Ironically, the loss of credibility which the media suffer in African societies has been traced to their inability to create the needed awareness necessary to cultivate a sense of national identity and define political agenda. As Bryant and Oliver (2009), Mcquail (2006), and Graber (1989) observed, the functions of the mass media should not be subjected to governmental controls if political development is to be realized in a democracy. Evidently, any form of control or interference will impede media's watchdog and oversight function that allows them to promote the political process and sustain constitutional democracies. These studies indicate if the mass media and governments enjoy an interdependent relationship, the ability of the former to serve as channels for ethnic and national integration, especially in developing countries, remains highly unlikely. Consequently, the existing negative perception of media systems in some societies raises a fundamental question   of their credibility to hold politicians accountable and to be seen as dependable and objective sources of information.

Independently but consistent with the views of other scholars, (Nwanko & Nwokeafor, 1993; Nwanko, 2000; Okigbo, 2000; Casmir, 1991) argue for media integration in Africa. In his collection of articles and monographs spanning over two decades, Nwanko maintains that traditionalism in Africa hinders the introduction and the effective functioning of modern institutions such as the media. He concludes that the "partial presentation of reality" which characterizes African media content grossly constitutes a weak political framework. He suggests that in order for the mass media to perform their role as channels of national integration and analyzers of political issues, the citizens of the developing nations should have access to information and should experience the type of communication needed to enhance their political awareness, intellectual sophistication, and democratic participation.

Mass Media and the Challenge of Democratization

Over the past several years, no issue has polarized political communication scholars more than the debate and analysis over what should be the appropriate role of the mass media in the democracies of the newly-independent nations of the Africa. Among the more persistent arguments dominating intellectual discussions and scholarly inquiries is the notion of refocusing national priorities and strategies to include the establishment of an independent media system. Empowering and strengthening indigenous media to provide and promote objective political discussions and analysis is critical in Africa's present and future development agenda and in its position in the twenty-first global society. The inclusion of the media in planning and implementing national development objectives eliminates the widespread perception of an adversarial relationship between the state and media channels presently existing in African countries.

It is no longer arguable that the current strategies of subjecting and subordinating media institutions in Africa to government controls have gradually generated a weak, self-interested, and largely dependent journalistic status quo that perpetuates a sense of insecurity, helplessness, and a lack of confidence among the citizens. The concept of "accountability news" which Entman (1989) discusses seems inconceivable in the face of a manipulated indigenous media. Based on The World Bank Report (1989) and UNESCO (1970), democracy of information is as important as political development itself, because the concepts are mutually supportive. Additionally, the analysis by The World Bank confirms that the backwardness in African societies was precipitated by the absence of a free and dynamic media system that can educate the growing population on the critical importance of politics and civic responsibility in nation-building. The World Bank report acknowledges that full participation of an independent media is a prerequisite to achieving sustainable political development as well as the integration of disparate and warring ethnic groups in Africa.

As political development becomes an overriding mission for most developing nations of Africa, an improved relationship between the media and governments is strongly suggested. Nationally-recognized experts (Megwa, 2009; Onwumechili, 2000; Nwokeafor, 1993) from a wide range of subject areas have maintained a consistent position that communication must be used to address and advance Africa's development agenda, and to encourage citizens' interest in political reforms. In the light of the preceding analysis, it becomes obvious that the autonomy of media systems can easily translate into accountability of news and increased stakeholders' commitment to nation-building. Studies by Nwanko (2000) and Graber (2006) show that the survival of democracies will depend on an established mechanism that checks leadership accountability, transparency, and commitment. More than four decades ago,

Ethel de Sola Pool (1963) described the functions of the media as decisive in terms of cultivating responsible and sensitive leaders, creating a forum for constructive discussions and criticisms, defining social values, and exposing political indiscretions.

Drawing heavily on the vast literature in political communication on Africa, the primary focus of this paper is to rekindle an awareness and sensitivity in the present and future governments of the critical importance of positioning and encouraging an independent media. Establishing a high level of political consciousness will enable African leaders to rise to the need, to redefine, and broaden their political directions and commitments. The theoretical framework provided by Robert Entman (1989), in his study "Democracy Without Citizens," provides an essential backdrop for recognizing the critical, informative, and educational role of the mass media in the creation of political reality in contemporary societies.

Collectively, Shoemaker & Reese (1991) Bryant & Oliver (2009) confirm that the mediating role of the media has sustained the participative democracy practiced in the United States and Great Britain. Further, stressing the concept of "market-place of ideas," Entman takes the position that a vigorous media system is indispensable for citizens to become knowledgeable, intellectually sophisticated, and capable of holding their elected officials and governments accountable for action, inaction, and decisions. Indeed, this line of argument seems most applicable to the developing nations' population who need factual and objective information to enhance their political commitment and to make independent choices and decisions.

Communication, Politics, and African Society

When considering politics, it becomes increasingly critical to examine the functions and characteristics of government to the general nature of the country. Political consciousness is dependent upon communication, because communication can determine the way in which the citizens relate to their social and political environment (Denton and Woodward, 1990). From the genesis of political rhetoric to the present day, researchers and world organizations have emphasized the role of the media as an instrumental influence as well as a major participant in the political reforms and development (Entman, 1989; The World Bank, 1990; Graber, 2006). In addition, African intellectuals (Ziegler and Asante, 1992: Nwanko, 1993) blamed the widespread failure of the post-independent development strategies in Africa on the deliberate exclusion, limited, and controlled functions of the mass media.

Based on the findings and suggestions of contemporary subject matter experts (McCombs and Reynolds, 2009; Megwa, 2009; McQuail, 2006), it is no longer doubtful that developing nations need effective new approaches to political development because the present process that involves media control has proven grossly ineffective and counter-productive over the years. Therefore, there is an urgent need for a sustained political change and philosophy in the application of democratic strategies in the developing African societies. Notably, the role of the press in the struggle for political stability is implicated in The World Bank's report (1989), "Long-Term Perspective Study." This critical study suggests that future development strategies in Africa need to recognize the increasingly awesome responsibility of the press in strengthening and sustaining constitutional political democracies. Charging that the presence of a free and dynamic press is uncommon and perpetuates under-development in the African nations, The World Bank's report repeatedly recommends the establishment and empowerment of an independent national press because it is an indispensable condition to achieving sustainable political reforms and future development.

New Media Technology and African Democracy

With the advent of new media technology in the twenty-first century, there is a strong speculation that this communication invention, especially the Internet, will be used to sustain public interest in politics and current affairs, and to increase participation in political strategies and commitment. Tambini (1999) postulated that the new media technology will have a tremendous influence on the processes of democratic communication within the appropriate regulatory and economic context with a specific focus on access to communications technologies. Contrary to the view that the traditional media (newspapers, radio, and television) distort, trivialize, and embellish information that diminish democratic communication, the new media technology (Internet, multimedia, and computer-mediated communication) can be utilized to encourage active political citizenship and promote effective debate, dialog, and critical analysis of the political process.

Further, Bhuiyan (2006) explains that rapid growth of new media technology including the Internet, interactive television networks, and multimedia information services will increase the potential for interactivity with the citizens as well as an instant access to news and information. Therefore, it is expected that the trend in the new media technology will certainly facilitate news dissemination in the democracies of developing nations, and will strengthen the viability of their democratic institutions. Additionally, the new media process is powerful in its outreach as it is constantly increasing public access to national and political issues, especially in Africa where it is believed that the media have limited capacity to perform their functions. Bhuiyan identifies the key advantage of the new media technology, particularly in the developing parts of the world, as enhancing the explosion of creativity and innovation, because people can emerge into an age of cultural richness and abundant choices that were never imagined.

It is noteworthy that the global advent of new media technology has great potentials to strengthen efficacy and dependability of African democratic establishments because of the potential for free speech and the free flow of communication. As studies (Graber, 2006; Gyimah-Boadi, 2004; Entman, 1989) have argued, political development would be difficult to attain in the absence of a robust media operations. It is also contended that some of the inadequacies of traditional media will be resolved by the sophistication associated with the new media technology. For example, the revolution of the media industry in the global marketplace has the advantage of enhancing the credibility of communication channels around the world. Much has been written in recent years about the growing citizen disenchantment with traditional media in reshaping the directions of democratic institutions in Africa, partly because of their limited capacity to play their role. However, Bhuiyan (2006) asserts that in the western democracy, there is a lot of emphasis on maximizing freedom of speech, free flow of information in online and interactive media environment, which has kept the citizens adequately informed and participating in various issues in the political process and reforms.

Mass Media, Human Rights, and Political Development
A number of studies have delineated the inability of the media to adequately publicize human rights abuses in the developing nations of Africa. Scholars consistently argued that in developing countries with authoritarian governments, the traditional role of the media has been to serve as advocate for justice and fairness (Mogekwu, 2009; Okigbo, 2000; Okoli, 2009). Over the years, the media have been expected to analyze abuses associated with human rights and personal privileges, employment opportunities, wrongful firing and dismissal, interracial relationships, equity and justice in the society, and to shape public opinion on a wide range of ethnic issues bothering on discrimination and disintegration. The ultimate goal of analyzing these issues and raising awareness of political activities relating to governance is to promote democratic process. All over the world, especially in the developing nations, governments' efforts to influence or intimidate the media is not only common to authoritarian administrations but also to newly established democracies. The abuse of human rights continues unabated in many parts of the world because of the failure of the media to perform their watchdog and oversight function, which is critical in order to achieve lasting and credible democratic governance. Sibley and Nadas (2006, p.56) identified the methods used by authoritarian governments to manipulate or minimize the performance of the media as "ownership of media firms by political elite, control of resources used by the media, taxes on circulation and value-added taxes on newsprint and advertising, extensive government advertising, bribes, censorship, violence or the threat of violence."

Additionally, constant subtle manipulation of the media is often as effective
as sporadic overt violent acts and intimidation. For example, Mattiace and
Cramp (1996) pointed out that, for a number of years, governments in Mexico
controlled the distribution of newsprint, which was sold only to cooperating
newspapers at low cost. This control mechanism made it difficult for
newspapers to criticize any human rights abuses, political indiscretions,
embezzlement, and other forms of systemic manipulations. Across Africa,
many women and significant minority groups have expressed strong opposition
about the extent of marginalization and under-representation taking place in the
political process, and these groups have also expressed frustration about the
inadequate media coverage of their problems or the insensitivity toward their
concerns.

Media Participation-Based Integrative Approach
In a study entitled "Press and politics in Nigeria: Toward a conceptual
framework for political development," Okoro (1993) offers a model for the
effective utilization of the media channels for political development. This
conceptual political framework was based on key development indicators in
African politics within the last three decades of democratic governance. These
indicators and reforms have resulted in an unprecedented surge for a civil
society, sustained political reform, and the quest for media sophistication.
Africa's continuing effort at political renewal, relaxation of media censorship,
and citizens' active involvement in democratic consolidation require the
establishment of a creative approach toward national development. Indeed, the
single most important requirement in achieving a lasting political reform and
citizen's participation is the strong presence of the media in the new emerging
republics. Seen against this background, studies (Okoro, 2009; Mazula, 2004;
Kpundeh, 2004) reached the consensus that the mass media must play the role of
a watchdog over the rights of citizens and democratic establishments in order to
create a political culture of democracy that can be fully established and
institutionalized.
The fundamental problem, therefore, was not the distortion of
communication or the inability of the media to carry out its oversight
responsibility within the political system, but to establish a credible governance
structure that allows the media, government, and citizens to work together
toward a common national development goal. Drawing considerably from
political development experiences of Africa and from research evidence by
African-focused scholars (Nwanko, 2000; M'Bayo, 2000; Nwokeafor, 1993)
among others, this paper found that political development objectives and
strategies of Africa are substantially deficient and would have been effective if:

(a)   the political establishments in Africa had allowed the media
adequate latitude to provide development information, address specific

political improprieties, and charge political leaders with accountability and transparency.

(b)   the press were allowed to make constructive criticisms of government decisions, activities, and programs; and

(c)   government ownership of the press did not translate into control and censorship of contextual information.

In responding to the preceding political development shortcomings, abuses, failures, and in the attempt to resolve the fundamental issues impeding political development delineated in this paper, the Media Participation-Based Integrative Model, which substantially derives from the General Systems Theory and Agenda-Setting, was framed. Implicit in this model is the idea that communication media must be considered an integral part of political development goals in the Sub-Saharan Africa. In addition, the concept reflects the need for collectivity and inclusivity in the design and implementation of development agenda in the region. It is a common knowledge that the democratic system in Africa appears grossly inadequate to foster sustainable political objectives; therefore, a new approach that would strengthen democratization in Africa is critically important as the twenty-first century evolves. As its name denotes, the Media-Participation Integrative Model operates on the axiom that development programs whether for political, economic, social, or national must involve the effective role of an independent media both in planning and implementing reforms and institutional improvements.

Conclusion

There is no doubt that political-national development objectives in Africa can be achieved, but the strategies for achieving them must include a robust, vibrant, and free media system. As a heterogeneous and pluralistic continent, a strong press that can address and redress the complex political issues must be present in order that a sustainable development is attained. Through an in depth historical/critical and content analysis across the African political landscape, it was established that colonialism heavily influenced the attitudes, behaviors, and orientation of leadership in the continent. The intimidation and suppression of the media in many African countries was rooted in their colonial experience. As Faringer (1991), Zigler and Asante (1992), and Asante (1996) noted, African leaders, many of whom were journalists, were apprehensive of the media because of the realization of media's effective role in challenging and transforming the status quo. Empirical evidence from past and current studies are consistent in their conclusion that to achieve political reform and development in Africa, governments should not divorce the media from performing their critical functions in democratic governance, especially in the twenty-first century global society in which the new media technology has redefined and expanded the functions of the media.

Significantly, developing an alternative conceptual framework makes it unnecessary to uncritically employ foreign ideas and models to address specific development issues of African societies. For example, the nature of relationship between the press in Africa and the political system must have been antagonistic because of external influences and the impracticable principles upon which such a relationship was based. Therefore, an indigenous development model that provides a sound and realistic basis on which to build a political system that recognizes the pluralistic character of the African society is needed to promote democratization. The model must be responsive to and inclusive of the values, history, cultures, and the contextual realities of Africans and their environment. In recognition of these desirable objectives, the media participation-based integrative approach, which is a holistic effort that seeks the full participation of indigenous media, is advanced to address the present-day political development problems and needs facing African nations.

REFERENCES

Agbaje, A. (2004). *Nigeria: Prospects for the fourth republic. Democratic Reforms In Africa: The Quality of Progress.* Edited by E. Gyimah-Boadi. Boulder, CO: Lynne Rienner Publishers.

Altschull, J. H. (1984). *Agents of power: The role of the news media in human affairs.* New York: Longman Publishers.

Asante, C. E. (1996). *The press in Ghana: Problems and prospects.* Lanham, MD: University Press of America, Inc.

Asante, M. K. (1980). *Afrocentricity: The theory of social change. Philadelphia,* PA: Temple University Press.

Asante, M. K., & Gudykunst, W. (1989). *Handbook of international and intercultural Communication.* Beverly Hills, CA: Sage Publications, Inc.

Awa, N. E. (1989). *National Development.* In M. Asante and W. Gudynst (Eds.) *Handbook of international and intercultural communication.* Newbury Park, CA: Sage Publications, Inc.

Bennett, W. L. 2003. *News: The politics of illusion*, 5th Edition, New York, Longman

Boas, N. K. (2009). *Social conflict, communication and youth in Tanzania. Communication in an Era of Global Conflicts: Principles and Strategies for 21st Century Africa.* Edited by Richard T. M'Bayo, Chuka Onwumechili, and Bala Musa. United Press of America: Lanham, MD.

Chick, J. (1971). The Nigerian press and national integration. *Journal of Commonwealth Political Studies*, 9, 115.

Collier, P, Soludo, S.C., Pattillo, C. (2008). *Economic policy options for a prosperous Nigeria. Palgrave,* Macmillan: New York, NY

Cummings, M., Niles, L., & Taylor, O. (1992). *Handbook on communications and development in Africa and the African diaspora.* Needham Heights, MA: Girin Press

Denton, R. E. , & Woodward, G. C. (1985). *Political communication in America.* New York: Praeger Publishers.

Diamond, L. (2004). *Promoting real reform in Africa. Democratic Reform in Africa: The Quality of Progress.* Edited by E. Gyimah-Boadi. Boulder, CO: Lynne Rienner Publishers.

Entman, R. M. (1989*). Democracy without citizens: Media and the decay of American Politics.* New York: Oxford University Press.

Epstein, E. J. (1974). *News from nowhere: Television and the news.* New York: Vintage Books.

Faringer, G. L. (1991). *Press freedom in Africa.* New York: Praeger Publishers

Graber, D. A. (1989). *Mass Media and American politics* (3rd ed.). Washington, D.C.: Congressional Quarterly Press.

Gyimah-Boadi, E. (2004*). Democratic reform in Africa: The quality of progress.* Boulder, CO: Lynne Reinner Publishers, Inc.

Halloran, J. D. (1981). The need for communication research in developing societies. In G.C. Whihoit, & H. de Bock (Eds.) *Mass communication review*, Vol. 2 (pp. 160-173).   Beverly Hills, CA: Sage Publications, Inc.

Hedebro, G. (1982). *Communication and social change in developing nations.* Ames, Iowa; Iowa State University Press.

Henry, P. (1989). *Newspaper as a source of political agendas in two Caribbean nations.* Unpublished doctoral dissertation, Howard University, Washington, D.C.

Jeffress, L. W. (1986). *Mass Media: Processes and effects* (preliminary edition). Project Heights, IL: Waveland Press, Inc.

Josyln, R. A. (1980). The content of political spot, advertisements. *Journalism Quarterly,* 57 92-98.

Lent, J. (1977). A third world news deal? Part one: The guiding light, Index on censorship, 6 (5)

Lin, C. A. (2009). *Effects of the Internet. Media Effects: Advances in Theory and Research.* Edited by Jennings Bryant and Mary Oliver. New York, N.Y.: Lawrence Erlbaum Associates, Inc.

Lerner, D. (1963).   Towards a communication theory of modernization In L. Pye (Ed.). *Communication and Development* (p. 348). Princeton, NJ: Princeton University Press.

M'Bayo, R. T. (2000). The African press: Prospects for freedom in the new millennium. *Press and Politics In Africa.* Edited by Richard Tamba M'Bayo, Chuka Onwumechili, R. Nwafo Nwanko. The Edwin Mellen Press, Lampeter, Wales.

M'Bayo, R. T. & Mogekwu, M. (2000). Political authority and the transformation of the Sierra Leone press. *Press and Politics In Africa.* Edited by Richard Tamba M'Bayo, Chuka Onwumechili, R. Nwafo Nwanko. The Edwin Mellen Press, Lampeter, Wales.

McCombs, M., Reynolds, A. (2009). *How the News Shapes Our Civic Agenda. Media Effects Advances in Theory and Research.* Edited by Jennings and Mary Beth Oliver. Lawrence Erlbaum Associates, Inc.: New York, NY.

McLeod, D., Kiosicki, G.M., McLeod, J.M. (2009). *Political Communication Effects. Media Effects: Advances in Theory and Research.* Edited by Jennings Bryant and Beth Oliver. Lawrence Erlbaum Associates, Inc.: New York: NY

Mogekwu, M. (2009). *Mass Media and the establishment of peace as path to sustainable development in Africa. Communication in an Era of Global Conflicts: Principles and Strategies for 21st Century Africa.* Edited by Richard T. M'Bayo, Chuka Onwumechili, and Bala Musa. United Press of America: Lanham, MD

Mukasa, S. G. (2000). Press and politics in Zimbabwe. *Press and Politics In Africa.* Edited by Richard Tamba M'Bayo, Chuka Onwumechili, R. Nwafo Nwanko The Edwin Mellen Press, Lampeter, Wales.

Martin, L. J., & Chaudhary, A. G. (1983). *Comparative Mass media systems.* New York: Longman, Inc.

McCombs. (1981). Setting the agenda for agenda-setting function of the mass media. *Public Opinion Quarterly,* 36, 176-187.

McCombs, & Weaver, D. H. (1977). Voters and the mass media: Information seeking, political interest, and issue agendas. Philadelphia, PA: *American Association for Public Opinion Research*

McQuail, D. (1992). Media performance: Mass communication and the public interest. Newbury Park, CA: Sage Publications, Inc.

Megwa, E. R., & Brenner, D. J. (1988). Toward a paradigm of media agenda-setting: Agenda-setting as process. *Howard Journal of Communication,* 1, 39-55

Megwa, E. R. (2009). *Agenda-Setting: African Media and Conflict. Communication in an Era of Global Conflicts: Principles and strategies for 21st century Africa.* Edited by Richard T. M'Bayo, Chuka Onwumechili, and Bala A. Musa. United Press of America: Lanham, MD

Mody, B. (1991). *Designing messages for development communication: An audience participation-based approach.* Newbury Park, CA: Sage Publications, Inc.

Ndolo, I. S. (1987). *Radio broadcasting and the language problems of socio-political integration in Nigeria.* Unpublished doctoral dissertation, Howard University, Washington, D.C.

Nimmo, D., & Swanson, D. L. (Eds.) 91990). *The field of political communication: Beyond the voter persuasion paradigm. In New directions in political communication: A resource book.* (p. 7-47). Newbury Park, CA: Sage Publications, Inc.

Nwanko, R. N. (1973a). Utopia and reality in the African mass media: A case study. *Gazette, International Journal of Mass Communication Studies,* 14 (3), 71.

——— (1973b). Communication as symbolic interaction: *A synthesis. Journal of Communication*, 23.

——— (1989, May 25-29). Communication research as intercultural discourse: Issues of intercultural communication theory, method, and pragmatics. Paper presented at the International Communication Convention in San Francisco, California

Nwanko, R. N., & M'Bayo, R. (1989). The political culture of mass communication research and the role of African communication researchers. *Africa Media Review*, 3 (2), 9-12.

Nwanko, R. N. Press, politics, and state in Africa (2000). Theoretical framework and overview. *Press and Politics in Africa.* Edited by Richard Tamba M'Bayo, Chuka Onwumechili, and R. Nwafo Nwanko. The Edwini Mellen Press, Lampeter, Wales

Nwokeafor, C. U. (1992). *Development communication in the Nigerian mass media: A study of selected publications.* Unpublished doctoral dissertation, Howard University, Washington, D.C.

Nwokeafor, C. U. (2000). The pan African news agency: Conduit to African press and political system. *Press and Politics in Africa.* Edited by Richard Tamba M'Bayo, Chuka Onwumechili, and R. Nwafo Nwanko. The Edwin Mellen Press, Lampeter, Wales.

Nwokeafor, C. U., and Nwanko, R. N. (1993). "Development information content in the African mass media: A Study of Two Nigerian Dallies." *African Media Review*, 7(3), 75-90

Nwosu, P. (1990). *Communication and agricultural development in Swaziland: Toward a need-based integrative model.* Unpublished doctoral dissertation, Howard University, Washington, D.C.

Nwosu, P. (1995). *Development theory and communication: An overview. Communication and the Transformation of Society: A Developing Region's Perspectives.* Edited by Peter Nwosu, Chuka Onwumechili, Richard M'Bayo. United Press of America, Lanham, MD

Obotette, B. E. (1984). *Mass communication for development in Nigeria: Analysis of content and structure.* Unpublished doctoral dissertation, Howard University, Washington, D.C.

Okigbo, C. (1992). Horse race and issues in Nigerian elections. *Journal of Black Studies,* 22, 3.

Okigbo, C. (2000). *Media, civil society, and politics in Africa. Press and Politics in Africa.* Edited by Richard Tamba M'Bayo, Chuka Onwumechili, and R. Nwafo Nwanko, The Edwin Mellen Press, Lampeter, Wales.

Okoli, E. J. (2009). *Mass media and ethnic conflict in Africa. Communication in an Era of Global Conflicts: Principles and Strategies for 21st Century Africa.* Edited by Richard T. M'Bayo, Chuka Onwumechili, and Bala Musa. United Press of America: Lanham, MD

Okoro, E. A. (1993). *The press and politics in Nigeria: Toward a conceptual framework for political development.* Unpublished doctoral dissertation, Howard University, Washington, D.C.

Omu, F. I. (1978*). Press and politics in Nigeria* 1880-1937. New Brunswick, NJ: University Press.

Onwumechili, C. (1990). *The roles of television in adapting African students to American Culture in the United States.* Unpublished doctoral dissertation, Howard University, Washington, D.C.

Onwumechili, C. (2000). Politics and communication training in Africa. *Press and Politics In Africa.* Edited by Richard Tamba M'Bayo, Chuka Onwumechili, and R. Nwafo Nwanko. The Edwin Mellen Press, Lampeter, Wales

Opubor, A. (1974). Communication and Nigerian identity. Lagos, Nigeria:
NBC lecture Series.

Parenti, M. (1986). *Inventing reality: The politics of the mass media.* New
York: St. Martin's Press.

Patterson, T. E. (Ed.). (1980). The mass media election. New York: Praeger
Publishers.

Patterson, T. E. (2000). Doing well and doing good: How soft news and critical
journalism   are   shrinking   the   news   audience   and   weakening
democracy—and what news outlets can do about it. Cambridge, MA.
Harvard University, Joan Shorenstein Center on Press, Politics, and
Public Policy, Kennedy School of Government.

Pool, I. (1963). The mass media and politics in the modernization process. In L.
Pye (Ed.). *Communication and political development.* Princeton, NJ:
Princeton University Press

Pye, L. W. (1963). *Communication and political development.* Princeton, NJ:
Princeton University Press.

Shoemaker, P. J., & Reese, S. D. (1991). *Mediating the message: Theories of
influences on mass media content.* New York: Longman Publishers.

Schramm, W. (1964). *Mass media and national development; The role of
information in the developing countries.* Stanford, CA: Stanford
University Press.

Shivute, M. (1995). The media in post-independent Namibia. In P. Nwwosu, C
Onwumechili, and R. M'Bayo (Ed.). *Communication and the
Transformation of Society: A developing region's perspectives.*
Lanham, MD: University Press of America, Inc.

Steward, D. W., Pavlou, P. A. (2009). *The effects of media on marketing
Communications. Media Effects: Advances in Theory and Research.*
Lawrence Erlbaum Associates, Inc. New York, NY.

Uche, L. U. (1991). Communication and development in military political
culture: A case study of a Nigerian pubic campaign for social change.
In F. L. Casmir (Ed.). *Communication in Development.* Norwood:
NJ: Abex Publishing Corporation

Ugboajah, F. U. (1980). Communication policies in Nigeria. Paris, UNESCO.

UNESCO. (1970).   Mass media in society: The need for research.   Paris:
    UNESCO

Unger, S. J. (1991). The role of a free press in strengthening democracy. In
    Judith Lichtenberg (ED.). *Democracy and the mass media.* (pp. 368-
    398). New York: Cambridge University Press

———— (1980). *Many voices one world.* Southhampton, London, England: The
    Camelot Press Limited.

United Nations. (2007/2008). *Human Development Report.   Fighting Climate
    Change: Huam Solidarity in a Divided World.*   United Nations
    Development Program (UNDP). New York: NY

Uzomah, D. A. (1989). *Mass media and national integration: Television and
    socio-political   integration   in   Nigeria.*   Unpublished   doctoral
    dissertation, Howard University, Washington, D.C.

Walle, N.D. (2004). *Economic Reform: Patterns and Constraints. Democratic
    Reform In Africa: The Quality of Progress.*   Edited by E. Gyimah-
    Boadi. Boulder, CO: Lynne Rienner Publishers

West, H. G., & Fair, E. (1993). Development communication and popular
    resistance in Africa: An examination of the struggle over tradition and
    modernity through media. *African Studies Review,* Vol. 26, I.

World Bank. (1989). Sub-Saharan Africa: From crisis to sustainable growth. A
    long term perspective study. Washington, D.C.: The World Bank.

———— (1990).   A long-term perspective study of Sub-Saharan Africa:
    Economic and sectoral policy issues (2). Washington, D.C.: The World
    Bank

———— (1991).   World Development Report: The challenge of development.
    Washington, D.C.: The World Bank.

———— (2001). Economic Freedom of the World. Annual Report. Edited by
    James Gwartney & Robert Lawson. The World Bank: Washington,
    D.C.

———— (2006).   World Development Indicators.   The World Bank.
Washington, D.C. The World Bank.

Ziegler, D., & Asante, M. K. (1992). Thunder and silence: The mass media in
Africa. Trenton, NJ: *Africa World Press, Inc.*

Chapter 11

The Use of Techno-media Strategies in Effective Healthcare Service Delivery in Nigeria and the Implications for Democracy Sustenance

Matthew Uzukwu
Bowie State University

Abstract

The Nigerian healthcare system, a two dimensional system consisting of the public and private sectors, historically has been ineffective in delivering healthcare services to users. Using survey and historical data analysis methodologies, this study examines the problems associated with this ineffectiveness, their potential impact on Nigeria's nascent democracy, and how a techno-media strategy can be successfully deployed to achieve effective, systemic healthcare services delivery with positive implications for the sustenance of democracy.

INTRODUCTION

Nigeria's latest practice of democratic governance commenced with the inauguration of its Fourth Republic on May 29th 1999 by the then military government headed by General Abdulsalami Abubakar. Devoid of democratic institutionalization for most of its existence as an independent nation chiefly due to too many military coups, Nigeria, as a nation, has not made meaningful progress on various fronts, including in the area of healthcare. Chazan (1996) emphasized the association of institutions with stability and continuity of ways of doing things in the context of an organization being able to make adjustments as needed, deal with difficulties, maintain freedom of action, and operate in a consistently logical manner.

In the context of Nigerian democracy, attempts at introducing these requisite elements of organizational institutionalization were made by Abubakar Tafawa Balewa, the first prime minister of Nigeria. The complexities of the Nigerian state, constructed by the British Sovereign, encompassing matters of history, language, culture and tradition created a combustible political situation within six years of independence. Idealistic young Turks in the army took advantage of the situation and staged a bloody coup which toppled the Balewa government in 1966.

Although the federal and regional governments which took control at independence in 1960 budgeted monies for healthcare services, there was no credible framework to guide nationwide strategic healthcare planning. Over time, the lack of sustained democratic institutionalization created political repercussions, in terms of decades long ruinous militarization of society (Butz and Metz, 1996). The result reflected negatively on the development of a democratic ethos and the development of other capacities of state indispensable to the creation of a dynamic socioeconomic society. The health sector was thus adversely affected.

Fundamentally problematic in the healthcare sector, consisting of both the public and private sectors, was inadequate funding. There was also low capacity development in human resources, obsolete equipment, low literacy rates and concomitant ignorance of health wellness strategies. Other areas of concern were lack of access or limited access to healthcare facilities, lack of access to beneficial health information as a consequence of poverty and/or illiteracy. This study professed that the survival of the Nigerian Fourth Republic was not dependent upon political processes alone, but also upon the wellness of her citizens, especially the elite class, imperiled by the scourge of HIV/AIDS (CIA, 2003).

The inadequacies of the healthcare system have been adumbrated. The scope of the problem for investigation in this study chiefly dealt with the ineffectiveness of the healthcare system, not only from political and socioeconomic factors, but also from the lack of systemic use of technomedia tools for healthcare delivery.

Han (2007) explained how technomedia involved the Internet and the applications of media technologies. Essentially, the combination of information technologies and the Internet facilitated rapid and convenient socioeconomic intercourse, such that effectiveness and efficiencies were achieved. As effective healthcare delivery is one of several elements indispensable to building a healthy, prosperous, and democratic Nigerian state, the study proposed the adoption of a systematized nationwide use of technomedia for healthcare delivery.

In summary, the problem was identified as the inadequate use of technomedia by healthcare practitioners, and the lack of nationally integrated technomedia architecture as a strategic interventionist tool in healthcare delivery to the citizens of Nigeria. As sustainable societal development depends on a healthy citizenry, the problematic Nigerian healthcare sector leaves the nation vulnerable to epidemics and other types of healthcare crises with dire implications for national progress. If national vulnerability to an epidemic can happen in Uganda and in Zimbabwe relative to HIV/AIDS (Feldman and Miller, 1998), it can happen in Nigeria too.

The constellation of challenging political and socioeconomic factors, with specific emphasis on the inadequacy of techno-media tools and the lack of a strategic, integrated techno-media strategy in the delivery of healthcare, are impediments to societal development and consequently a long term threat to Nigeria's Fourth Republic.

The problem statement was the basis for the following research questions:
1. What are the threats to Nigeria's democracy attributable to its ineffective healthcare system?
2. What role, if any, does techno-media currently play in healthcare delivery?
3. What are the potential benefits of a techno-media strategy as a component of healthcare delivery in Nigeria and in strengthening and stabilizing Nigeria's democracy in the long term?

Theoretical and Conceptual Bases for the Research

Eisenhart (1991) described a theoretical framework as "a structure that guides research by relying on a formal theory... Constructed by using an established, coherent explanation of certain phenomena and relationships" (p. 205). Theoretical frameworks must consist of values and beliefs commonly shared with other scholars, and must constitute a platform upon which the researcher aligns the perspectives undergirding his/her research with other researchers. The associational research type is a theoretical framework suitable to conducting research about phenomena occurring in Nigeria. Gliner and Morgan (2000) stated that "the specific purpose of associational approach includes finding associations, relating variables, and also making predictions from the independent or predictor variable," (p. 79). Alubo (1990) and Ityavyar (1987) among many others gave credence to the use of the associational framework approach to conduct social science research in Nigeria. Alubo (1990) found that power and privilege had a relationship with access to high quality medical care. Ityavyar (1987) in studying health service inequalities reported a relationship between healthcare service inequalities with a low socioeconomic status.

A contrast to the associational approach is the distinctive type where political, economic and social issues are studied separately from one another. The distinctive framework which deemphasizes associational relationships has limitations. Mainly, the research design and methodology may yield new knowledge relative to the specific phenomenon being studied; however, use of that knowledge could be of limited value to policy makers and stakeholders who must contend with varied political and socioeconomic issues requiring good decision making.

This study followed the theoretical framework consistent with investigating associational relationships between phenomena. Specifically, the relationship between the inadequacy of techno-media tools in the healthcare delivery system as well as the lack of a nationally integrated techno-media strategy, and the healthcare system. What is the nature of this relationship and what improvements or adjustments, if any, are necessary to deliver effective healthcare to Nigerians? The alignment of this study with related research of Nigeria's socioeconomic evolution, as a matter of historical perspective, necessitated a brief discussion of the investigations and findings of a few of these.

A CIA report released in 2003 regarding the spread of HIV/AIDS in Nigeria and consequent threat to the survival of the Nigerian state was illustrative of the associational approach to social issues research in Nigeria. In its report, the CIA revealed the results of an AIDS epidemiological study which showed that the spread of the disease within the Nigerian elite was a threat to the survival of the Nigerian state. It asserted that the elite controlled the political and economic levers of the Nigerian state; as such a destruction of the elite class by HIV/AIDS would constitute a long term catastrophe relative to the survival of the Nigerian state. The CIA's analysis of the threat of AIDS to the viability of the Nigerian state melded elements of politics and healthcare in arriving at its conclusions. It did this by linking the failure of the political leadership to recognize the threat of HIV/AIDS; as such the absence of containment strategies allowed HIV/AIDS to spread to the level of constituting a national threat.

Okafor (1991), in writing about the inadequacies of the healthcare delivery system in Nigeria, attributed most of the failures of the system to corruption in government. The healthcare system was seriously underfunded as a consequence of contrived leaks in the budget and funds allocation process. Like a sieve, appropriated funds were stolen by government officials. As a result, facilities were underequipped and healthcare personnel were underpaid or were forced to work without pay for months at a time. In Okafor's approach, there was a linkage of politics and healthcare issues, which showed the influence of one on the ineffectiveness of the other, in this case the ineffectiveness of the healthcare system due to the corruption in government.

Akukwe (2001) adopted a similar approach in linking governmental failure, specifically the lack of a coherent national HIV/AIDS response strategy to contain the spread of the disease, with a failure of the political leadership to do its job. Warning of a ticking time bomb as a result of this failure, Akukwe raised an alarm to spur action before it was too late.

From a common thread of associational relationships, this study adopted a similar approach in linking ineffective healthcare delivery with a lack of techno-media, while recognizing the failure of government to address national healthcare challenges. The conceptual basis for the study was to justify the use of techno-media as an effective strategy in improving healthcare delivery to Nigerians. ·Eisenhart (1991) described a conceptual framework as "a skeletal structure of justification, rather than a skeletal structure of explanation" (p. 209). The idea that techno-media could be a powerful tool in improving healthcare delivery, thus ensuring a healthier citizenry, a requisite for national socioeconomic progress and by extension political stability is the distinctive conceptual basis for the study. Justification was underscored by the research methodology which applied a blend of historical and descriptive statistical approaches with the use of a self administered survey (SAS). This approach yielded information that was used as a basis to buttress the techno-media concept in the conclusion of the study.

Historical Background

Butts and Metz (1996) stated that, "few African nations have more potential than Nigeria but few have experienced greater trauma in attempts to build democracy" (p. 11). The Nigerian state at its creation by the British Monarch in 1914 became a hodgepodge of ethnic groups and nationalities with varying histories, traditions, cultures and customs. Whereas historically, the northern region's political and social structures were basically feudal, in the Yoruba dwelling western part of the country, non feudal kingdoms flourished (Smith, 1969). In the east, Basden (1921) observed that the Igbos, spread out on both sides of the River Niger, in western Nigeria but predominantly in eastern Nigeria, practiced a mix of monarchical and autonomous communal governance, the autonomous structure being the most widely practiced. Living among the Igbos for an extended period in the early 1900s, Basden, a British subject, recorded that "Every town... stands by itself. With the exception of the king of Onitsha, there are no kings in these parts" (p. 81-82). Among the Igbos, feudalism was unknown.

After independence in 1960, intractable political and ethnic issues overheated the polity for several years, culminating in a vicious Civil War from 1967 to 1970. The military establishment in trying to forestall an unraveling of the state fostered a praetorian paradigm of national existence which affected the development of democracy. Engel (2005) observed that the Nigerian state became "an instrument for competing ethno-regional elites to maintain disorder and use the state as the prime avenue for capital accumulation" (p.55). The corrosive influence on socioeconomic growth that was the emanation from militarization had a most profound salience in corruption and embezzlement of public funds. Basedau and Mehler (2005) pointed out that in Nigeria "minerals and other natural resources have been linked to systemic corruption and the weakness of state institutions" (p. 17). The healthcare sector and its constituent institutions most certainly were negatively impacted.

Rumors were always rife about the management of the country's huge revenues from crude oil exports. In the arguably rumor prone country, where, anecdotally, the leader of Nigeria's first military coup—Major Patrick Chukwuma Kaduna Nzeogwu—just out of months-long detention for his role in the coup, had responded "Good gracious! ...It is not true," to a reporter's question that rumors were rife about the pending release of a book he had written while in detention (Ejindu, 1967), there was nonetheless physical evidence of embezzlement of public funds by military officers and conniving high level bureaucrats, as the ostentatious edifices where they resided and their lavish life styles were not supported by their public salaries.

Nigeria has lurched from one political tension and /or crisis to another since 1963: the census crisis of 1963; the federal elections crises of 1964/65; the bloody coups of 1966; the Civil War of 1967-1970; the consolidation of the militarization of society after the Civil War and further continuation of military rule until 1979; the spectacular failure of President Shagari in the Second Republic (1979-1983) and the return of the military in 1983; more coups and executions of dozens of military officers for coup plotting; an aborted attempt at a return to democratic governance in 1993 and the imposition of an illegitimate interim government; yet another coup and the emergence of the most brutal dictator yet to govern the country; a military handover to an elected government in 1999 in controversial elections; a transfer of power from an outgoing president to a new one in 2007, in elections contested all the way to the Nigerian Supreme Court which upheld the election of Umaru Musa Yar Adua, vindicating the Professor Maurice Iwu-led Independent National Electoral Commission (INEC), which was unfairly vilified for the conduct of the elections, despite the fact that the political class, which wanted to win by all means, using such methods as violence, created severe impediments for INEC to hurdle.

Nigeria's health policy was based on a three-tier framework consisting of primary, secondary and tertiary levels of care in the public sector Okafor (1991). Clients/users of the system initially encountered this system at the primary level through outpatient visits at any number of facilities throughout the country. Thereafter, referrals, if needed, were made to secondary level care facilities, which consisted of specialists, for further treatment of the illness. Included at the secondary level care were pharmacies and laboratories for special services pertaining to the filling of prescriptions and laboratory tests respectively. Additional specialized care beyond the secondary level, such as psychiatric care, were referred to the tertiary level.

In the three-tier structure, oversight responsibilities were divided among the federal, state, and local government authorities such that the federal government minded the university teaching hospitals and the federal medical centers located in each state of the federation. The state governments were responsible for general hospitals, and the local governments exercised administrative responsibility for much smaller health facilities (Okafor, 1991). Although the framework was laudable and the mission statement of the ministry of health, which reads in part "...to bring about the improved health of Nigerians to serve as the engine for the pursuit of accelerated economic growth and sustained development," (Nigeria Federal Ministry of Health, 2005) was equally good, the annual resources committed by the federal government to the ministry to enable it do its work was paltry. Prior to 1991, total expenditure on healthcare did not exceed 4.6 percent of the gross national product (Okafor, 1991). In 2007, total expenditures budgeted for healthcare by the federal government, as contained in a presentation to a joint session of the Nigerian National Assembly by President Umaru Musa Yar Adua on November 7, 2007, amounted to N138 billion naira ($ 1.1 billion at a currency conversion rate of N127 to $1 in 2007) just about 5 percent of a GDP of $220 billion (CIA, 2008).

Confronted with the issue of HIV/AIDS in the healthcare system (Uzukwu, 2005) and a resurgence of polio in parts of the northern states, as well as a dire need to carry out facility improvements and increased capacity training for healthcare personnel serving a nation with an estimated population of 149 million people (CIA, 2008), the government only budgeted $1.1 billion.

Inadequate funding of the healthcare system has led to a deterioration of healthcare facilities and caused morale problems among healthcare workers (African Development Bank "ADB" and Organization for Economic Cooperation and Development "OECD," 2002). The deterioration in healthcare facilities and services were angrily mentioned by Brigadier Sani Abacha in his broadcast on national radio on December 31st 1983 announcing the overthrow of the Second Republic. Though additional reasons were stated for the coup, and Abacha was later to become a despot, who jailed and ordered the assassination of political opponents, his accusation of the political leaders of the Second Republic causing health services to be "in shambles as our hospitals are reduced to mere consulting clinics without drugs, water and equipment," (Abacha, 1983) resonated with the public at large.

There was a national health policy that lacked comprehensiveness due to the absence of a national death certification system, a credible vital registration system, mortality surveillance of adult risk behaviors, and mortality data as they pertain to communicable and non communicable diseases. The World Health

Organization (WHO, 2000) defines health as being disease free and attaining physical, mental, emotional and social well being. In rating the health systems of nations in terms of performance, Nigeria was rated 187 out of 191 nations (WHO, 2000). The mental health component of the Nigerian healthcare system, active strictly in the public sector as there is virtually no private practice, suffered from the effects of the brain drain involving the migration of providers to industrialized countries (WHO, 2005). Although there are eight regional psychiatric centers, in addition to medical schools of major universities where psychiatric services are provided (Ayorinde and Gureje, 2004), the shortage of qualified personnel and the pull of traditional herbalists and faith healers, who staked unscientific claims to healing powers, affected the effective delivery of mental healthcare.

Literature Review

Han (2007) defined techno-media as "media technologies that are defined by interoperability between devices, usually using the Internet as the connective medium,"(p.10) Techno-media thus enables fluid interaction across various media using multiple technologies. In the age of globalization, issues pertaining to politics, economics, war and peace, diseases, and social transformation have assumed more complex dimensions; as such, available information on these issues have become vast. Assembling, processing and making this information available for decision making have involved techno-media as an indispensable tool, with technology a major component. Hans (2004) indisputably avers that technology touches upon everything that's important to humankind's existence. In techno-media, there is a synergy of media and technology, and this conceptually and technically represent a powerful paradigm shift in how knowledge is acquired and brought to bear in dealing with a whole range of issues, including politics (Han, 2007).

An estimated two billion people worldwide use mobile phones, and one billion use the Internet (Han, 2007). The Internet revolution has enabled an explosion of information in the techno-media era, enabling quick access to data within a vast network that is global, yielding benefits by facilitating solutions to a wide array of issues. The efficiencies of the Internet are enormous. It is a tool for research, e-mailing, improved production processes, employee training, and many other things (Kreitner and Kinicki, 2008). Internet connectivity and interoperability with cell phones, desktops, personal assistant devices (PADs), laptops and many other emerging media related technologies substantially enhance the influence of techno-media over a broad spectrum of issues dealing with politics, economics, education and healthcare. Its adoption as a key strategy in healthcare services delivery in Nigeria could revolutionize healthcare by bringing effectiveness and efficiency to a chronically deficient system. Lemert (2007) defined techno-media as the generation of technologies in the post television era—cell phones and the Internet. Lemert explained the transformative nature of these technologies relative to the users of techno-media and their social environment. Social intercourse has been transformed with the speed and convenience of cell phones and the Internet. Efficiencies have thus been created in terms of time and monetary costs. In the context of healthcare efficiencies facilitated by techno-media, computerization of healthcare records, quick and ready access to communicative tools such as the Internet, cell phones and other hand held devices by both providers and users enable the achievement of these efficiencies. On both micro (individual) and macro (nationwide) levels, especially in developed countries, savings to the healthcare system derived from the use of techno-media have been enormous.

That mass media and information technology have combined to transform contemporary society was elucidated by Thompson and Hickey (2005). Especially in what they described as the post industrial world, the advent of techno-media has enabled profound change in many respects. Societal progress is fueled by rapid advances in technology, and information technology has certainly contributed to the rapidity of processes in industries of various types, in the context of the overall economy. Usage of techno-media in the healthcare services of a developed nation such as the United States, for example, featured online doctor's appointments, review of test results by e-mail, and refill requests of prescription drugs online. These activities were impossible just a decade or so ago. Mendes (2002), observed that the negative side of techno-media on youth and adolescents is fraught with subjective influences serious enough as to require psychoanalyst intervention. Detrimental or irresponsible use of techno-media occurs in a number of ways. But two of the most commonly misuses of techno-media resources are texting and checking e-mail while driving or operating other mechanical equipment. As the consequences of being distracted could be severe injury or death, some states and localities in the United States have outlawed texting and other dangerous behavior with techno-media equipment or gadgets while operating machinery or driving.

The Internet as a techno-media resource, is an invaluable tool in learning. For healthcare professionals, online courses are accessible toward course completion. Sklar (2003) underscored the necessity of physicians earning continuing medical education credits to maintain licensure and retain hospital privileges. Whereas physicians used to earn these medical credits through home study or by attending live meetings and conferences, today the convenience of online continuing medical education saves physicians money and time (Sklar, 2003).

Anderson (2004) reported in a study of consumers of e-health in 2002, that 80 percent of adults in the United States sought health information and/or services online. 10 percent communicated by e-mail and 50 percent showed an interest in using the Internet for clinical purposes. Barriers to the use of the Internet for health related purposes were found by Anderson (2004) to have been related to privacy, evaluation of services and reliability of the information. Although there were concerns, the positives outweighed the negatives in the usage of the Internet for health-related purposes.

Although Miller and West (2009) found that digital technology and healthcare in the Internet age in the United States was overblown, as few people were using digital technology to obtain healthcare information, they observed that less well educated people and lower income people living in rural areas used healthcare Internet less. Miller and West (2009) did recommend a number of policy initiatives, such as technology familiarization and access to appropriate equipment to encourage increased usage. Consumer satisfaction with techno-media as a tool in healthcare outcomes depended on familiarization with how to navigate the Internet to search for the beneficial material or information. Problems regarding effective navigation of websites were found by Toms (2007) in a study of consumers searching for health related topics. This finding underscored the need to implement technology familiarization as a matter of public policy.

Stolley, Thompson, Sharp and Fitzgibbon (2009) found that mobile phone texting was a useful tool in promoting healthy behaviors. In a study of women participating in a weight management program, they found that text messaging the participants with tips about proper eating and physical activity, as well as reminders about other aspects of the program, was successful in keeping the women consistent with the weight management regimen. This demonstration of text messaging as a powerful techno-media tool in healthcare management has implications for effective and efficient systemic healthcare management. Its popularization as a medium of communication between providers and users in any healthcare system could make a significant difference in the delivery of healthcare.

Research Design and Methodology

This study aimed to investigate a problem identified as being of a social science nature. A mixture of quantitative and qualitative research design was employed in the inquiry. This approach recognized the influence of the past on the present and shed light on the implications of this past influence on the implementation of healthcare policies over the years, starting from 1960, the year of Nigeria's independence from British colonial control, to 2009. In short, the historical aspect of the methodology allowed a systematic evaluation and synthesis of relevant material relative to the historical effectiveness or otherwise of healthcare delivery. The descriptive statistical aspect in the methodology was for the purpose of obtaining key data from a sample population of healthcare providers, specifically physicians, with the use of a survey. As these healthcare providers are important players in the healthcare system, data obtained from them were deemed indispensable to the success of the study, particularly in the recommendations phase. As the study aimed to propose techno-media as a strategic tool to improve healthcare delivery, it was deemed relevant to obtain data from the healthcare providers that pertained to their understanding of techno-media, their familiarity with it, use of or lack of use of techno-media resources in their respective practices, their opinions about the healthcare system and implications for democracy sustenance, and their views about the future of healthcare delivery if techno-media were to be an added component. Descriptive statistical procedures were used to organize, describe and summarize the data. As Glenberg (1995) explained, because the entire scores of a population are rarely done, samples are typically obtained and subjected to descriptive procedures to provide a platform from which educated guesses of the entire population can be made.

Healthcare practitioners, specifically physicians, were the target population. The city of Lagos, Nigeria's largest commercial city, with the most medical practices, was chosen as the accessible population area for the purposes of a random selection of respondents for the study. Three elements of the sampling frame were: practitioners in well to do areas; those in the middle and low income class areas; and those who practiced at the largest public facility, the Lagos University Teaching Hospital (LUTH). Respondents were randomly selected from this sampling frame. The survey instrument was distributed to 30 respondents by field assistants and 20 were returned. For the purposes of collecting data for analysis, the sample size of 20 respondents was deemed sufficiently representative of the 52, 408 medical practitioners on the Nigerian medical register as of 2007, though only 14,000 paid their practicing licensing fee for that year (Labiran, Mafe, Onajole & Lambo, 2008).

The aim of this study was to prescribe an approach to deal with the effective delivery of healthcare and to contextualize the prescription in a political sense by linking it with sociopolitical stability, an essential element of democratic sustenance. The study remained consistent with the associational theoretical framework in establishing an associational relationship between techno-media inadequacies and the quality of healthcare delivery, with implications for democracy longevity. Ultimately, a credible prescription could not be made without soliciting the views of healthcare practitioners in the Nigerian healthcare system, both in the public and private sectors, hence use of a survey instrument in obtaining these views. As Ghosh (1982) explained, the survey approach enabled a researcher to take the pulse of a given population on a phenomenon through data collection and analysis of the data, and was especially useful in socioeconomic matters. Uzukwu (2005) in a study of degrees of AIDS knowledge and their associational relationships with high risk sexual behavior in Nigeria, have demonstrated that the survey instrument is indispensable to obtaining pertinent data for use in analysis to guide recommendations.

In summary, the methodological blend of: a) using a Likert (1932) scale survey to gather data from healthcare providers, identified as major players in the healthcare system, then subjecting the data to descriptive statistical analysis;

and b). historical analysis of material, enabled the attainment of credible answers to the research questions as well as guided the recommended solutions to the problem.

Findings and Analysis:

The problem was stated as being the continual ineffectiveness of the Nigerian healthcare system in delivering services to users due to a number of factors, including the lack of a techno-media strategy to deliver care. The research questions were thus constructed with the aim of finding answers about how to deal with the problem. Historical analytical and descriptive statistical methodology with the use of a self administered survey (SAS) which applied the Likert model was used in eliciting answers to a set of declarative statements. The survey consisted of two sections. Part A gathered data relative to whether the respondent was in the public or private sector, whether they had access to the Internet and if so whether access was limited or always available, and whether the respondent's practice was computerized. The aim of this section of the survey was to determine computer and Internet familiarities of the respondents, considering those elements were crucial to establishing the reliability and validity of the study. Part B, the second part of the survey featured statements relevant to the problem and the research questions. As consistency and stability in any data are essential in establishing reliability, just as validity must be predicated upon accuracy and the generalizability of a study's findings (Potter, 1996), the survey instrument, choice of physician respondents for the study, and the random selection process were deemed consistent with the research principles of reliability and validity.

The survey was administered through the self administration method to a sample of healthcare providers, selected because of their key role in the functioning of the healthcare system. The declarative statements elicited responses in varying degrees of agreement or non agreement regarding the effectiveness of the system, to wit: whether governments had historically devoted adequate attention to healthcare, and whether the system as it currently exists threatens Nigeria's democracy. The sample of 20 physician respondents was randomly drawn. There was equal representation of providers in the public and private sectors.

The Healthcare System and Threats to Nigeria's Democracy

Pertaining to threats to Nigeria's democracy attributable to the ineffective healthcare system, analysis of the data on one of three relevant declarative statements in the survey which stated that the healthcare system was a threat to Nigeria's democracy (see Table 1) showed that 60 percent of the respondents were in agreement that the inadequacies of the system were a threat to democracy.   The second statement which sought to ascertain the respondents' professional assessment of the healthcare system elicited a 55 percent unfavorable assessment of the system as currently exists. Forty percent had a favorable opinion of the system. Considering bigger majorities agreed that the system was a threat to democracy and that successive governments did not give adequate attention to healthcare, the 40 percent favorable assessment of the system was significant and may speculatively have been influenced by an unwillingness of the respondents to indict a system of which they are an integral part. That 55 percent did not have confidence in the system and believed the system was a threat to Nigeria's democracy buttressed the historical analysis which showed ineffective healthcare delivery partly attributable to political and socioeconomic factors.

There is a nexus of the overall health of any nation's labor force and its productivity. A decline in labor hours as a consequence of illness drives productivity down. Economic decline, a bad healthcare system and political instability were conflated by the military when it overthrew the Second Republic in 1983 (Abacha, 1983). Myriad wellness issues pervade healthcare in Nigeria. Afflictions, many numerically significant in the population, cover the gamut and they include malaria, TB, malnutrition, HIV/AIDS, parasitic infections, typhoid fever, strokes, hypertension, cancers, diabetes, sickle cell disease, yellow fever, leprosy and polio. For the scope of the study, analysis of the findings were limited to five salient but ineffectively addressed healthcare challenges namely, epidemic control, malaria, polio, leprosy, and HIV/AIDS. .

Episodic epidemics have caught the government unawares at times, placing the citizenry at risk of massive deaths. In 1985, an outbreak of yellow fever killed 1,000 people in a town, even though a vaccine for yellow fever has been around since 1930 (Vogel, 1999). A lack of readiness to deal with a massive public health emergency could be destabilizing. In the context of the ongoing low level military conflict in the oil bearing Niger Delta region pitting militants against the federal government over control and sharing of oil revenues, the inadequacies of the healthcare system can adversely impact the government's ability to deal with a biological attack by extremely radical elements within the ranks of the militants. .

Malaria is one of the leading causes of morbidity and mortality in Nigeria. The yearly national economic loss attributable to endemic malaria is N132 billion naira (Over $900 million) (Malaria Consortium, 2008). The disease is an enormous obstacle to Nigeria's social and economic development, as 90 percent of Nigerians live in malaria endemic areas, where malaria causes 25 percent of infant mortality, 30 percent of childhood mortality, 50 percent of outpatient consultation, and 15-31 percent of hospital admissions (Rollback Malaria, 2001). The healthcare system's inadequacies, shown in the findings, present significant challenges to controlling this disease. Leprosy and polio, debilitating afflictions largely wiped off the face of the earth, are yet to be eradicated in

Nigeria. In the state of Kano, misinformation about the contents of a polio vaccine in 2003 led to political and religious posturing by political and religious leaders while an outbreak of polio went unchecked. There was no effective vaccine program until 2004 (Disease Infection News Report, 2004).

Nigeria is one of 10 countries in the world (Nigeria, India, Nepal, Congo, Ethiopia, Brazil, Indonesia, Bangladesh, Mozambique and Tanzania) with the highest rates of leprosy, accounting for 96 percent of 296,000 newly diagnosed cases in 2005 (WHO, 2009). Tackling polio and leprosy in the context of the current ineffectiveness of the healthcare system revealed in the findings will be an enormous task.

HIV/AIDS prevalence is estimated to be slightly over 3 percent (CIA, 2008), an infection rate considered an epidemic level. The CIA (2003) estimated the number of deaths from HIV/AIDS in 1999 to have been 250,000, and the number of people living with HIV/AIDS numbered 2.7 million. By 2001, the Joint United Nations Program on AIDS (UNAIDS) and the World Health Organization (2002) estimated this figure to have grown to 3.5 million people, an increase of 800,000 infected people in just two years. The onslaught of HIV AIDS was such that the federal ministry of health estimated that deaths from AIDS would surpass deaths from malaria, long the leading cause of mortality in the country. Juxtaposed with the findings that show a lack of confidence in the healthcare system, the situation appears dire relative to societal stability.

Summarily, the lack of confidence in the healthcare system, its inadequacies being a threat to democracy as presented in the survey, showed that a significant portion of Nigeria's population is susceptible to ill health at any time from malaria, polio, leprosy, and HIV/AIDS. This situation made Nigeria vulnerable to upheavals, including military takeovers, and consequent demise of democracy.

Computerization of the Role of Techno-media in the Healthcare System Today

The survey showed that only 25 percent of respondents had a computerized practice, though all had access to the Internet in either a limited or unlimited manner. A computerized practice was defined as one with an electronic database of patient medical records combined with capabilities of the Internet, such as e-mail. A significant 75 percent of respondents did not have a computerized practice. Data about computerization and access to the Internet were considered crucial to the eliciting of reliable opinion regarding the adoption of techno-media as a tool for healthcare services improvement. In Table 2, on the question of whether respondents' believed that computerization would improve service, a solid 100 percent were in agreement. On whether use of techno-media as a component of the healthcare system would improve delivery, 100 percent indicated that it would. All the respondents (100 percent) believe a healthy citizenry is useful to sustaining Nigeria's democracy.

That a majority of the respondents did not have a computerized practice was understandable, especially for practitioners in the public sector, in the context of the less than adequate funding of that sector of the healthcare system. Historically, one of the banes of healthcare effectiveness has been poor funding of the system, which not only affected the modernization of facilities, but also the purchase of updated equipment, including computers. As Onwujekwe, Chima and Okonkwo (2000) observed, reduced overall budgeting to the health sector affected the performance of the healthcare sector in critical areas such as malaria control.

The lack of widespread computerization inhibited creative innovations such as the application of electronic resources to improve overall efficiency. For example, tele-health—the use of telecommunications technologies to deliver health related services and information that support patient care, administrative services and education (Agency for Health Research and Quality, 2004)—has been shown to be effective in connecting doctors and patients far away, such that patients' illnesses were managed with medical advice and the patients were saved potentially high transportation costs.

The fact that 100 percent of respondents agreed that computerization and techno-media would improve healthcare services delivery provided an aperture into the thinking of these providers, that they were amenable to working in a computerized environment with techno-media tools, in spite of being currently hampered by a lack of access to those tools. The lack of computerization in the practices of 75 percent of the respondents presented stark evidence about the extremely limited use of techno-media resources in the healthcare system, assuming a system wide inference of the 75 percent finding in the sample. Yet techno-media could be very useful, as it would enable patient information sharing among providers to ensure better care. The recommendations phase details other advantages of techno-media.

Table1.   Healthcare   providers'   assessment   of   techno-media, computerization, healthcare, and implications for democracy sustenance.

Number of Respondents N=20	Strongly Agree	Agree	Undecided	Disagree	Strongly Disagree	% in agreement	% in disagreement
Your professional assessment of healthcare in Nigeria is favorable	3	5	1	5	6	8 (40%)	11 (55%)
The current healthcare system is a threat to democracy	2	10	2	6	0	12 (60%)	6 (30%)
Historically, governments have not given adequate attention to healthcare	7	6	4	3	0	13 (65%)	3 (15%)
A computerized practice can improve effectiveness of healthcare delivery	10	10	0	0	0	20 (100%)	0
Access to techno-media resources as a component of the healthcare system can help improve service delivery	12	8	0	0	0	20 (100%)	0
A healthy citizenry can help the sustenance of Nigeria's democracy.	10	10	0	0	0	20 (100%)	0

Table 2. Healthcare providers' practice computerization and Internet access.

N=20	In private practice	In public practice	Access to Internet	No access to Internet	Limited Internet access	Internet access always ready	Computerized practice	No computerized practice
Providers In private or public practice.	10	10						
Public providers with access to the Internet.			10	0				
Private Providers with access to the Internet.			10	0				
Providers whose Internet access is limited or always ready.					13	7		
Have or do not have a computerized practice.							5	15
Totals	10	10	20 (100%)	0	13 (65%)	7 (35%)	5 (25%)	15 (75%)

Recommendations and Conclusion

The problem was identified as an ineffective healthcare delivery system due to a lack of techno-media strategy. The research questions enquired into whether the healthcare system was a threat to Nigeria's democracy, the current role or non role of techno-media in healthcare services delivery, and the potential benefits derivable from its use as a tool to improve services delivery. The research design incorporated elements of quantitative and qualitative research, relying on a historical analysis and a descriptive analysis of the data. The survey instrument was constructed using the Likert scale and was administered to a random sample of healthcare providers, considered key players in the healthcare system thus of necessity to obtain information from them regarding computerization in their respective practices, and their views about whether techno-media could be an effective tool in improving service delivery.

The findings broadly revealed that the healthcare system's ineffectiveness undermined the overall health of the general population, a necessary factor in economic productivity and societal stability in the long term. The population was at risk of disease outbreaks as the federal government, which has consistently underfunded the healthcare sector, appeared to be unprepared to handle such public health emergencies. Malaria disease in the population caused an annual economic loss of over $900 million (slightly less than the total federal budget for the healthcare sector in 2008). And debilitating diseases like polio and leprosy, eradicated in most countries, continued to remain a threat to the population. The findings further showed that healthcare providers were optimistic about techno-media playing a positive role in improving services, though computerization, a facilitator of techno-media usage, was found to exist in the practices of only 25 percent of the respondents.

On the basis of the findings, recommendations regarding the strategic use of techno-media to improve service delivery follow. Of pertinence in the successful use of this strategy is adequate funding. In this respect, an increase in government funds and from global stakeholders such as the World Health Organization (WHO) to procure the needed equipment will be of the utmost necessity. With available funds, the techno-media strategy should be implemented with the setting up of a system wide infrastructure, with equipment and accessories, to cover the entire country. This should consist of Internet accessible computers and the requisite hardware and software to establish intranets and extranets, subsidized cell phones with Internet capability for healthcare workers, and video conferencing equipment. Private sector providers will be a part of this country wide strategy through favorable government loans for the purchase of equipment.

When fully set up, a techno-media architecture will link up primary, secondary and tertiary healthcare facilities, both public and private, in a nationwide network. This network should revolutionize the gathering, storing and access of healthcare information. From a provider's vantage point, this network should facilitate quick access to a patient's medical records and clinical reports, irrespective of geographical location, upon which medical decisions can be made, such as referral to a secondary or tertiary facility. For instance, a trader from Onitsha in Lagos on a business trip who suddenly fell sick would have a good chance of receiving proper treatment if the provider had access to his medical records, fed into the network by his primary care provider in Onitsha. Healthcare providers will be able to more effectively monitor prenatal and neonatal care, keep track of immunization histories and improve the collection and centralization of morbidity and mortality data. Providers will also transmit lab test requests, test results and x-rays to one another through the network, saving patients precious time and money in transportation costs. The network should also be useful as an educational tool in enabling the imparting of health education to rural dwellers where governments at the local level would mobilize biweekly or monthly gatherings at selected locations wired for Internet connectivity so educational materials (films and lectures) on wellness issues could be fed in.

Malaria, chronic diabetes and hypertension are prevalent in large numbers in the population. Dahiru, Jibo, Hassan and Mande (2008) in a study conducted in a northern Nigerian village, found a two percent prevalence of diabetes Mellitus. The study was consistent with similar prevalence rates across Nigeria. When extrapolated to the entire population of 140 million, the national prevalence rate in raw numbers reaches 2.8 million people. Hypertension rates in the population range from 10 percent to 20 percent, or 14 to 28 million people in raw numbers (Ike and Ikeh, 2006).

Internet connectivity to reach remote areas, enabling healthcare professionals to provide health information and education in real time streaming media can make a huge difference in life style changes, preventative behaviors and disease management. From a studio in Abuja, Lagos or Enugu, a healthcare professional's presentation can be streamed in to selected Internet equipped locations in all 775 local government areas of the country. Internet access can be facilitated through local government authorities who would be mandated to build and equip selected locations and would disseminate information to residents in their respective domains about health program schedules and access times.

In this way there would be no onerous burden on those without the financial wherewithal to obtain a computer and Internet access. The network should prove invaluable to providers for research, participation in discussions, professional updates, and e-emailing. An e-mailing capability will enhance the provider's services in being a tool to provide patients with lab test results and follow up advice about wellness and saving the patients time and money in transportation. The network should enable providers to log on and share professional information and advice, thereby mutually enriching one another's experience. As a tool for training, the network should promote capacity building for healthcare workers. A survey of physicians in the US showed 96 percent of the respondents agreed that computerization and Internet connectivity improved the practice of medicine and the quality of care (Health Technology Center, 2001). Although Nigeria is a developing nation without comparable resources as the US, but an increase in the federal healthcare budget from the current four percent of GDP to say 15 percent can finance a techno-media paradigm shift in healthcare services, and the gains in ensuring a much healthier population will have enormous positive implications for economic growth. It can be done if there is the political will to do it.

A nationwide integrated computerization of healthcare facilities will be beneficial in creating efficiencies, eliminating waste and duplication, and saving the government money. Computerization and the creation of a network with Internet connectivity will ensure the efficient deployment of resources. For instance, scarcity of drugs or specific equipment, or oversupply in any given facility in any part of the country can be quickly determined and appropriate action taken by authorized personnel to remedy the situation by accessing the computer database and using e-mail. Reduced costs achieved through efficiencies would free up funds for use in further enhancing the system.

Limitations in executing the recommendations exist in the cost of implementation, especially in the critical area of the requisite hardware and software, as well as in the political will to embark on what would undoubtedly be a revolutionary path in changing the heath care system for the better. There needs to be access to techno-media resources to both providers and users (patients), where users can be granted access on a limited basis to obtain useful healthcare information. To minimize overall costs, implementation can be carried out in phases. Under such a plan, urban areas where Internet access is common (in homes and in Internet cafés) and where cell phone usage is high can be linked up on the nationwide health network before the rural areas, where network linkage can occur later, perhaps with the savings derived from reduced costs gained from a successful implementation of the urban network linkage phase. Considering computers and Internet access are inexpensive compared to a few years ago, the budgetary outlay for the recommended techno-media strategy should not be an onerous one for the federal, state and local governments. To create the political will needed for the adoption and implementation of these recommendations, healthcare advocates, organized labor, progressive politicians, other civic leaders, and the general public must prevail on the political authorities for action.

REFERENCES

ADB & OECD. (2002). *African economic outlook.* Paris, France: OECD Publishing/African Development Bank.

AHRQ. (2008). *Using telehealth to improve quality and safety: Findings from the AHRQ health IT portfolio.* Rockville, MD: Agency for Healthcare Research and Quality.

Akukwe, C. (2001, May). AIDS in Nigeria: the ticking time bomb [Electronic version]. *Africa Economic Analysis.* Retrieved April 1, 2004 from http://www.africaeconomicanalysis.org/articles/gen/aidsnigeriahtm.html

Alubo, S.O. (1987). Power and privilege in medical care: An analysis of medical services in post-colonial Nigeria. *Social Science and Medicine*, Vol 24 (5), 453-62.

Anderson, J.G. (2004). Consumers of e-health. *Social Science Computer Review*, Vol. 22 (2), 242-248

Ayorinde, O., & Gureje, O. (2004). Psychiatric research in Nigeria. Bridging tradition and modernization. *The British Journal of Psychiatry,* 184, 536-538.

Basden, G.T. (1921). *Among the Ibos of Nigeria.* Philadelphia, PA: J.B. Lippincott Company.

Basedau, M., & Mehler, A. (2005). Conceptualizing the "resource curse" in sub-Saharan Africa (PP17-). In M. Basedau & A. Mehler (Eds). *Resource politics in sub-Saharan Africa.* Institute of African Affairs, Hamburg African Studies, 14. Hamburg: Scientific Association, German Overseas Institute.

Butts, K. H, & Metz, S.(1996). Armies and democracy in the new Africa: Lessons from Nigeria and South Africa: *Strategic Studies Institute, US Army War College Report,* 1-36.

Central Intelligence Agency. (2003). *Report on AIDS.* Retrieved October 15, 2003 from http://www.cia.gov/cia/publications/factbook/geo/ni.html.

Central Intelligence Agency. (2008). *The world factbook.* Retrieved March 20, 2009 from http://www.cia.gov/library/publications/the-world-factbook/print/ni.html

Chazan, N. (1983). *An anatomy of Ghanaian politics: Managing political recession,* 1969-1982. Boulder, CO: Westview Press.

Dahiru, T., Jibo, A., Hassan, A.A., & Mande A.T. (2008). Prevalence of diabetes in a semi urban community in northern Nigeria. *Nigeria Journal of Medicine,* Vol 17 (4), 414-416.

Disease Infection News Report. (2004). *Nigeria resuming polio immunizations.* Retrieved March 24, 2009 from http://www.news-medical.net

Eisenhart, M.A. (1991). Conceptual frameworks for research circa 1991. Ideas from a cultural anthropologist: implications for mathematics education researchers (PP 202- 219). In R.G. Underhill (Ed). *Psychology of mathematics education.* Blacksburg, VA: Group for the Psychology of Mathematics Education.

Ejindu, D. (1967). *Interview with Major Nzeogwu..* Retrieved March 20, 2009 from http://maxsiollun.wordpress.com/2008/02/20/interview-with-major-nzeogwu/

Engel, U. (2005). The Niger delta region—a strategic conflict analyses of conflicts around oil (PP 20-30). In M. Basedau & A. Mehler (Eds). *Resource politics in sub-Saharan Africa.* Institute of African Affairs, Hamburg African Studies, 14. Hamburg: Scientific Association, German Overseas Institute.

Feldman, D., & Miller, J. (1998). *The AIDS crisis: A documentary history.* Westport, CT: Greenwood Press.

Ghosh, B.N. (1982). *Scientific method and social research.* New Delhi: Sterling Publishers Private Limited.

Glenberg, A. M. (1995). *An introduction to statistical reasoning.* Hillsdale, NJ: Lawrence Erlbaum Associates.

Gliner, J.A., & Morgan, G.A. (2000). *Research methods in applied settings: an integrated approach to design and analysis.* Mahwah, NJ: Lawrence Erlbaum Associates, Inc.

Han, S. (2007). *Navigating Techno-media.* Lanham, MD: Rowman and Littlefield.

Hans, J. (2004). Towards a philosophy of technology (P17). In D.M. Kaplan (Ed) *Readings in the philosophy of technology.* Lanham, MD: Rowman and Littlefield.

Health Technology Center. (2001). *Physicians welcome increased role for the Internet.* Retrieved March 19 from http://www.mentalhealthabout.com/library/sci/0301/blmamt301.htm? terms=internet+physicians.

Ike, S.O., & Ikeh, V.O. (2006). The prevalence of diastolic dysfunction in adult hypertensive Nigerians. *Ghana Medical Journal,* Vol 40 (2), June, 55-60.

Ityavyar, D. (1988). Health services inequalities in Nigeria. *Social Science and Medicine,* Vol 27 (11), 1223-35.

Kreitner, K., and Kinicki, A. (2008). *Organizational behavior.* New York, NY: McGraw- Hill/Irwin.

Labiran, A., Mafe, M., Onajole, B., & Lambo, E (2008). *Health workforce country profile for Nigeria.* Nigeria: Africa Health Workforce Observatory.

Lemert, C.C. (2007). *"Resetting the temperature: Are techno-media cool or hot or others?" Navigating techno-media: Caught in the web.* New York: Rowman &Littlefield.

Likert, R.(1932), "A Technique for the Measurement of Attitudes", Archives of Psychology 149: 1-55.

Mendes, E.R.P. (2002). Contemporary adolescence and the crisis of ideals. *International Forum of Psychoanalysis,* vol. 11(2), June, 125-134 (10)

Miller, A.M., & West, D.M. (2009). Where's the revolution? Digital technology and healthcare in the Internet age. *Journal Health Politics, Policy and Law,* 34 (2), 261-284.

Okafor, S.I. (1991). Spatial aspects of healthcare provision in Nigeria. In R. Akhtar (ed). *Healthcare patterns and planning in developing countries* (pp. 263-276). New York, NY. Greenwood Press.

Onwujekwe, D.I., Chima, R., & Okonkwo, P. (2000). Economic burden of malaria illness on households versus that of all other illness episodes: a study in five malaria holo-endemic Nigerian communities. *Health Policy,* 54, 143-159.

Rollback Malaria. (2001*). Facts and figures from some African countries— Nigeria.* Retrieved March 18 from http://rollbackmalaria.org/docs/amd/africa_facts.htm

Sklar, B.M. (2003). Introduction to Online CME. *Internet Health: Journal of Research, Application, Communication & Ethics*, 1:4

Smith, R.R. (1969). *Kingdoms of the Yoruba*. London: Methuen.

Stolley., M.R., Thompson, A.L., Sharp, L.K., & Fitzgibbon, M.L. (2009). Mobile phone text messaging to promote healthy behaviors and weight loss maintenance: a feasibility study. *Health Informatics Journal*, Vol.15 (1), 17-25.

Thompson, W.E., & Hickey, J.V. (2005). *Society in focus: An introduction to sociology*. New York: Allyn & Bacon.

Toms, E.G. (2007). How consumers search for health information. *Health Informatics journal*, Vol. 13 (3), 223-235

Uzukwu, M. (2005). Factors influencing the spread of HIV/AIDS from high-risk sexual behavior within three economic status/income level groups in Owerri, Nigeria. *Dissertation Abstracts International*, 66 (7B), p.3623. (Proquest—formerly UMI—#3182191)

World Health Organization. (2000). *Health systems: Improving performance.* Geneva: WHO.

World Health Organization. (2002, July). *Report of Integrated management of cardiovascular risk* to WHO meeting in Geneva.

World Health Organization. (2005). *Mental health atlas.* Geneva: WHO

World Health Organization. (2009). *Leprosy fact sheet.* Retrieved March 18 from http://www.searo.who

Yar' Adua, U.M. (2007, November). *Budget presentation*, to the national
assembly in Abuja, Nigeria

Chapter 12

Concepts, Dimensions in New Media Technology: Reinforcing the Contest Against Financial Crimes in Nigeria

Isika G. Udechukwu and Assay B. Enahoro
Delta State Polytechnic
Ogwashi-Uku, Nigeria

Abstract

It was Marshall McLuhan, a Canadian communication scholar, who said that the emerging satellite communication technology would turn the world around to become one global village. This world, which he conceived would be likened to the community life of old, where families sit together to share tales under moonlight; where everyone would know what everyone else was saying and doing; and communities far apart would affect one another in vicarious ways. With this prediction coming through, the new information technology responsible for shrinking the world as it were has become accessible to fraudsters who sit on the Internet to perpetrate all manners of financial crimes. The challenge thus posed by this trend is now a global concern which this paper sets to reinforce by proposing appropriate strategies, including techniques to discourage and check fraudulent practices, especially among youths in Nigeria.

INTRODUCTION

Three major landmarks preceded the evolution of what could be referred to as communication technology. They are the birth of electrical technology in about 1800 when Volta discovered primary battery; the academic feat wrought by Clark Maxwell, who developed the concept of electro-magnetic radiation in his classical work, *The Dynamic Theory of the Electro Magnetic Field* in 1864. That work remained in the shelves as a theory until 1887, when Heinrich Hertz validated it and debuted yet another discovery — the radio wave frequency modulation for which he is known today. The third epoch has to do with the discovery of electrical impulses through wires, which made communication across land distances possible, perfected by Samuel Morse in 1939 and thus, the birth of communication technology had begun. This brief survey reinforced the deliberate determination of science to surmount all possible barriers in the way of realizing an emergent communication world.

The Internet is the newest word on the ICT lexicon; that is to say, it is the latest technology. It is actually the realization of McLuhan's dream. The world today is Internet based. Every bit of information required by the modern man is at his beck and call. All that he needs to do is push the buttons and the information will be there waiting to be accessed. The Internet has advanced beyond imagination so much that there is hardly any area of human endeavor that it cannot be applied. It is sometimes referred to as the "information super highway." Severin and Tankard (2001, p. 336) described the Internet as a worldwide collection of computer networks. Unlike the old system of communication that requires wires for transmission, the Internet is a multimedia form. Multimedia is a technology that presents information in more than one medium such as text, still images, moving images and sound (Williams & Sawyer, 2003, p. 5).

Today, the global wave of information and communication technology development has become a strong driving force in almost every aspect of life. As a powerful tool for the realization of this purpose, any effort in the direction of critical assessment of its impact, in our own opinion, may be worthwhile. Paradoxically, the Internet is a double-edged sword, providing many opportunities for persons and organizations to develop, but at the same time, it has brought with it opportunities for crime mongers. Cybercrimes are now everywhere with increasing sophistication as a result of development in ICT.

The overall impact of this problem can be felt on the global economy. One of the greatest problems of the Internet is the magnitude of scam activities on the web. Since the early 80s, a worldwide scam has been running on the net. The Nigerian version of this is referred to as the advance fee fraud (aka 419). The term "419" comes from a section of the Nigerian Criminal Code which outlaws fraudulent activities. It is estimated that over US$550 billion may have been swindled by cyber scams. Scam operations are not limited to Nigeria alone.

Other West African nations such as Togo, Ghana, Liberia, Sierra Leone, Cote d' Ivoire, to name only a few are involved in e-mails and other variations of scams. The typology of these scams will be considered in subsequent units of this chapter.

It must be noted that countless individuals, companies, and institutions are falling prey to this scheme. It was reported by Agence France Presse in 2005 that a Brazilian businessman was duped US$181 million. That same report also carried information about a Florida-based business mogul, Prince Tampa, who lost US$400,000 to a Nigeria scam, while a New Zealand paper reported in November, 2007 that a businessman was duped of US$4m. The most pathetic of these reports involved a clergyman, the Bishop of Los Angeles, who in 2006 in response to a fictitious scam letter for aid to distressed children and women in war torn Sudan lost US$2m to the scam (http://www.gabrielsawma. blogspot.com). All of these signify the unintended purpose of which the Internet has now been made to serve.

Faced with the protuberant problem of financial scams, many nations are wary of their dealings with others especially countries which are quite prone to Internet crimes. This scenario has image implications and challenges that gear toward creating adequate awareness of prevalence among citizens and foreigners. Nigeria has developed a very bad image due to malfeasances on the net. Considering the powerful influence of the Internet, no government worth its salt would allow honest citizens to fall prey to cybercrimes. Part of the measures to control this has been the establishment of Economic and Financial Crimes Commission (EFCC) and renewed effort toward the provision of adequate information on the Nigerian web on the possible dangers of Internet crimes.

Problem Statement

The impact of ICT on contemporary global information flow is quite overwhelming. In view of this amazing dimension, it would be safe to say that the world has really shrunk into one global family. ICT as it is has greatly enhanced global neighborhood in terms of immediate access to information, views and opinion around the globe. What is, however, worrisome is the global trend of dysfunctionality of the Internet technology as a result of emergent economic and socio-political dimensions of our time. It has been the view that since technology development is a western ideology, a few powerful and wealthy nations of the West who also control the production and distribution of this latest technologies, and use them to idealize western political philosophies and values to the detriment of numerous poor developing nations (Inayatullah, 1999, Obe et al, 2008). Despite the threats to Afro-centric ideologies from massive influx of western media content, the case of ICT is like the hunter being hunted. Internet crime is not a problem peculiar to poor and unindustrialized nations, it is a global problem, which also requires a global panacea (Maras, 2002, p.106). The focus of this paper is to provide an insightful frame work that will address the immediate menace where censorship of data on the Internet is near impossible.

In the light of the above, we intend to propose strategies and measures which will be proactive enough to address some of the values and nuances inherent in human nature.

Methodology

The researchers relied on the historical research design to obtain data for this study. This involved extensive review of published research work which provided both theoretical and empirical evidence that helped to shape the perspective of the study. The work subjected data collected from the Internet, textbooks, newspapers, and magazines to extensive evaluation and determined their validity and reliability. From this we were able to draw some logical deductions, which formed the thesis of this paper.

Theoretical Framework

This study is hinged on the technological determinism theory. The theory states that media technology shapes how we as individuals in a society think, feel, act, and how society operates as we move from one technological age to another. Technological determinism is often associated with Marx's assertion that "The windmill gives you society with the feudal lord: the steam-mill, society with industrial capitalist" ("The Poverty of Philosophy," 1847).

Technological determinism has been defined as an approach that identifies technology, or technological advances, as the central causal element in processes of social change (Croteau and Hoynes, 2003, p. 305-307). As a technology is stabilized, its design tends to dictate users' behaviors, consequently diminishing human agency. This stance however ignores the social and cultural circumstances in which technology was developed. Fischer (1992) cited in Croteau and Hoynes (2003) characterized the most prominent forms of technological determinism as "billiard ball" approaches, in which technology is seen as external force introduced into a social situation, producing a series of ricochet effects.

Rather than acknowledging that a society or culture interacts with and even shapes the technologies that are used, a technological determinist view holds that "uses made of technology are largely determined by the structure of the technology itself, that is, that its functions follow from its form" (Postman, 1992, p. 3-20). However, this is not to be confused with the inevitability thesis (Chandler, 1995), which states that once a technology is introduced into a culture, what follows is the inevitable development of that technology.

Most interpretations of technological determinism share two general ideas namely: that the development of technology itself follows a predictable, traceable path largely beyond cultural and political influence, and that technology in turn has effects on societies that are inherent, rather than socially conditioned or that the society organizes itself in such a way to support and further develop a technology once it has been introduced.

The exponent of the technological determinism theory is believed to be Thorstein Veblen (1857-1929), an American sociologist. Veblen's contemporary, popular historian, Charles Beard, provided this apt determinist image: "Technology marches in seven-league boots from one ruthless revolutionary conquest to another, tearing down old factories and industries, flinging up new processes with terrifying rapidity." But technological determinism is often misinterpreted. What is largely bypassed as a result of technology as part of culture as a whole is the different uses and assessment of human potentials. In other words, in terms of possible uses and application of technology, a person who searches for and obtains financial information from the Internet and applies the information to foster his business interest has been helped by the technology to move forward. This is what Smith (1994) meant by saying that the idea of progress is centralized around the idea that social problems can be solved by technological advancement and this is the way society moves forward.

Technological determinists believe that "You cannot stop progress," implying that you are unable to control technology (Green, 2001, p. 15). It is the set of ideas in the above assertions that drive this study.

Literature Review
Concept of ICT
Information and Communication Technology is a relatively new technology and its effects on many areas of human endeavor are still to be fully identified. At enterprise level, technological innovations have some effect on the quality and quantity of products as well as in relation between the machines and workers on their jobs. Communicating new ideas through ICT shows that ICT is capable of stimulating small and medium scale enterprises. In the academic sphere, higher institutions of learning must be encouraged to use ICT in designing their curriculum content, especially in communication where computer-assisted reporting may be used to transform the rural environment (Okpoko, 2007, p.153).

From what has been said, the introduction of ICT into any sphere generally engenders unprecedented levels of transformation. This assertion has been reiterated in politics, culture, education and economy to mention but a few. According to Brown (2000, p. 89), the development so far is just a tip of the enormous iceberg. The advanced countries are using ICTs to enhance their competitiveness at most alarming rate. It is perhaps for this reason that Okunna (2002, p. 293) has advocated the need for development partners to come together by communicating development messages in order to bring faster development.

ICTs have the capacity of bringing about changes in communication. Such changes are usually for the best. Assembling, processing, and storing information are not only easy but also fast. Rodney (2005, p.145) noted that advancement in telecommunication networks relays massive volume of voices, video, and print products along digital circuits at very high speed. In addition, the capacity of computers, communication networks, and information storage and retrieval systems has grown faster than any technology in history (Souter, 1999, p. 406).

Using ICTs in communication has a capacity of potential empowerment of poor communities, which will in turn help in reducing the imbalance between developing and developed countries. This is what McPhail (2006, p. 290) calls "global communication dimension." In fact, ICTs have empowered poor communities through the creation of job opportunities. For example, mobile phones and GSM operators have created vast job opportunities in Nigeria. Souter (1999, p. 406) has alluded to the range of services that can be provided by ICTs in the areas of fax, mobile phones, e-mail, and private networks as well as software in PCs and computer networks. ICTs have also created a digital divide between technological advanced and backward countries. The divide manifests in uneven access to the new technologies and the opportunities they bring. Factors such as economy, ICT contents, infrastructure, literacy, culture, non-implementation of ICT policies, and politics, among others have made developing countries to trail behind in the information age and to explore the potentials of ICT more fully (Mehra, et al, 2004).

Internet and its Structure

The most prominent of the ICTs is the Internet. Its ability to maintain open standard for transmitting digitalized data-voice, video or text from one computer to another has constituted its single most important reason for success. According to Baran (2004, p. 215) the Internet is most appropriately referred to as "network of networks." It is growing and expanding at increasingly fast rates. These networks consist of Local Area Networks (LANS) and Wide Area Networks (WANS). LANS connect two or more computers, usually ones within the same building, while WANS connect several LANS in different locations. Consequently, the Internet serves as a connection for WANS. The Internet therefore connects the individual user to a complex network whereby information can be accessed irrespective of time and space. The vastness of the Internet makes it impossible to specify the number of users in the net. However, according to statistics obtained from Miniwatts Marketing Group, the number of Internet users worldwide stood at 1,463,632,361 as at June 30, 2008 (Internetworld Stats–www.internetworldstats.htm). If this statistic is broken down to usage by world regions, Africa has 51,065,630 representing 5.3 percent of the world population of users. (See table and chart below.)

World Internet Users by World Regions
Source: Internet World Stats:
www.internetworldstats.com/stats.htm
1,463,632,361 Internet users for June 30, 2008
Copyright © 2008, Miniwatts Marketing Group

NIGERIA
NG — 138,283,240 population — Country Area: 923,769 sq. km
Capital City: Abuja — population 1,129,345 ('08)
10,000,000 Internet users as of Mar/08, 7.2% of the population per

ITU 500 broadband internet subscribers as of Sept 07, per ITU.

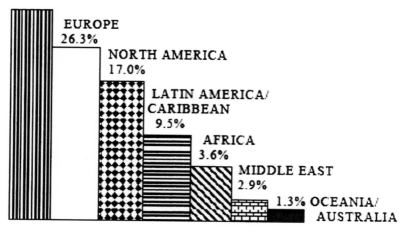

ASIA
39.5%

EUROPE
26.3%

NORTH AMERICA
17.0%

LATIN AMERICA/
CARIBBEAN
9.5%

AFRICA
3.6%

MIDDLE EAST
2.9%

1.3% OCEANIA/
AUSTRALIA

Structure

The Internet shares the features made possible by digitalization. These features lie in their interconnectedness, their accessibility to individual users as senders and/or receivers, their interactivity, their multiplicity of use and open-ended character, their ubiquity and "delocatedness."

The Internet is a combination of thousands of computer network sending and receiving data from all over the world with competing interests joined together by common purpose (Biagi, 2003, p. 39). The Internet structure is a channel which holds enormous amounts of useful information (much of it consisting multi-media) stored by individuals, government, educational and research establishments, as well as commercial outfits. The affordability of this mass of structure or network makes a person an instant publisher with access to millions of Internet users who create a new class of mass communicators (Dominick, 2002, p.303-304).

In relation to freedom of expression, media and societal control, the Internet has been both a help and hindrance. It has generated a lot of solutions and a lot of problems and has impacted a lot on society and our existence. The issues of problems including information overload arising out of prevalence of data available, in Payne's opinion, has created a new set of problems and new issues concerning the use of the "gadgets" available to us — Internet makes it an avenue for any idea good or bad and thus, a powerful tool for individuals who may want to use it for good or evil. The Internet has given solutions as well as created problems because it is a free-zone where everything goes (2001, p.108). Morris and Ogan (1996, p.25) had earlier amplified the panics of Payne thus:

> *The net beauty is that it is uncontrolled...it is information by everyone, for everyone, there is racist stuff, bigoted, hate-group stuff filled with paranoia, bombed recipes; how to engage in various kinds of crimes, electronic or otherwise, scams and swindles. It is all there. It is all available.*

As there are views of the Internet as a free for all zone when it comes to evil ideas, so also are views about the Net being a tool for development and enhancement of human beings. McNair cited by Briggs and Cobley (1998, p.182) captures this dichotomy when he discussed the freedom and the varying views about the potentials of the Internet thus:

> *In relation to the commercial and political constraints which accompanied all previous communicative media, the Internet combines accessibility and interactivity, making it a uniquely democratizing technological innovation: a medium which evades censorship, regulation and commercialization like no other. An opposing 'dystopian' view (however) sees the 'Internet' as latest in the long line of dehumanizing technological development, producing a population of 'computer-nerds' who, if they are not watching television or fiddling with their play stations are addictively 'surfing' the*

*net. The Internet it is argued encourages not communication
but isolation in which one talks not to real people but
disembodied screens. It's most enthusiastic advocate often
base concerns about the implications of the Internet on a fear
of its anarchic, uncontrollable character-precisely the
qualities welcomed by its most enthusiastic advocate.*

The above sheds light on the ability of the Internet, a unified electronically-based computer system in human interactiveness, in accomplishing many activities and actions.

Internet Crime

Internet crime is a kind of organized crime. By definition crime consists of the following: (1) activities that involve breaking the law (2) an illegal act or activity that can be punished by law (3) an act that is immoral. Organized crime refers to forms of activity that have many of the characteristics of normal business, but are illegal. Organized crimes embrace smuggling, gambling, drug trade, prostitution, large-scale theft, and protection rackets, among other activities. It often relies on threats of violence to conduct these activities. While organized crime has traditionally developed within individual countries in culturally specific ways, it has become increasingly transnational in scope. Slapper and Tombs (1999, p.232) posit that:

*The reach of organized crime is now felt in many countries
throughout the world, but historically it has been particularly
strong in a handful of nations. In America organized crime is
a massive business rivalling a number of major sectors of
economic enterprise. National and local criminal
organizations provide illegal goods and services to mass
consumers. Illicit gambling on horse races, lotteries and
sporting events represent the greatest source of income
generated by organized crime.*

The activities of organized crime groups have become international in scope. Internationally organized crimes are greatly facilitated by the Internet-narcotics trade, counterfeiting, human trafficking and so on. Despite the extremely high level of sophistication of Internet and advancement in its technology, which has provided exciting new opportunities and benefits, vulnerability to crime has become heightened. While it is difficult to quantify the extent of crime, it is possible to highlight some of the major forms it has taken.

❖ Illegal interception of telecommunications systems (which means that eavesdropping has become easier). This has implications ranging from spouse monitoring to espionage.

❖ There is heightened vulnerability of electronic vandalism and terrorism. Western societies are increasingly depending on computerized systems; interference with such systems could pose serious security hazards.

❖ The ability to steal telecommunication services means that people can conduct illicit business without being detected or simply manipulate telecom and mobile phone services in order to receive free or discounted telephone calls.

❖ Telecom privacy is a growing problem. It has become relatively easy to violate copyright rules by copying materials, soft ware, film and CDs.

❖ It is difficult to control pornography, offensive content in cyberspace. Sexually explicit materials, racist propaganda and instructions for building incendiary devices can all be placed on and down load from the Internet. "Cyber-stalking" can pose not only virtual, but real threats to on-line users.

❖ Telemarketing fraud has been noticed of late. Fraudulent charity schemes and investment opportunities are difficult to regulate.

❖ There is an enhanced risk of electronic funds transfer crimes. The widespread use of cash machines, e-commerce and "electronic money" on the Internet heighten the possibility that some transactions will be intercepted.

❖ Electronic money laundering can be used to "move" the illegal proceeds from a crime in order to conceal their origins.

❖ Telecommunications can be used to further criminal conspiracies. Because of sophisticated encryption systems and high speed data transfers, it is difficult for law enforcement agencies to interpret information about criminal activities. This has particular reference to new international criminal activities (Grabosky and Smith, 1998, p. 234).

Today cyber or Internet crime is on the rise. It used to be the fastest going category of crime in Britain in the late 90s. Then fraud and forgery rose by 29 percent — an increase of 70,500 offenses over the period of one year. This phenomenal development has been attributed to Internet based crime. The global reach of Internet crime poses challenges for law enforcement, since criminal acts perpetrated in one country have the power to affect victims across the globe (Giddens, 2001, p. 234).

Nigeria's reputation as a cybercrime hub is quite unfortunate considering the various efforts toward encouraging our teeming youths to be ICT compliant. It will be very dangerous for our society to allow considerable leeway for people to engage in non-conformist pursuit. With high rate of unemployment and increasing criminal violence, Nigeria can ill afford these deviant actions. Any society that tolerates deviant behaviors would suffer social disruptions. Let us now look at the various dimensions of Internet fraud and the extent of participation among youths.

Forms of Internet Fraud

Internet fraud comes in various guises. Most scams usually begin with a letter or e-mail sent to the web making an offer that will ultimately result in a large payoff for the intended victim. The details vary, but the usual story is that a person, often a government or bank employee, knows of a huge sum of unclaimed money or gold, which he cannot accessed directly, usually because he has no right to it. Most times the people involved may be real, but impersonated or fictitious characters. It could be wife or son of a deposed African or any other leader from any part of the world, usually a dictator who has amassed a stolen fortune, or a bank employee who knows of a terminally ill wealthy person with no relatives, or a wealthy foreigner who had deposited money in the bank just before dying in a plane crash (leaving no will or known next of kin).

Another variation is one in which fictitious documents bearing official government stamps and seals are displayed on the net. The scammers often mention false addresses and use photographs taken from the Internet or magazines to represent themselves. But these photographs are by no means representations of the persons involved. At a certain point in the transaction the scammer will introduce a delay or monetary hurdle to prevent the deal from occurring as planned, such as "in order to transmit the money we need to bribe a bank official, could you please help us with a loan?"

Some other scams are perpetrated through the website. Such websites are imitations of real sites — e-Bay, Paypal, or a banking site like Bank of America in order to lend credibility to the scammer's story. Another common variation comes with invitation to visit the country. Sometimes victims are invited to meet with fake or real government officials. Some of the victims are instead held for ransom or killed. This form of fraud is similar to what online predators do to children and teenagers in the West. An increasing number of advance-fee fraud is for con scammers to answer an advertisement for products and services. The scammer will offer to send a bank draft to cover the cost of the items for sale. The bank draft arrives with a large surplus and the victim is asked to cash the checks. Some schemes are based solely on conning the victim into cashing fake checks.

A variation that is quite prevalent in Asia is what we call charity scam. The scammer poses as a charitable organization soliciting donations to help the victims of a terrorist attack (such as the September 11 World Trade Center attack), regional conflict or natural disaster — hurricane Katrina and the 2004

Tsunami were popular targets of scammers perpetrating charity scam. The scammer asks for donations often linking to online news articles to strengthen their story of fund drive. The victims are charitable people who believe they are helping a worthy cause and expect nothing in return. Once sent, the money is gone and the scammers disappear (http://www.snopes.com/crime/fraud/nigeria.asp).

Typical Nigerian Scam

Aside from the con works by blinding the victims of an imaginable fortune, the Nigerian scammers have the unique feature in the slangs and modes it employs. They use such terms as "fall mugu to," and "flash of account."* A dimension which has not been fully uncovered but is commonplace among Ibo-speaking scammers of Nigeria, and to some extent the Yorubas, is the use of voodoo power. A scammer was reported to have used such power against his victim by placing both legs on a live tortoise while surfing the net (Korie, 2005, p. 19). The question remains whether such incantations can go through the net to their victims. Nevertheless, it is a common practice, the truth of which may be the subject of another academic inquiry.

A typical Nigerian scam letter reads thus:

Request for Urgent Business Relationship

First, I must solicit your strictest confidence in this transaction. This is by virtue of its nature as being utterly confidential and 'top secret.' I am sure and have confidence of your ability and reliability to prosecute a transaction of this great magnitude involving a pending transaction requiring maximum confidence.

We are top officials of the federal government contract review panel who are interested in importation of goods into our country with funds which are presently trapped in Nigeria. In order to commence this business we solicit your assistance to enable us transfer into your account the said trapped funds.

The source of this fund is as follows: during the last military regime here in Nigeria, the government officials set up companies and awarded themselves contracts which were grossly over-invoiced in various ministries. The present civilian government set up a contract review panel and we have identified a lot of inflated contract funds which are presently floating in the central bank of Nigeria ready for payment.

*However, by virtue of our position as civil servants
and members of this panel, we cannot acquire this money in
our names. I have therefore, been delegated as a matter of
trust by my colleagues of the panel to look for an overseas
partner into whose account we would transfer the sum of
USS 21,320,000.00 (Twenty one million, three hundred and
twenty thousand U.S. dollars). Hence we are writing you this
letter. We have agreed to share the money thus:*
1. 20% for the account owner
2. 70% for us (the officials)
*3. 10% to be used in settling taxation and all local and
foreign expenses.*
        *It is from the 70% that we wish to commence the
importation business.*
        *Please, note that this transaction is 100% safe and
we hope to commence the transfer latest seven (7) banking
days from the date of the receipt of the following information
by Tel/fax: 234-1-7740449, your company's signed, and
stamped letterhead paper. The above information will
enable us write letters of claim and job description
respectively. This way we will use your company's name to
apply for payment and re-award the contract in your
company's name.*
        *We are looking forward to doing this business with
you and solicit your confidentiality in this transaction.
Please acknowledge the receipt of this letter using the above
Tel/fax numbers I will send you detailed information of this
pending project when I have heard from you* (Korie, 2005,
p. 19).

"Fall mugu (to)" means to be fooled or to become a victim of
advance-fee fraud. "Flash of account" means to cause a victim's bank
account to show large credit. This is intended to induce the victim to
believe in the deal and send money. The credit gets reversed by the
bank when it is discovered that the original check or electronic
transfer was fraudulent.

Control Measures
Since Internet fraud was discovered, various governments, agencies and
institutions have taken some measures to put the activities of scammers to
check. Organizations like Microsoft are in partnership with governments, banks,
and other financial institutions to track down Internet surfers who perpetrate
financial crimes. Operators of *Moneygram* or *Western Union** services in major

locations have developed technologies which are constantly warning Internet users to be wary of fraudsters.

In October 2006, the Dutch Police launched "Operation Apollo" in Amsterdam, Netherlands to fight Internet fraud scams operated by West Africans and notably Nigerians (www.worldlawdirect.com/.../5939-advance-fee-fraud.html). The governments of Netherlands and Sweden have put in place fraud detecting machines capable to identifying scam motivated letters and their perpetrators, especially those having to do with financial transactions through the banks.

The Nigerian government is not left out. After a scam involving a forged signature of President Olusegun Obasanjo in the summer of 2005, Nigerian authorities raided a section of Oluwole Market in Lagos. This development provoked the then president who directed the Economic and Financial Crimes Commission (EFCC) to intensify the manhunt against offenders. The position of the former president has demonstrated Nigeria's willingness to fight cybercrime. Hitherto, authorities in Nigeria have been slow to take action and that may have exacerbated cybercrimes in the country, especially with the reputation of criminals being able to avoid convictions through bribery. Since 2003 the EFCC has been able to wage serious war on scam activities, and it has equally made a couple of successes.

Recently, a bill seeking the establishment of a special agency to battle Internet-related crimes in the country was put together and would soon be on the floor of the House of Representatives for debate and passage into law (Salem, 2009, p. 6).

The establishment of Youth Focused Initiative named the Internet Safety, Security and Privacy Initiative for Nigeria (ISSPIN) is one, out of many other campaigns, aimed at engaging and educating young people on the dangers of cybercrime and to provide opportunities for them to use their skills positively in identifying potential threats (Usigbe, 2009, p. 7).

Conclusively, a developing economy like Nigeria and other African countries have every reason to fight cybercrimes. It is crucial that governments, organizations, and institutions work together to address the problem of cybercrime, particularly among young people. More importantly, these organizations should show commitments toward developing healthy environments where youths can put their talents to use in positive ways.

*They are involved in international money transfer from one location to another. But of late, this business has become highly susceptible to cybercrime attacks in form of wire transfer interception, identity theft and credit card fraud. To checkmate this, the operators have been providing relevant information to their customers and the public about the activities of scammers through the Internet. They have also put in place devices to guard against currency counterfeiting.

Rebuilding Africa's Democracy: An Internet Perspective

The essence of democracy, in our own opinion, is to make government popular and for the press to be strong, but this is a direct antithesis from experience. It is rare in Africa to find where a government put in place by the people, which pursue policies that are not tailored to meet the needs of the people. Because of the failure of our democracy, which as a concept of government in our contemporary world is so bastardize or prostituted, the dividends of democratic systems are hardly realizable. No wonder Crick (1983, p. 56) observed:

> Democracy is perhaps the most promiscuous word in the world of public affairs. She is everybody's mistress and yet somehow retains her magic even when a lover sees that her favours are being in his light, illicitly shared by many others. Indeed, even amid our pain at being denied, her exclusive fidelity, we are proud of her adaptability to all sorts of circumstances, to all sorts of companies.

We said that people have needs (personal, information, psychological or emotional, and so on) in situating the theoretical framework of this study. It is from here that we can now draw the correlation between democratic opportunities and realized or relatively unrealized expectations leading to deviant behaviors - Internet fraud, corruption, electoral malpractice and so on.

The problem with the practice of democracy in Africa is complexity arising from political power acquisition and end-use of political power. This phenomenon is responsible for violent change of government and conflicts of various dimensions.

Now that the Internet has provided a free medium for popular expression of opinion as against the denials and stringent control of the conventional press, it is up to us to use the Internet to rebuild the ruins of our democratic experience.

It is necessary to emphasize the relationship between democratic process and information and communication technology. This relationship most often involves well-defined tenets and media democratic processes (Obasanjo and Mabogunje, 1992, p.43). Thus, achieving the goal of participatory democracy within the framework of national aspiration and development requires well informed citizens through information delivery systems.

The new media have shifted from printing and television to computer mediated technology. Joanne (2007) discusses the linkage between democracy and Internet. While describing the system as a vehicle for mass communication and political participation, she argues that information dissemination online can influence the system users to participate in the democratic process.

In Africa, corruption is a major problem undermining democracy and most corrupt practices are perpetrated in government offices due to the nature of bureaucracies. With e-payment, where every transaction is consummated through banks, corrupt tendencies are mitigated and confidence in government is restored. Through e-governance, information relating to government activities is open to public scrutiny and government business is no longer a secret meant for top government officials and their associates. Already, the e-payment has reduced the level of bribery in government offices and it is possible to extend this to bids for government contracts, which will further make the process transparent.

Conclusion and Recommendations

Remarkably, it is fascinating to observe that information delivery, which uses to be the unique role of the press, is being complemented by ICT. This is an attestation of how the new media technologies are influencing our lives. As clearly illustrated by the bourgeoning discussion, the potentials of the ICT continue to be realized as new ground is broken. The pessimism/fatalism which has characterized technological transfer has given way to massive development of varying equipment,   and hardware of new media technology. The opportunities for generating and receiving mass-mediated messages are staggering in this information age.

All over the world young people constitute probably the most volatile group in every society. They are in the forefront of the crusade for rights, which from the perspective of Nigeria's "lost generation" revolve around rights to education, employment, decent living, security, and opportunities for the realization of individual potentials. The same youths are also responsible for deviant behavior which is expressed in cybercrimes. Thus, the problem of any social sector raises many issues — degeneration of moral values, respect and dignity, erosion of loyalty to the nation, lack of commitment and patriotism at a larger scale. Crisis between government and the people at various levels arises from lack of confidence by the people, while resentment against established rules and regulations points to the lack of political will to arrest the decadence in society.

This work has profited greatly from numerous information sourced from the web. On reflection, it could not have been possible years back to put all the opinions together poring through text. This affirms the relevance of Internet in today's world.

In this work, we examined the evolution, development, and use of ICTs as well as its dysfunctional effects, in which we observed that the spate of Internet crime across the globe, as a result of the failure of institutional systems, is alarming. From varying experiences of scam activities, it is imperative that a holistic approach to cybercrimes has become an emergency. Perhaps, a forthright approach may be to call attention to the need to secure the cyberspace by setting up a commission, which will work with all the stakeholders to develop appropriate strategies and control measures necessary.

Much as the paper agrees that the cyberspace is open, unmanned, and therefore vulnerable to all kinds of practices, it will be the duty of the proposed commission to identify technical possibilities and solutions to this problem. The magnitude of the work ahead of this commission may be visualized from the following:

❖ How can we discourage cybercrimes?
❖ How can the apathy of the civil society be transformed into interest and participation in the control of cybercrimes?
❖ How can we arouse global disdain for crime mongers on the web?

The current global problems the paper highlights may be quite challenging. But the multiplicity of the media involve in ICT can be the bulwark against the forms of abuses which the paper had identified.

Scam activities affect a nation's image. Presently, the complex interplay of international trade and diplomacy point to the fact that the nations that are able to attract international finance and expertise in sufficient quantum possess stronger economies. America is presently using the H1 visa program to attract the best brains around the world. It is our thesis that she could not possibly allow cybercrimes to mess up her economy. Considering the level of Internet crimes in Nigeria, it may not be possible for the nation to benefit from foreign investment where national reputation is a pre-condition for the assessment of such dividends.

A number of strategies are proposed:

❖ Address national image by creating capacities for enduring economies
❖ Use available media to discourage scam activities
❖ Need for inter-government collaboration against crime using security agencies
❖ Technical assistance mobility from ICT hardware and software manufacturers
❖ Education and promotion of public order and morality

In summary, although this paper has identified a number of concepts on ICT as well as the dimensions to which it has been put, it remains that there is so much to do, share, and gain when democratic institutions are working efficiently and effectively. It is this social exchange that transforms the world.

REFERENCES

Baran, S.J. (2004). Introduction to mass communication: Media literacy and culture. Boston: McGraw-Hill Inc.

Biagi, S (2003). Media Impact: An introduction to mass media.   Boston: Wadsworth Publishing Company.

Briggs, A. and Cobley, P. (eds) (1998). The media: An introduction. Essex: Addison Wesley Longman limited.

Brown, M.M. (2000). The challenge of information and communication technology for development. Tokyo: UN. Chandler, D.(1995).Technological or media determinism. http://www.aber.ac.uk/media/Documents/tecdet/tecdet.html. Retrieved on June 25, 2009

Crick, B. (1983). In defense of politics, 2nd edition. Middlesex: Penguin.

Croteau, D, & Hoynes, W. (2003). Media society: Industries, images and audiences. Thousand Oaks: Pine Forge Press.

Dominick, J.R. (2002). The dynamics of mass communication: Media in the digital age. Boston: McGraw-Hill.

Folarin, A.B. (1998). Theories of mass communication: An introductory text. Ibadan: Stirling-Horden Publishers.

Giddens, A. (2001). Sociology, 4th edition, Cambridge: Polity Press.

Grabosky, P.N. and Smith, R.G. (1998). Crime in the digital age: controlling telecommunications and cyberspace illegalities. New Jersey: Transaction.

Green, L. (2001). Technoculture. Crows: Allen & Unwin Inayatullah, S. (1999). Transforming communication: Technology, sustainability and future generations. Westport, CT: Praeger and Adamantine Studies on the 21st century.

Joanne, J. (2007). "Democracy and the Internet." Available at http://abcnet:au/p/a/citizen/interdemoc/democ/html, retrieved March 27th, 2009.

Korie, N. (2005). Internet fraud; be warned! The Pointer, Wednesday, June 22.

Maras, S. (2002). "The medium as a platform: An emerging sense of medium" in the Journal of New Media and Culture. Vol 1. No. 2 September.

Mehra, B., Merkel, C. & Bishop, A.P. (2004). "The Internet for empowerment of minority and marginalized users" Journal of New Media and Society Vol. 6.

McPhail, T.L (2006). Global communication: Theories, stakeholders and trends, 2nd edition. Austria: Blackwell.

Morris, M. and Ogan, C. (1996).The Internet as a mass medium in Journal of Communication Vol. 46. No 1.

Obasanjo, O. and Mabogunje, A. (1992). Elements of democracy Abeokuta: Alf Publication.

Obe, J., Ayo, C.K., & Odukomaiya, S. (2008). The Nigerian press, and ICTs and the MDG initiative on Nigeria's development in Mojaye, E.M., Oyewo, O.O., M'Bayo, R. and Shobowale, I.A. (eds.) Health communication, gender violence and ICTs in Nigeria. Ibadan: Ibadan University Press.

Okpoko, J.I (2007). ICT and agro-allied industries in Nigeria: A case study of Federal Super Phosphate Fertilizer Company, Kaduna in the Nigerian Journal of Communications. Enugu: ACCE.

Okunna, C.S. (2002). A quick look at development communication in Okunna, C.S (ed). Teaching mass communication: A multi-dimensional approach. Enugu: New Generation Books.

Payne, J. (2001). Application communication for personal and professional contexts. Topeka: Clark Publishing.

Postman, N. (1992). Technopoly. New York: Vintage.

Rodney, C. (2005). Modern communication technology and the new world information order in Okoro .N. (ed) International Journal of Communication No. 2.

Salem, T. (2009). Anti-cybercrime agency bill under way. Vanguard, Monday, January 19.

Severin, W.J., and Tankard, J.W. (2001). Communication theories: Origins, methods and uses in the mass media. New York: Longman.

Slapper, G. and Tombs. S. (1999). Corporate crime. Essex: Longman.

Smith, M.R. & Leo, M. (eds) (1994). Does technology drive history? The dilemma of technological determinism. Cambridge: MIT Press.

Souter, D. (1999). The role of information and communication technologies (ICTs) in democratic development In Journal of Policy Regulations and Strategy for Telecommunications, Information and Media Vol.1 No.5. UK: Crawford.

Strangelove, M. (1994). The Internet as catalyst for a paradigm shift in Computer Mediated Communication Magazine, Vol.1 No. 8.

Usigbe, L. (2009). Fighting cybercrimes: the executive, legislative and judiciary collaboration approach. Vanguard, Monday, January 19.

Williams, B. and Sawyer, C. (2003). Using information technology: A practical introduction to computer and communication. New York: McGraw-Hill.
http://www.gabrielsawma.blogspot.com.
www.worldlawdirect.com/.../5939-advance-fee-fraud.html
http://www.snopes.com/crime/fraud/nigeria.asp.

Contributors

Adele M. Mda was born in South Africa. She has always liked communication technologies, women and children's issues. She was especially interested in education, communication, and finance. Luckily, her family and teachers encouraged those interests. She graduated from National University of Lesotho and earned a degree in Education for Development. Soon after, she graduated from St Michaels College in Vermont and Rand Afrikaans University in South Africa with Masters Degrees. In 1995, Adele went back to South Africa and worked for the non-profit organization and later for government. Her biggest dream was to work with UNESCO and the South African Broadcasting.

Assay B. Enahoro is the Coordinator, Department of Mass Communication, Delta State Polytechnic, Ogwashi-Uku, Nigeria. He holds BA and MA degrees in Mass Communication from Delta State University, Abraka and University of Nigeria, Nsukka respectively. Currently, he is a doctoral candidate of Mass Communication, Benue State University, Makurdi, Nigeria. His area of research interests include development communication, public relations and advertising, population communication, media and governance, international communication and media theory. He has published articles in reputable national and international journals, as well as contributed chapters to local and international books. He is a member of several professional bodies, including African Council for Communication Education (ACCE), Nigerian Institute of Management (NIM), Nigeria Institute of Public Relations (NIPR), Association for Promoting Nigerian Languages and Culture (APNILAC), National Association for Research Development (NARD), among others.

Cosmas U. Nwokeafor, Ph.D., is a full professor of mass communication at Bowie State University, where he currently serves as the Interim Dean of Graduate School. He has served as a provost fellow and assistant provost for graduate studies at Bowie State University. Prior to his current position, he served as the assistant dean and dean of the college of Arts and Sciences respectively as well as chair of the department of communication. His professional experiences include leadership training at Harvard University and the Oxford Roundtable workshop at Oxford University, London. He has conducted research on development communication, new communication technologies and development in Africa, conundrum of autism, retention studies among students in historical black colleges and universities, and effective leadership in student retention. Currently, he serves as the dissertation reviewer for Council of Historically Black Colleges and University Graduate School. Dr. Nwokeafor was the past associate editor of the Journal of African Communication (JAC), a scholarly journal currently housed at the department of English and Communications at California State University, Bakersfield, California. He has been involved in some funded and unfunded grants among which is the multimillion dollar project learning community (Project LINC), National Science Foundation (NSF) proposal titled "Prince George's Partnership for Innovation and a 4.5 million dollar National Science Foundation (NSF) grant titled "Training Institute for Practicing Mathematics and Sciences Teachers. He has published/co-published six book chapters and is the author of numerous scholarly articles. His most recent books include *My Father's Journey: A True Story*, Instant Publishers Company (2008), and *When Cultures Collide: The Challenges of Raising African Children in a Foreign Country*, Instant Publishers Company (2008). He has also reviewed John Merrill's book, *Global Communication.*

Ephraim Okoro, Ph.D. is an assistant professor in the Department of Marketing, School of Business at Howard University. He teaches business communication, marketing communication, management communication, and principles of marketing. Formerly administrative dean, acting chair, and professor of management and marketing at Southeastern University in Washington, D.C. Dr. Ephraim Okoro has taught at the University of Maryland University College, Strayer University, and Bowie State University. His primary research interests focus on business/organizational communication, mass communication, intercultural communication, and global marketing/consumer behavior. He has authored book chapters and research proceedings, and co-authored articles in peer-reviewed journals, including *Business Communication Quarterly*, and *Journal of Innovative Marketing.* He is a member of the American Marketing Association, the Association for Business Communication,

Eastern Communication Association, and the International Communication Association. Dr. Okoro may be contacted at eaokoro@howard.edu.

Gado Alzouma, Ph.D. is associate professor of anthropology at the School of Arts and Science, American University of Nigeria, Yola. He did his undergraduate and graduate studies in France. He also holds a Ph.D. from Southern Illinois University, Carbondale, USA. Before joining AUN, Dr. Gado Alzouma taught sociology and anthropology courses for twelve years in Abdou Moumouni University of Niamey, Niger. He later worked as coordinator, evaluation and learning systems, in the Africa and the Information Society Program of the International Development Research Center, (IDRC, Dakar, Senegal) and as a research fellow in the Global Media Research Center (SIU, Carbondale, Illinois). His research and publications focus on information and communication technologies for development, on science, technology and society as well as globalization and identities. He is the author of numerous evaluation studies and several peer-reviewed papers, including "Identities in a 'fragmegrated' World: Black Cybercommunities and the French Integration System"; *African and Black Diaspora: An International Journal*, Vol. 1, Issue 2, 201-214 (2008); "Myths of Digital technology in Africa: Leapfrogging Development?"; *Global Media and Communication*, Vol. 1, No. 3, 339-356 (2005); "Islamic Renewal in Niger: From Monolith to Plurality" (with Abdoulaye Niandou Souley), *Social Compass*, 43(2), 249-265 (1996).

George Gathigi, Ph.D. (Ohio University, Athens) is the Andrew W. Mellon Postdoctoral Fellow in African Expressive and Material Arts at Hampshire College at Amherst, MA. George teaches courses on African popular culture and media for social change. His research is on broadcast media, media and everyday life, youth and popular culture, and media for social change. George previously worked in East Africa on various development communication projects on health, education, and leadership. He has been involved in the design and implementation of media for social change projects in Kenya, Uganda, Sudan, and Botswana. He has also been involved in designing communication for social change training materials for development practitioners.

Isika G. Udechukwu teaches Mass Communication at Delta State Polytechnic Ogwashi-Uku His research interest includes: expressive Communication, Media research and development communication. His foray into mass communication actually began in the 80s as one of the pioneering students of Mass Communication Department of Auchi Polytechnic, Auchi, Nigeria. He thereafter graduated with BA. (Hons) in Communication Arts at University of Uyo and a master's degree in the same University. Isika has severed local and international publications to his credit and belongs to some international organizations including African Council for Communication Education (ACCE) International Public Relations Association (IPRA), among others. He is happily married to Philomena, and blessed with four lovely children.

Hala A. Guta is a doctoral candidate in the School of Media Arts and Studies, Scripps College of Communication, Ohio University. She holds dual Master's degrees in Communication and Development Studies and Cultural Studies in Education from Ohio University. Her research interest is communication for development and social change with special emphasis on peace and conflict transformation. She has special interest in East Africa and the Horn of Africa region. She is also interested in peace education, cross-cultural communication, media representation and identity formation Corporation in 13 African countries on media and children. She came back to the U.S. to complete her Ph.D. in Mass Communication at Ohio University in 2009. Her research interests are in media policy and management, ICT, race and gender. She encourages women of all races and young people to work together for a common goal.

Kehbuma Langmia, Ph.D. is an assistant professor of communications at Bowie State University where he teaches research and other media related courses in the Department of Communications. A graduate from the Television and Film Academy in Munich, Germany, Dr. Langmia has extensive knowledge and training in media productions and management. After earning his Ph.D. in Mass Communication and Media Studies from Howard University in 2006, he has written and published fiction and non-fiction books, book chapters and research articles in prominent national and international journals. They include: *An Evil Meal of Evil* (Michigan State University Press, 2009); *Minorities and Video Production* (Kendall Hunt Publishers, 2008); *The Internet and the Construction of the Immigrant Public Sphere: The Case of the Cameroonian Diaspora* (University Press of America, 2007);*Titabet and Takumbeng* (Michigan State University Press, 2008); *Harnessing the Power of African Traditional and Modern Media Systems to Avert Conflicts in Africa* — book chapter in *Communication in an era of global conflict* (University Press of America, 2009). Dr. Langmia has had several awards the most recent being profiled in Montclair's "Who is Who in North American Universities" 2009-2010.

Matthew Uzukwu, Ph.D. is an adjunct professor in the Department of Management, Marketing and Public Administration of the College of Business at Bowie State University. Dr. Uzukwu has published articles in both print and electronic media, and is the author of three books—*Across Cultures, Out of the Slave Coast,* and *Scammers of the Dictators' Realm.* An avid promoter of his native Igbo language, he has also published two titles; *Ezi Ndu Ka Nma* and *Naijiria: Mgbe Ochie Rue Taa* in Igbo language.

Victor A. Aluma, Ph.D. is a senior lecturer at the Department of Mass Communication, University of Lagos, Nigeria. He holds the Ph.D. (Communication) of the University of Ibadan, Nigeria and is an alumnus of the International Institute for Journalism, Germany. He has published internationally in the areas of cultural, political and development communication as well as on broadcast and digital media. In 2008, he edited a volume on investigative journalism commissioned by the Wole Soyinka Centre for Investigative Journalism. He has consulted on development communication for the United Nations Children's Fund, the International Labour Organisation, the News Agency of Nigeria, the Nigerian Television Authority and the Human Development Initiatives, receiving the latter's Certificate of Appreciation in 2007. He maintains an interest in the creative arts expressed through original electronic media productions and poetry publications. vayedun-aluma@unilag.edu.ng.

The Authors/Editors

Cosmas U. Nwokeafor, Ph.D., is a full professor of mass communication at Bowie State University where he currently serves as the Interim Dean of Graduate School. He has served as a provost fellow and assistant provost for graduate studies at Bowie State University. Prior to his current position, he has served as the assistant dean and dean of the college of Arts and Sciences respectively, as well as chair of the department of communication. His professional experiences include leadership training at Harvard University and the Oxford Roundtable workshop at Oxford University, London. He has conducted research on development communication, new communication technologies and development in Africa, conundrum of autism, retention studies among students in historical black colleges and universities, and effective leadership in student retention. Currently, he serves as the dissertation reviewer for Council of Historically Black Colleges and University Graduate School. Dr. Nwokeafor was the past associate editor of the Journal of African Communication (JAC), a scholarly journal currently housed at the department of English and Communications at California State University, Bakersfield, California. He has been involved in some funded and unfunded grants among which is the multimillion dollar project learning community (Project LINC), National Science Foundation (NSF) proposal titled "Prince George's Partnership for Innovation and a 4.5 million dollar National Science Foundation (NSF) grant titled "Training Institute for Practicing Mathematics and Sciences Teachers. He has published/co-published six book chapters and is the author of numerous scholarly articles. His most recent books include *My Father's Journey: A True Story*, Instant Publishers Company (2008) and *When Cultures Collide: The Challenges of Raising African Children in a Foreign Country*, Instant Publishers Company (2008). He has also reviewed John Merrill's book, *Global Communication*.

Kehbuma Langmia, Ph.D. is an assistant professor of communications at Bowie State University where he teaches research and other media related courses in the Department of Communications. A graduate from the Television and Film Academy in Munich, Germany, Dr. Langmia has extensive knowledge and training in media productions and management. After earning his Ph.D. in Mass Communication and Media Studies from Howard University in 2006, he has written and published fiction and non-fiction books, book chapters and research articles in prominent national and international journals. They include: *An Evil Meal of Evil* (Michigan State University Press, 2009); *Minorities and Video Production* (Kendall Hunt Publishers, 2008); *The Internet and the Construction of the Immigrant Public Sphere: The Case of the Cameroonian Diaspora* (University Press of America, 2007*); Titabet and Takumbeng* (Michigan State University Press, 2008); *Harnessing the Power of African Traditional and Modern Media Systems to Avert Conflicts in Africa* — book chapter in *Communication in an era of global conflict (*University Press of America, 2009). Dr. Langmia has had several awards the most recent being profiled in Montclair's "Who is Who in North American Universities" 2009-2010.

Breinigsville, PA USA
27 August 2010
244359BV00003B/2/P